D0617181

LUFTWAFFE: A HISTORY

LUFTWAFFE: A HISTORY

Edited by Harold Faber

Times
BOOKS

Contents

FIGURES

ILLUSTRATIONS

Following pages 78 and 198

Preface

THIS BOOK is a condensation of twelve volumes written by former key officers of the German Air Force for the United States Air Force Historical Division on why the legendary Luftwaffe disintegrated under wartime pressures in World War II. With one exception, an historian, all the authors are former Luftwaffe generals who held important staff positions before and during the war.

Based on personal experience and knowledge, the perspective of the authors is neither unbiased nor history in the ordinary sense of the word. Instead, their insight into the rise and fall of the Luftwaffe—intimate, reflective, and in many ways incomplete—constitutes a vital part of the story of the air war over Europe, fascinating in itself and an essential part of any comprehensive history of World War II.

As their story unfolds, the reader is constantly reminded that these are Germans recalling, reporting, and analyzing decisions made and actions taken in Nazi Germany, a dictatorship under the complete sway of Adolf Hitler. As military officers, they accepted the political decisions—war or peace—made by Hitler. As Air Force officers, they were aghast at some of the military decisions by their leaders and at the internal politics, personality conflicts, and planning mistakes made at high levels in the years preceding the war and during the war itself.

In preparing these studies, the authors did not depend on their memories alone, according to our Air Force historians. They supplemented their knowledge with a collection of Luftwaffe documents now housed in the Archives Division of the United States Air Force Historical Division. The collection consists of directives, situation reports, war diaries, personal diaries, strength reports, minutes of meetings, aerial photographs, and other material derived mainly from three sources: the Captured German Documents Section of the Adjutant General in Alexandria, Virginia; the Air Ministry in London; and private German collections donated to the project by participating authors and contributors.

The authors also made use of the records of the Nuremberg Trials, manuscripts prepared by the Foreign Military Studies Branch of the Air Force Historical Division, the official military histories of the United States and the United Kingdom, and the voluminous literature on World War II that has appeared in books and military journals since 1945, both in English and German.

Among the authors of the works used extensively in this condensation were Dr. Richard Suchenwirth, historian, author and teacher who was professor of history at the University of Munich as the war ended; Generalleutnant Andreas Nielsen who saw active service in Spain, Poland and France before occupying numerous staff positions; and Generalleutnant Klaus Uebe who commanded a fighter squadron against England and then served in Africa and Russia. In addition two other high-ranking German generals, General der Flieger Paul Deichmann and Generalleutnant Hermann Plocher, acted as control officers during the research and writing phases of the project. Numerous United States Air Force historians, both military and civilian, also were involved in revising and editing the original manuscripts.

The overall purpose of the series was, according to the United States Air Force, threefold: 1—to provide it with a comprehensive and insofar as possible authoritative history of a major air force that suffered defeat in wartime; 2—to provide a history of that air force prepared by many of its principal and responsible leaders; 3—to provide a firsthand account of that air force's combat in war with the Soviet Union.

For the American reader, one of the surprises will undoubtedly be the emphasis by the German generals on the war with the Soviet Union. Six of the twelve original volumes concern the fighting on the Eastern front, in which the Luftwaffe became, for all practical purposes, tactical flying artillery rather than a diversified air arm. Moreover, the German generals' reports on the recuperation of the Russian Air Force, the survival of its aircraft industry, the development of its planes, and the changing strategy and tactics of the Russian fliers in World War II may, to some extent, contain some lessons for today.

The twelve volumes were published by the United States Air Force Historical Division in the 1950's and 1960's. They were republished in the 1960's and 1970's by Arno Press, with the cooperation of the Department of Defense and the Air Force Historical Division.

In preparing this one-volume condensation, following the pattern set earlier by the Air Force translators and editors, I have used the words and style of the authors (except for a handful of connective words or phrases). At the risk of repetition, it must be remembered that this is their version of what happened, not the views of the United States Air Force nor an objective history of the air war over Europe.

I have also retained the German military titles and so the following list of comparisons to American rank may be helpful. However, there is no American equivalent for the title of Hermann Goering, the top commander of the Luftwaffe. In German, he was Reichsmarschall des Grossdeutschen Reiches. Translated, that is Reichs Marshal of the Pan-German Reich.

Under him were generalfeldmarschalls (generals of the Air Force, which were the same as our five-star generals); generalobersts (or our four-star generals); generals der flieger (or our three-star lieutenant generals); generalleutnants (or our two-star major generals); and generalmajors (or our one-star brigadier generals).

HAROLD FABER

Introduction

(EDITOR'S NOTE: This introduction by Telford Taylor was written for the entire series of books prepared for the United States Air Force Historical Division's studies of the Luftwaffe, most of which is condensed in this book.)

THE PUBLICATION of this series of official historical studies is at once a most significant contribution to our knowledge of the Second World War and a landmark in the development of commercial publishing.

So much is published nowadays—far beyond the capacity of any individual even to screen—and so much is printed that ought never to see the light of day, that one tends to forget the considerable amount of writing well worth reading which rarely or never gets published at all. These volumes are an excellent example. Military monographs by foreign officers whose names are unknown to the public are not attractive items to most commercial publishing houses. But sometimes, as in the present case, they are unique sources of information which should be available in public if not in private libraries. Less often, and again as in the case of these volumes, they are surprisingly well written, and in many parts fascinating to the general reader as well as to the historian or military specialist.

Not the least remarkable feature of the series is its authorship. With the single exception of Dr. Richard Suchenwirth—a one-time Austrian Army officer and more recently a historian and educator in Munich—they are all former Luftwaffe generals, of low to middling seniority, who were intimately and responsibly involved with the events and problems of which they write. All seven were born within the decade 1891-1901, and thus in their forties or early fifties during most of the war years. Lieutenant-colonels or colonels when the war began, they filled a wide variety of staff and administrative assignments. Only two

(Deichmann and Drum) attained three-star rank (*General der Flieger*), and only one (Deichmann) was ever given a major field command.

In military parlance, accordingly, they are all "staff" rather than "command" types, and for present purposes that is a good thing. Staff officers are responsible for the smooth functioning of the military machine; they must anticipate and provide for contingencies, and are expected to possess good powers of analysis and imagination. They spend much time drafting orders, which requires the ability to write with clarity and brevity. All these qualities are reflected in their product; our seven generals must have been good staff officers.

Banned by the Treaty of Versailles, the German air arm was condemned to a clandestine and embryonic life until 1933, and the Luftwaffe's existence was not publicly acknowledged until 1935. Hermann Goering and his colleagues in its command thus had only six years prior to the war in which to assemble and organize an officer corps. Its younger members—those who were lieutenants and captains when the war came—were recruited and trained during those years (1933-39), but the upper reaches of the corps had to be manned in other ways.

The need for experienced staff officers was especially acute, and this was met largely by transferring army (and a few navy) officers to the newly established air arm. Thus it is not surprising to find that all but one of our generals were professional soldiers who made their careers in the *Reichsheer* of the Weimar Republic, and received general staff training at the time Adolf Hitler was coming to power. So far as possible, the officers to be transferred were selected from those who had served in the air arm during the First World War, as had Deichmann and Drum.

Morzik alone represents the other principal type of senior Luftwaffe officer. He was not of the "officer class"; he had been a noncommissioned officer in the air arm during the First World War. Between the wars he led an adventurous and varied life as a commercial pilot, a successful competitor in aviation contests, a Junkers test pilot, and a flying instructor. Like his more famous superiors—Udet, Loerzer, von Greim, and Goering himself—Morzik was a free-lance knight of the air, and one of a considerable company commissioned from civil life in the 1933-35 period.

These generals are writing about events of which they were a part, in the course of a war in which Germany was catastrophically, and the Luftwaffe even ignominiously, defeated. What they have written is certainly not objective in the sense that it is detached; they see with the eyes and speak the language of the air arm, and readily find explanations for their own failures in the mistakes of the Army leadership—often with good reason, to be sure. But their work is objective in the sense that it is dispassionate. Their studies bespeak a deep curiosity about their conduct of the war and the causes of their defeat, and they have, on the whole, endeavored to put the record straight by the lines they are able to perceive.

There is, however, a great deal that they did not perceive. Few, if any, are those who can write at length about other men without revealing a great deal about themselves, and our authors are not in this respect exceptional. At least during this century, the German military profession has been rightly celebrated for its technical and tactical competence, but its record in the field of grand strategy has been abysmal. By and large these studies do not often venture into the rarefied atmosphere of the highest levels of command, and when they do, the results are unimpressive. Plocher's account of the reasons for the German attack against the Soviet Union, for example, is superficial and diffuse. Of course he was not party or privy to the decision, but in telling us what he has heard there is little effort to winnow fact from fable, or to assess the considerations and alternatives.

In other respects, these volumes are not to be faulted so much for what is said as for what is left unspoken. Describing the Russian soldier, Uebe tells us that it is his "inherent character" to be "ruthless" and to place "a relatively lower value on human life" than "Western" peoples do. For myself, I am inclined to discount popular stereotypes about national characteristics, and to judge rather upon a record of behavior. Beyond question the Russian soldier was often ruthless and worse, but what of the German soldier in Russia? Neither Uebe nor any of his colleagues carries the story in that direction. To be sure the Luftwaffe, by nature of its operations, was not much involved in the exterminations, forced labor impressments, and other atrocities in which the Army was extensively implicated. But this hardly justifies Plocher's chest-thumping conclusion that: ". . . the incomparable performances of the individual German soldier in combat in the East are above criticism. This applies to all ranks, from the lowest private to general officers, on the land, in the air, and on the seas." Unhappily, the German military records tell quite a different story.

Fortunately such departures from the factual dimension are rare, and the authors have given us a unique and invaluable fund of information. Two of these studies concern the high command of the Luftwaffe, and two more cover particular Luftwaffe functions—airlift and ground support. The remaining six all concern the fighting on the eastern front between the German and Russian forces—a ferocious conflict on a scale greater than any other in human history.

Three of the eastern front studies, all by Plocher, constitute a chronological account of Luftwaffe operations on the eastern front in 1941, 1942, and 1943, one year to each volume. It is a mammoth undertaking of nearly 1,200 pages, well-organized, and abundantly supported and illustrated with maps, charts, and photographs.

Plocher was chief of staff of an air corps on the southern part of the front, and remained in the east until the middle of 1943. Thus he witnessed at firsthand the Luftwaffe's highly successful operations during the first few days of the campaign in July 1941, in the course of which the entire Russian Air Force was virtually annihilated, as well as the great encirclements at Minsk, Kiev, Bryansk, and elsewhere, which netted over two and a quarter million Russian prisoners and drove the Soviet attack forces back to the gates of Leningrad and Moscow and the banks of the Don. No doubt the Wehrmacht's failure to achieve decisive success was more the fault of the Army leadership than of the Luftwaffe, but the air generals made serious mistakes of their own, of which Plocher stresses two of major strategic proportions: (1) failure to carry out strategic bombing attacks on Russian armaments industries, and (2) dispersion of the slender air strength at the extreme northern end of the front, so that Murmansk and Archangel remained in Russian hands, as ports through which the western Allies could help the Russians to recover, following their nearly disastrous losses in the opening months of the campaign.

With the Russian air arm largely destroyed and strategic operations neglected, the Luftwaffe became, in practical terms, part of the German army—"flying artillery," supplemental transportation, additional ground forces. There were few Russian aircraft for the German *Flak* to shoot at, so the antiaircraft units became front-line artillery.

Later on, as the Army got into even deeper trouble, the Luftwaffe was pulled in after it. Bombers were misused on ground-attack and airlift assignments; efforts to supply encircled German armies by air caused the Luftwaffe catastrophic losses. New Russian aircraft began to appear on the scene, and the balance gradually shifted so that by the end of 1943 the Germans no longer enjoyed air superiority, and the Luftwaffe became, as Plocher puts it, a "fire brigade," constantly on emergency call to plug up holes or salvage hard-pressed Army units.

How the Russians responded to the Luftwaffe's operations is the subject of Uebe's report. Except for the first few days, when the Soviet planes were destroyed in close array on their own airfields, like our own aircraft on Clark Field in the Philippines in December 1941, the Russians reacted to the overwhelming German superiority with great adaptability, and skill in the arts of camouflage and deception. Rails laid on ice did not sink with the thaw, for supports had been built under the ice; ships that appeared half-sunk and useless were under repair, with the bow flooded to elevate the stern. "As events show," writes Uebe, "Russian reaction to German Air Force operations, however primitive and makeshift in character, and however crude they might have first appeared to be to their more enlightened Western opponents, proved throughout the course of the war to be highly efficient, effective, and ultimately an important factor in the defeat of Germany."

These same qualities were strikingly manifest in the Russian partisan operations behind the German lines, as described in a short but vivid study by General Karl Drum. The partisan units depended on air transportation for reinforcements, leadership, supplies, evacuation of wounded, and other necessary assistance, and all this was accomplished with obsolete aircraft and improvised equipment, utilizing airdrop or well-concealed airstrips. Upon occasion, men were "delivered" to the partisans by parachuteless airdrop, wrapped in straw and dropped from low-flying planes into deep snow. The Germans, counting on a blitzkrieg victory, had made no preparations for antipartisan warfare. No aircraft were earmarked to deal with the Russian air supply, no single antipartisan command was established to deal with the problem as a whole. Brutal occupation policies boomeranged by driving the population into the arms of the partisans. The German failure to take effective countermeasures is a striking demonstration that overwhelming superiority in heavy weapons and a sophisticated military tradition are no guarantee of success against surprise and deception.

Perhaps the most interesting and valuable of the eastern front volumes is Schwabedissen's extensive and perceptive study of the Russian Air Force as it appeared to the Germans. Through interchange of equipment and manufacturing and training facilities during the Weimar period, the antagonists were well known to each other. The Russian air performance in Spain and Finland had not been impressive, and in 1941, just prior to their attack, the Luftwaffe had a pretty accurate picture of the opposing force: it was far larger than the Luftwaffe, but much inferior in equipment, leadership, and training. The Germans expected to smash it to bits, and they succeeded.

What the Germans failed to reckon with was the Russians' recuperative powers. Most of their aircraft were destroyed on the ground rather than in the air, so that personnel losses were not high. The armament industries were rapidly moved eastward, and an early winter hampered Luftwaffe operations and gave the Russians a badly needed respite. By the winter of 1941-42 new Russian air units, better equipped, were beginning to appear at the front.

Still vastly superior in operational capacity, the Luftwaffe remained dominant in 1942, but in 1943 Russian numerical superiority, and techniques improved by experience, began to tell. During the last two years of the war, general air superiority passed to the Russian side of the front. But superior German technique enabled them to operate and achieve local successes right up to the end of the war; the Russians never achieved the total superiority enjoyed by the Allies on the western front.

German military air transport operations were opened by spectacular successes in the West. By parachute, glider, and landed aircraft, German airborne units descended on the major airfields of Norway and Denmark, on the airfields and tactically crucial bridges in Holland, and on the famous fort Eben Emael in Belgium.

The transport workhorse of the Luftwaffe was the three-engined Junkers 52, opposite number to our C-47's (otherwise known as DC-3's, Dakotas, "gooney birds," and in Vietnam as "dragonships"), and well known to all European travelers of ancient enough vintage to have flown Lufthansa during the thirties. A sturdy and versatile airplane, it was turned out by the thousands, but by the end of the war there were less than two hundred left. Most of the rest lay shattered and scrapped in Russia, near Demyansk and Stalingrad.

Morzik's account of the Demyansk and Stalingrad airlifts is gripping and enlightening. Retreating from the Moscow sector, the German Second Corps (roughly 100,000 men) was encircled at Demyansk in February 1942. Hitler forbade a breakout to the rear, and decided to supply the Corps by air. This was accomplished, but at a cost of 160 railway trains of gasoline, 265 Ju-52's, and consequent loss of trained crews and disruption of the pilot-training program. The psychological cost was even higher, for the apparent success of the operation made spuriously credible Goering's promise, ten months later, to supply Paulus' Sixth Army of over 300,000 men, encircled at Stalingrad. By then the Luftwaffe had only 750 Ju-52's left; half of them, and many bombers pressed into service as transports, were lost in the futile effort.

Airlift operations were the product of special circumstances, and strategic bombing the Luftwaffe neglected from birth to death. Day in and day out, its basic role was direct support of Army operations: attacking enemy troop columns, strong points, and tanks; impeding the flow of enemy reinforcements or cutting off their avenues of retreat; general intelligence reconnaissance. After 1941, Army support comprised over 75 percent of the Luftwaffe's operational activity—too large a proportion, as General Deichmann points out.

In "The German Air Force General Staff," Nielsen takes us into the weird world of the Luftwaffe high command, well stocked with colorful characters, many of them adequately unattractive. Hitler was not much interested in air power and left Goering a free hand as long as things went well. After the period of spectacular initial success, Goering suffered a sharp decline in influence, and the Fuehrer interjected himself into the Luftwaffe's management. He was not helpful; his decisions were the product of ignorance and favoritism and simply completed the process of demoralization.

Nielsen's study is focused on the general staff—i.e. the group of specially trained officers who held staff assignments—but its perspective is much broader, and includes the interplay of personality and rivalry at the top. Until his fall from grace, Goering's domination was complete, with one exception—Erhard Milch, his second-in-command, who had his own contacts and standing with Hitler and the Nazi Party. A former director of Lufthansa and a man of great energy and administrative ability, Milch was ambitious to the point that his attitude on proposed measures was governed less by the merits than by his estimate of their probable effect on his personal situation. Thus he initially opposed the creation of a general staff, and, when overruled, bent his energies to ensuring that the chief of the general staff would not impair his status as the No. 2 man. The consequence was a running battle between Milch and the succession of chiefs—seven during the Luftwaffe's less than twelve years of life—who served, basically, as Goering's advisors in the field of combat operations.

The results of his jerry-built command structure and riven leadership are graphically portrayed in Professor Suchenwirth's "Historical Turning Points in the German War Effort." Since the Luftwaffe ended the war in a state of total disintegration, the title postulates a study of crucial decisions which proved disastrous.

Perhaps the worst mistakes were made before the war began, and were the almost inevitable consequence of the personal shortcomings of the Luftwaffe leaders. Hans Jeschonnek—a career army officer barely old enough to have had a bit of flying experience at the very end of the First World War—was the Luftwaffe chief of staff from early 1939 to his suicide in 1943. Blindly devoted to Hitler and, until near the end, to Goering, he swallowed whole Hitler's assurances that the war would be a short blitzkrieg. Accordingly, he took no interest in training, neglected air transport, opposed the development of a long-range bomber, and focused all of his considerable ability on army support, and especially on the dive-bomber. During the first year of the war these weaknesses did not show, but the Luftwaffe's failure over Britain and its inadequacy to the sustained demands of the eastern front were the direct result of such miscalculations, of which Jeschonnek was by no means the only author. Udet, Milch, Goering, and Hitler himself all contributed greatly to the Luftwaffe's misconstruction, misuse, and miserable fate.

In 1936, when Francisco Franco asked Hitler for help in moving his forces from Africa to Spain, Ju-52's were sent to do the job. Nine years later, as the Third Reich crumbled, Ju-52's—what was left of them— were still the standard Luftwaffe transport aircraft, and in this circumstance the Luftwaffe's intrinsic weakness is strikingly reflected. Messerschmitt 109's and 110's, Dornier 17's, Heinkel 111's, Ju-87 "Stukas," and Ju-88's were all on hand before the war began. With the sole exception of the Focke-Wulf 190—somewhat but not significantly superior to the Me 109—not a single new major aircraft type was added to the Luftwaffe until the last year of the war. Then came the first jet aircraft and the V-weapons, but it was too little and too late.

In retrospect, it is apparent that the Luftwaffe reached its peak of effectiveness before the war had even begun. Germany's bloodless conquest at Munich was achieved largely by the fear of Goering's bombers —a threat that was real enough, though exaggerated far beyond its true dimensions. Spectacular as they were, the Luftwaffe's triumphs in Poland, Norway, Holland, and even against the French (whose air force was woefully decrepit) were not scored against major opponents. As early as Dunkirk the veil was torn, and from then on the story is one of decline, gradual until the winter of 1941-42, rapid thereafter.

And so it came about that the story told, and well told, in these volumes can be fairly summarized in just seven words: how not to run an air force.

TELFORD TAYLOR

PART I
Command and Leadership

1
The Legend of the Luftwaffe

AT THE BEGINNING of World War II the German Air Force attracted the attention of the entire world as a completely invincible force. German armies, supported by the Luftwaffe's relentless attacks on enemy positions and marching columns, were able to carry out a blitzkrieg which resulted in the conquest of Poland, Norway, and France. Airborne operations, particularly the daring assault leading to the capture of the almost impregnable Belgian fortress on the Meuse, Eben Emael, filled the world with amazement. Although the Luftwaffe did not succeed in gaining a clear aerial victory against Great Britain, it was able to achieve occasional air superiority over the Channel and to put this to a successful test in February of 1942, when the German battle fleet carried out its escape dash from Brest to its home ports in Germany. The campaign in the Balkans required Luftwaffe participation in a blitz operation over extremely difficult terrain. The air landings in Crete and the eviction of the British fleet from the waters surrounding the island brought new laurels to the Luftwaffe. In the Mediterranean area, General der Flieger Hans Geissler's X Air Corps and (later) the Second Air Fleet under Field Marshal Kesselring maintained air superiority for a long time.

Even in the first year of the Russian campaign (until the summer of 1942) the Luftwaffe managed to maintain air superiority and often to achieve air supremacy against a dangerous and rapidly recovering adversary. The Russian Air Forces were simply unable to prevail against the German Air Force whenever it appeared in a highly concentrated action, and Field Marshal Wolfram Freiherr von Richthofen, a ruthless but scrupulously fair head of the VIII Air Corps and the Fourth Air Fleet, was a past master at this sort of operation. A very small number of German fighter units were able to successfully defend the home area by day and night during 1940, 1941, and early 1942, or until the first devastating attacks upon Luebeck, Rostock, and Cologne. Even after this time the Luftwaffe remained a stubborn enemy, worthy of being taken seriously by the British, and after 1942 by American bomber forces, although the latter, because of their range and efficiency of radar equipment, were undeniably far superior.

Nevertheless, in the course of this rise to fame over nearly all of Europe, large parts of Africa as far as the Suez Canal, and the northern tip of the Red Sea, the German Air Force lost some of its most valuable personnel, including carefully trained aircrews and outstanding individual aces, men such as Werner Moelders and Hans-Joachim Marseille.

The Russian theater of operations, because of its poor airfields, the dreadful winter of 1941-42, and the muddy periods, swallowed up a great amount of materiel. In addition, inordinately large quantities of equipment and huge numbers of personnel were lost in missions conducted in direct support of ground operations in the East. Air operations in support of the Army were carried out to an unusual extent there because of the fact that the Russians, fatalistically inclined, terribly stubborn, and capable of enduring great suffering, were not as easily terrorized by aerial attacks as were, for example, the French. The Russians almost invariably stood their ground and fired away with whatever they had at hand. Though ineffective as individuals, the sheer mass of fire was dangerous, and aircraft such as the He-111 bomber offered an all too easy target.

It was principally the air supply operations (which had to be carried out because of the adverse course of events on the ground) which were to become the ruin of the Luftwaffe. Air logistical undertakings such as those at Kholm, Demyansk, and finally Stalingrad (not one of which was really imperative from the point of view of military necessity and the last of which was the result of a tragically faulty decision) cost the Luftwaffe not only most of the Ju-52's, but a great many He-111's, a few He-177's, and certain other models which had been pressed into service as transports. A vast amount of highly valuable Luftwaffe materiel, including aircraft, was lost through the untimely advent of the Russian winter of 1941 and through the catastrophe which overtook Army Group Don in November of 1942, with the large-scale withdrawals and hasty evacuations which followed in its wake. Apart from a relatively short period during the spring, the year 1943 was characterized by a continual redeployment of forces, usually accompanied by a loss in territory. It was not always possible to carry out systematic, timely, and complete evacuation operations, and all of this became a serious headache for the Quartermaster General of the Luftwaffe.

The Russian theater, which Goering was so reluctant to enter with his Luftwaffe, turned out to be a land of costly sacrifices for both the Luftwaffe and for the Army. This situation was further aggravated by the fact that since the autumn of 1942 the enemy had gradually been winning air superiority in Africa and, after the successful Allied landings at Casablanca, Algiers, and Oran, in the entire Mediterranean as well. This led to particularly heavy losses for the German Air Force in Italy, where von Richthofen's last concentrated, large-scale operation for the purpose of throwing back the landing at Salerno (September 1943) failed in the face of superior Anglo-American air units. Thereafter, the Second Air Fleet was reduced to a feeble remnant of its former strength, and German air power in this theater of operations shrank to insignificance. The large Italian airfields at Foggia and elsewhere in southeastern Italy soon fell into enemy hands and shortly thereafter were in use as bases for American bomber wings for their harassing attacks on southern and southeastern Germany.

During 1943 the Allies penetrated ever more deeply into the home territory of the Reich, despite the fact that they often had to pay a heavy penalty in four-engine bomber losses at the hands of German fighters. This was the case in both of the attacks upon Schweinfurt. Nevertheless, it could no longer be denied that the once proud German Luftwaffe had entered a period of decline. Its numbers were too small to provide effective protection for the German armies in the East in their struggle against the relentless assaults of the Russian forces. Thrown into the invasion front with its hastily organized fighter reserves and freshly trained young pilots, it had hardly any chance of being able to relieve the ground forces in the face of the overwhelming enemy superiority. Its units were literally flying to their deaths, and knew it.

The German Luftwaffe was facing collapse—only a few years after it had gained a reputation as invincible. What happened?

2
The Command

THERE IS CONSIDERABLE TRUTH in a saying which was current in Germany after 1945 that in World War II Germany had "an Imperial Navy, a Prussian Army, and a National Socialist Air Force." The German Luftwaffe, a new branch of service, was composed of a greater number of younger officers than was true of either the Army or the Navy, but lacking the time-honored traditions and stability of the senior arms, it was from the first more receptive to the influence of Hitler and National Socialism.

During the Weimar period, the German Army, retaining the life-blood of the old Prussian Army, quietly reestablished itself as an instrument of national power, cautiously attempting to keep itself above the machinations of politics. The Navy pursued a similar course, assisted by the remoteness of its installations and a devotion to the principles of the old Imperial Navy. But the Luftwaffe, a new entity, was entrusted to the command of Hitler's closest Party associate, Hermann Goering, a man who was sufficiently ruthless and ambitious to secure preferential treatment for the air arm. Without question, Goering exercised tremendous influence in the Third Reich, especially upon those who were so casually associated with him that they could afford to be indulgent with respect to his weaknesses and vices. And there is no doubt but that in the early days of the German Air Force he provided the energy and drive that brought the Luftwaffe into the forefront as a full-fledged branch of the German Armed Forces and into a premier position among the world's air forces.

In the beginning the Luftwaffe was beset by problems stemming from a shortage of leaders. It was relatively simple to secure former fliers who yearned for the adventurous life in the air, but, without an institution comparable to the Army General Staff, it was difficult to find personalities capable of creating a "nerve center" to organize and administer the affairs of a great new service. This situation was resolved by transferring a number of Army General Staff officers to the Luftwaffe.

Of these officers, the most significant was Generalleutnant Walther Wever, a man still revered in German aviation circles. He was a person of great quickness and flexibility of mind, and a natural leader, but he was also devoted to Hitler and his ideas for a greater Reich. Wever's work for the German Air Force was terminated by his untimely death in 1936, so that he knew only the most favorable aspects of the Third Reich and saw only a bright future for the Luftwaffe, which he envisioned as a sword destined to strike a powerful blow for the future of Germany.

Following Wever's demise, the second and third officers taken from the Army (Colonels Albert Kesselring and Hans-Juergen Stumpff) succeeded, in turn, to Wever's post as Chief of the Luftwaffe General Staff. However, neither of them exerted a lasting influence upon it, and were, in short, merely interim Chiefs of the General Staff.

Along with Wever, four general officers immediately stand out as the most important and decisive personalities of the Luftwaffe: Goering, Erhard Milch, Ernst Udet, and Hans Jeschonnek. Their ideas and decisions were largely responsible for raising the Luftwaffe to a foremost position among the world's air forces, and their leadership, or lack of it, was likewise a major cause for the German Air Force's decline and fall. Three of these men committed suicide, one died in an air crash, and only one survived the war to live into retirement. Wever, of course, did not live to see the ominous future which lay ahead. Udet and Jeschonnek both experienced a shattering of their faith in German arms, in the eventual victory of National Socialism, and, betrayed and isolated by their associates, found it impossible to face what appeared to be a disastrous end. Goering early abdicated most of his responsibilities to the Luftwaffe by lapsing into a selfish epicurean existence, absorbed in the enjoyments of the gourmet and the art collector. At Nuremberg, after the war, he was still strongly impressed with the importance of his position and his fabulous honors, and continued to play the confident, and even blustering, Reichsmarschall. Mustering a defense that was cool, and at times even brilliant, he appeared more like the real Commander in Chief of the Luftwaffe than he had during most of the war itself. Although sentenced to death, he cheated the gallows by taking poison, leaving Milch as the sole survivor of the top echelon of the German Air Force.

German Air Force commanders became victims of self-deception. The surprising successes in Czechoslovakia (1939), and the blitz victories in Poland (1939) and in the West (1940), created an air of excessive optimism which completely obscured the sobering reality that the Luftwaffe had failed to establish itself in depth, to prepare organizationally and logistically for a long-term war, to mobilize the means of production, and to carry out a logical program of aircraft development.

Udet, a famous World War I ace, and an internationally renowned stunt pilot, was selected to head up the Luftwaffe's Technical Office and the Office of Supply and Procurement, but he lacked the prerequisites of training and personality which the job demanded. No one was more aware of this than Udet himself, who protested his appointment from the beginning. As his tasks rapidly expanded in scope, he became increasingly depressed with his inability to handle his massive and complicated assignment. Without adequate support from Goering, and deeply suspicious of the one man who could have been of assistance to him, Milch, his position became more and more untenable. The unsatisfactory outcome of the Battle of Britain and criticism of the Technical Office proved to be more than Udet could bear. Suicide seemed to be his only escape. Here, as in many other instances, Goering made no concerted effort to correct grave organizational and personnel problems, but preferred, instead, to allow one office to work against another.

Jeschonnek was the youngest General Staff Chief of any of the German services and a faithful devotee of Hitler and National Socialism. He failed to understand both the value of strategic air power and the inherent dangers from the air from the coalition of enemies ranged against Germany. He thus failed to provide for an adequate air defense organization. His exemplary conduct and adherence to all of the Prussian military virtues meant little in the face of his inability to properly assess the significant events and turning points in the war. A silent and bitter rivalry developed between him and Milch, which further hampered the operation of his office and delimited his influence. By 1942 he had also become the whipping boy of Goering, the frustrated Commander in Chief of the Luftwaffe. Still devoted to his Fuehrer, Jeschonnek found himself trapped between Hitler and a vindictive Goering, who was rapidly falling from grace. Burdened with the additional knowledge that he had failed to act correctly or decisively in numerous crucial situations, that the Luftwaffe had proved to be incapable of accomplishing its mission (especially after the disastrous Stalingrad airlift), and that Germany could not defend itself against the destructive Allied air attacks such as those of August 1943, he decided to end his life. Believing that his death would light the way to fresh thinking in the Luftwaffe High Command, he tragically proved once again that he was unable to clearly assess the situation and to draw the proper conclusions.

Until the collapse of Germany's air defenses in the period 1943-44, Milch united under his personal command all of the important officers of the Luftwaffe, with the exception of the General Staff and the Personnel Office, which remained within Goering's province. Milch was an energetic and able leader who brooked no interference with his policies. Because of this, as well as his great talents in the technical field, it was not surprising that his influence soon became so extensive that the General Staff was relegated to a minor role in Luftwaffe affairs. He was able to increase aircraft production and to streamline organization to some extent, but he could not hope to compensate for the many deficiencies of the Luftwaffe, some of which dated back to the 1930's. Even had he been able to accomplish such a task, it was impossible to do so during the course of a war which had grown out of all conceivable proportions. With his strong personality and his undoubted ambition, it was probably inevitable that he would eventually run counter to the domineering, but pleasure-addicted Goering, and even to Hitler. This resulted in his removal from office in 1944. Thereafter there was a futile attempt by the Luftwaffe General Staff to strengthen Germany's air defenses and to stabilize the Luftwaffe. This eleventh hour effort, despite amazing successes in certain areas, notably aircraft production, did little more than postpone the inevitable end.

In retrospect, it seems incredible that the Luftwaffe High Command could have presumed to defeat, let alone cope with, the great powers of the world. Obviously, Germany's supremely confident air leaders never envisioned any such prospect, nor did they allow themselves to speculate seriously about the possibility of a war of great dimensions. Instead, they moved rapidly along with the political leadership and the resulting flow of events, falling from one debacle into another, solving critical problems by improvising and scraping the barrel, without pausing for a sober consideration of the air force's proper role in a long-term, multi-front engagement. Even worse was their failure to act promptly and decisively in carrying out necessary modifications within the areas of organization, training, development, and production which could have given the Luftwaffe a chance to fulfill its mission within the framework of the Wehrmacht.

Behind these failures lay a mosaic of peculiar personalities, many of them possessing character weaknesses which hampered them during times of severe stress and crisis when sober and responsible action was imperative. As the war progressed, the Luftwaffe became filled with interdepartmental rivalries and strife, vicious intrigues, and an inordinate amount of currying of favor. Various factions lined up behind the individual whose cause they favored, or who seemed most likely to advance their own particular fortunes, taking the side of Goering, of Hitler against Goering, Milch or Jeschonnek against Goering, Udet against Milch, Milch against Jeschonnek, or Jeschonnek against Milch. Within Goering's headquarters there was the so-called "Little General Staff," a cabal of officers who issued Reichsmarschall orders, including matters pertaining to the Luftwaffe General Staff, without the knowledge or the assent of the Chief of Staff himself. Added to all of this was the almost unbelievable fact that in the closing days of the war, when Germany's back was to the wall and the nation required absolute internal solidarity, many of the Luftwaffe's leaders were avidly engaged in empire building and status seeking. Perhaps the best example of this was the rivalry for Goering's office in 1945, when there was virtually no longer any air force to command.

In 1933, after his party—the National Socialist—had come into power, Goering, the President of the National Parliament, was appointed to the position of National Commissioner of Aviation. It soon became obvious that this energetic man, who had been a successful fighter pilot during World War I, would not be content with directing the administration of Germany's commercial aviation alone. Those in a position to know were well aware of the fact that his goal was the establishment of an independent air force.

On 10 May 1933, the Reichs Minister of Defense announced that Paul von Hindenburg, President of the Reich, had authorized, on 27 April 1933, the establishment of an Air Ministry, to be under the National Defense Ministry. Thus, on 15 May 1933, the Air Defense Office and its staff moved from the Reichs Ministry of Defense to the Air Ministry.

Goering, a political revolutionary, realized instantly the potential significance of a strong and independent air force in a future war. In his capacity as Chief of the new Air Ministry, he did everything in his power to assure that all the resources available to the nation were fully exploited in order to build up a strong air force as rapidly as possible. President von Hindenburg conferred upon him the rank of an infantry general, so that he might possess the authority necessary to push through his plans for the new Armed Forces branch despite possible opposition from those of his own officers who came from the Army or Navy General Staffs. Unofficially, von Hindenburg's action was tantamount to his endorsement of the Luftwaffe as an independent Armed Forces branch, having the same rights and privileges as the other two.

During the period following its establishment on 15 May 1933, the Reichs Air Ministry assumed the functions of a Luftwaffe High Command for the units being activated under camouflage designation. The most important offices and branches of this Ministry, insofar as they were concerned with the activation and administration of the new Luftwaffe, were staffed by former General Staff officers taken over from the Army and, to a lesser extent, from the Navy. The mission assigned to these officers and their staffs was a challenge to their ability as military men, and a very rewarding one. Even the great General Staff itself had never been faced with a challenge of such scope during peacetime. The establishment of the Luftwaffe had literally to be undertaken from the ground up; the desultory preparations accomplished during the Reichswehr period were hardly worth mentioning. Thus the challenge could be met only with the untiring devotion of every single member of the staff and with smooth coordination with the other branches of the Armed Forces. These other branches, however, were also occupied with the preliminary preparations for enlarging the Armed Forces, and it was inevitable that conflicting interests often made coordination extremely difficult. The final reviewing authority, charged with the settlement of these differences of opinion, was the Reichs Minister of War; however, his Armed Forces Office, later the Armed Forces High Command, lacked the authority necessary to enforce its recommendations. Its role in these conflicts was that of an honest broker who does his best to see that each party receives its due. Thus, the inevitable arguments regarding strategic, organizational, and economic matters had to be settled at a lower echelon by discussions between the parties concerned and by their more or less sincere attempts to find a basis for agreement.

Throughout the period of preliminary preparations and up to the outbreak of the war, each Armed Forces branch had to depend pretty much upon its own initiative. During this period the Luftwaffe enjoyed comparative freedom in carrying out its plans, inasmuch as Hitler still had a great deal of confidence in Goering. The position of the Luftwaffe officers and their assistants, however, was not an easy one, for a certain amount of coordination with the other Armed Forces branches was inevitable. In fact, the heterogeneous composition of the Luftwaffe officer corps rendered its position very difficult during the conferences necessitated by this minimum coordination. The Luftwaffe negotiators were usually younger in point of time in rank than their Army and Navy colleagues, and for this reason were at a certain disadvantage. Whereas the insignia of the Army General Staff officers had an aura of traditional authority about it, the Luftwaffe officer had no special insignia of his own. Unless he was personally known to his Army colleagues, he could be assumed to belong to any one of the many categories represented in the Luftwaffe officer corps and thus was often treated with the disdain and irony commonly employed with up-starts. One should not generalize, of course, but on the other hand it is clear that this attitude made the negotiations with other Armed Forces branches, and especially with the Army, unnecessarily difficult.

Under these circumstances, it is not surprising that the Luftwaffe officers stemming from the Army General Staff, the younger ones par-ticularly, began to press for the establishment of an independent Luftwaffe General Staff with an insignia of its own, equal in impor-tance to that of the Army General Staff. It is possible, of course, that personal ambition may have played a role in isolated cases, but there can be no doubt that the motivating factor was the urgent desire to equate the status of the Luftwaffe to that of the other Armed Forces branches and thus to give it more influence in the joint planning and negotiations.

The Luftwaffe's desire for a general staff of its own met with bitter resistance on the part of Goering's deputy, Milch, the officers recruited from the commercial airlines, and the members of Goering's circle. They feared, quite correctly, that the formation of a Luftwaffe General Staff would mean a decrease of their own influence, for the older ones among them possessed neither the military training nor the mental agil-ity which would enable them to become members of such an elite staff. Inasmuch as the thoroughly trained, active Luftwaffe officers who had been taken over from the Army General Staff had, in any case, already moved into most of the key positions of the Reichs Air Ministry and the higher-level troop staffs, it was clear that their influence would grow even greater if they were granted the right to wear the traditional General Staff uniform and that they might well become annoying rivals to the reactivated and activated officers from other walks of life.

Wever, Chief of the Air Command Office, was also unenthusiastic at first regarding the formation of a Luftwaffe General Staff, chiefly be-cause he felt strongly that the homogeneity and unity of the Luftwaffe officer corps would be jeopardized unnecessarily by such a step. He feared that it might result in the development of a separate caste within the corps, which—in any event—was anything but homogeneous. It was his hope that the officers needed for missions of command and organi-zation might be recruited from the ranks of the outstanding pilots in the troop units, and he was convinced that this method of selection was best suited to the preservation of the indispensable mutual confidence between the front units and the command staffs. He ignored one important fact, however; it was precisely the best pilot personnel in the units who were the least ambitious for transfer to command staffs, especially since such transfer did not offer tangible compensation in the form of a distinctive uniform, preferential consideration for promotion, etc., as was traditional with the Army General Staff. Apart from this, the past—particularly the last war—had provided proof enough of the fact that personal courage and a talent for flying aircraft were not always an indication that their possessor also had the strength of character and the mental vision required for effective service in the responsible and often unrewarding positions within the Ministry or the command staffs.

The postwar writings of well-known fliers whose medals were considered (especially by Goering) to be sufficient qualification for service on the General Staff or in high-level command positions offer sufficient proof that leadership ability and military knowledge cannot always be adequately measured by decorations alone. The qualities which enable a man to function effectively in a higher position of command or on a general staff ordinarily presuppose years of military training and experience as well as a certain amount of worldly wisdom and personal maturity. The widespread disregard of this maxim within the Luftwaffe led not infrequently to orgies of dilettantism in Luftwaffe command agencies; Goering himself was an excellent example of this sort of thing. An officer corps capable of top-level performance is possible only if the method of selection guarantees the recruitment of the best officers, in point of strength of character, mental ability, and past performance, and if the training and orientation given them is of the type to assure homogeneity in their attitude towards their mission and in their accomplishment of it. Successful service in a troop unit is, in any case, an indispensable prerequisite.

Stumpff (later Generaloberst), Chief of the Personnel Office of the Luftwaffe and a recognized authority in questions pertaining to military personnel administration, was of the opinion that sooner or later the Luftwaffe would have to be given a general staff of its own. In his capacity as Chief of Personnel, he was fully aware of the fact that the choice of officers to fill higher-level Luftwaffe posts would become increasingly difficult without the preliminary orientation and selective elimination provided by a.general staff. Only by service on the general staff could the younger officer, who had already made his mark in combat, acquire the knowledge needed to apply his experience to the mission of command over large groups of forces. Experience had shown that the General Staff, itself composed of officers who had distinguished themselves in services at the front in World War I, provided the best opportunity for the development of a new generation of military leaders. There were sporadic exceptions, of course, but perhaps these served to prove the rule. The formation of a Luftwaffe General Staff also seemed imperative for another reason: the administration of such a complex and many-sided force as the highly technical Luftwaffe demanded the services of officers with thorough training in a large number of fields. The Luftwaffe technical people even submitted the suggestion—through the Chief of the Air Command Office—that a Technical General Staff be formed, because an officer trained in the field of military operations could not possibly possess the specialized technical knowledge necessary for effective accomplishment of the over-all mission.

Prior to 1936, however, the thinking in regard to these problems was largely theoretical, and they were far outweighed by other, more important problems connected with the establishment of the new Armed Forces branch. The officers most intimately concerned with them, particularly the Chief of the Air Command Office, were so busy with other tasks that they had neither the time nor the opportunity to give any thought to the future form of the command apparatus of the Luftwaffe. It was not until the induction of officer flying personnel completing their courses at the Army War Academy and a number of other officers without flight training of the class of 1936, who had volunteered for transfer to the Luftwaffe, that the question of their future assignment became acute. Their training for General Staff work and their future careers were matters which required an immediate solution. The question of the coming generations of officers was also one which needed thought, for it did not seem reasonable to continue sending Luftwaffe officer candidates to the Army War Academy for training; it was obvious that the training they received there could not be specialized enough to fit them for the highly specialized missions involved in the administration and command of the Luftwaffe.

For these reasons, the decision to create an Air War Academy ripened gradually during 1935. At the same time, plans were discussed for the founding of an Air Technical Academy in order to provide technically trained specialists within the Luftwaffe officer corps to take over the positions in the Reichs Air Ministry and in the command staffs which required familiarity with the technological aspects of the Luftwaffe.

Realizing that the establishment of these two academies would be pointless until a solution had been found for the problem of a Luftwaffe General Staff, Wever finally agreed to the preliminary planning necessary to set up such a staff. The difficulties experienced by officers from the Ministry and the Luftwaffe command staffs during negotiations with the other two branches of the Armed Forces, and with civilian agencies, certainly influenced his decision, as did the persistent efforts of Milch and Goering's personal circle to increase their own influence and to eclipse those Luftwaffe officers who had been taken over from the Army General Staff. Thoughtful and responsible Luftwaffe officers all saw in these efforts a serious danger for the development of the new force, which could be made into an effective military instrument for the defense of the nation only if it could be kept free of intrigue and from undue influence on the part of civilian and political circles. The only possibility seemed to be the creation of a firmly established command apparatus akin to the Army General Staff.

Goering, his own opinion wavering from one moment to the next, finally allowed himself to be persuaded by the arguments of the Luftwaffe officers. The thought that his own prestige among the public and among his fellow Commanders in Chief would be greatly enhanced by the presence in his entourage of general staff officers in their distinctive uniforms certainly played just as important a role in his final decision as his recognition of the military necessity of establishing a Luftwaffe General Staff.

Wever, the man who created the Luftwaffe General Staff and who must be considered its first—although anonymous—Chief, was not destined to witness the birth of his intellectual child; he was killed shortly before in an air crash which occurred during a routine troop inspection trip.

The order for the formation of the Luftwaffe General Staff was issued to become effective on 1 August 1936.

The Luftwaffe's top-level command adapted itself well to existing conditions until 1937-38. It is true that Goering, burdened with a plethora of other offices and duties, often had to withdraw from active participation in the affairs of the Luftwaffe—which he termed "his" service—but at such times he was very adequately represented by his permanent deputy, Milch. At no time during its history did the Luftwaffe command organization function so smoothly and with such unity of purpose as under the aegis of Goering during his most energetic period. The death, on 3 June 1936, of Wever (first chief of the Luftwaffe General Staff) marked the beginning of hostilities between Milch and the Luftwaffe General Staff, the latter chafing under the solicitous interference to which Milch, as Goering's permanent representative, felt himself not only entitled but obliged.

The Luftwaffe General Staff championed a kind of equality of authority to begin with, although it is likely that its ultimate goal was the exclusive right of command within its own organization, which means that the Chief of the General Staff—and not Milch—would have become Goering's permanent deputy. There was undeniably something to be said for this plan, but its realization was bound to involve a struggle with Milch who, after all, was already in possession of the deputyship. Since there could be no thought of deposing Milch because of incompetence, and since he was by no means a man of submissive character, the struggle was inevitably a long and hard one. Goering, as Reichs Air Minister, may have interpreted the struggle between Milch and the Chief of the General Staff as no more than healthy opposition; in any case, the solution which he decided upon to end the conflict was the worst possible one, because it was no more than a half measure; its only virtue being that it was the easiest solution and made the least trouble for Goering himself. He made the General Staff directly subordinate to himself, as he did later on with a number of Luftwaffe offices, and restricted Milch's permanent deputyship—which would have given the latter both insight into General Staff policies and a certain degree of influence over them—to those periods when he was himself absent from the Ministry.

Neither protagonist was satisfied with Goering's solution; they subsided into a relationship of grudging cooperation, and the silent struggle for top authority continued. Fearful of losing still more of his influence, Milch tried to strengthen his position by taking over first the office of the Inspector General (in 1939) and then (in 1941) the office of the Chief of Luftwaffe Procurement and Supply. His efforts were doomed to failure, however, and as the war progressed, he was forced to watch his position—both as State Secretary and as Inspector General—crumble into insignificance until 1944, when, in the words of Generaloberst Loerzer (Goering's friend and Luftwaffe Chief of Personnel from 1943 to 1944), the once all-powerful deputy was "organized out" of the Luftwaffe. With this the General Staff had finally gained its victory, but there was little cause for rejoicing for by this time the final defeat of the Luftwaffe had already begun, and one of the factors bringing about this defeat was surely the lack of inner unity in the ranks of the Luftwaffe's top commanders.

Quite apart from the friction and uncertainty which it caused, the end effect of Goering's reorganization was to leave the Luftwaffe without a leader. For he had weakened Milch's position without increasing his own participation in Luftwaffe affairs. His old, easy life continued; in fact, as time went on, it became easier. He no longer held the reins firmly, but took hold of them gingerly and only when he happened to be in the mood.

Lack of leadership is one of the worst evils which can befall a military organization. This is just as true in peacetime, and laxity then may well give rise to wartime defeat. During wartime, lack of leadership is an almost certain guarantee of failure.

Within the Luftwaffe the lack of firm leadership spread like a slow poison. It showed in the failure to plan and—even more—to carry through systematic programs of air armament, pilot training, and personnel assignment; and it was revealed ultimately in the total lack of any consistent delineation of the role of leadership itself. For the most part, as time went on, the concept of command gradually degenerated into mere administration. No body of authority, but least of all a military one, can afford this sort of degeneration.

It was without doubt one of the factors contributing to the demise of the Luftwaffe.

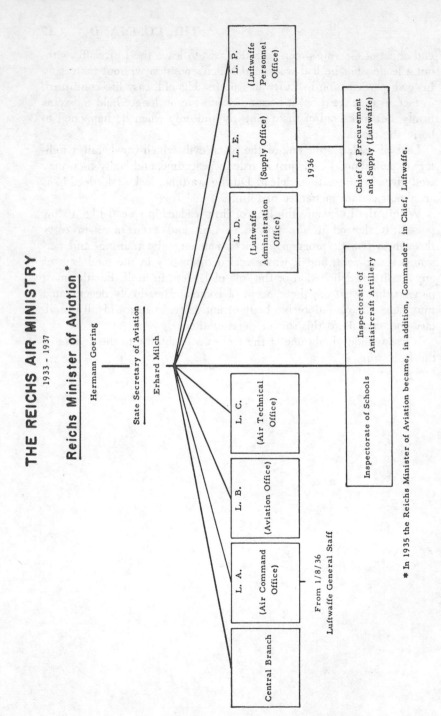

THE REICHS AIR MINISTRY
1933 - 1937

Reichs Minister of Aviation *

Hermann Goering

State Secretary of Aviation

Erhard Milch

Central Branch

L. A.
(Air Command Office)

L. B.
(Aviation Office)

L. C.
(Air Technical Office)

From 1/8/36
Luftwaffe General Staff

L. D.
(Luftwaffe Administration Office)

L. E.
(Supply Office)

L. P.
(Luftwaffe Personnel Office)

1936

Chief of Procurement and Supply (Luftwaffe)

Inspectorate of Schools

Inspectorate of Antiaircraft Artillery

* In 1935 the Reichs Minister of Aviation became, in addition, Commander in Chief, Luftwaffe.

FIGURE 1

ORGANIZATION OF THE REICHS MINISTER OF AVIATION AND COMMANDER IN CHIEF, LUFTWAFFE

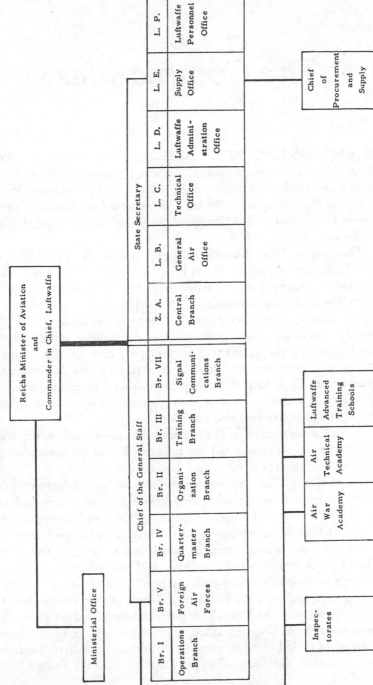

FIGURE 2

3
The Commanders

IF FACTORS CANNOT BE ALTERED, they assume the proportions of fate. If one has only a certain sum of money, for example, one cannot use it to buy something which costs three times as much, even if one's life depends upon it. Similarly, if a man is born blind one cannot expect him to have a clear concept of the phenomena of color and artistic form.

The human being himself represents one such unalterable, and therefore, "fate-ful" factor. He is like the leopard who cannot change his spots no matter how much he would like to have the stripes of a tiger! The inclinations and talents inherited by each individual, molded by the training he receives during his formative years, or by the traditional mores of his chosen profession, are determining factors throughout his life. For this reason it is tremendously difficult, if not impossible, to guide men into directions opposed to their own inclinations, to expect them to perform tasks they have never learned, or, once they have formed a clear opinion of their own, to try to convince them of the rightness of someone else's opinion.

Every human institution has to cope with factors such as the above, and the greater the scope and the responsibility of the institution, the greater their chances of exerting a lasting influence.

The Luftwaffe had more than its share of human factors to cope with, far more than the other two service branches. It lacked completely the decades of formative experience which had created a certain type of individual for the Army, for example. The Luftwaffe had to be called into being almost overnight, and it had to be built from scratch. The top-level organization formed during World War I—not very large to begin with—had disintegrated completely. And the new group of leaders entrusted with the buildup of Germany's air force lacked that sense of tradition which develops automatically with long service in a particular branch. Goering, Milch, and—later on—Udet were originally assigned to their Luftwaffe posts on an almost provisional basis. It is true, of course, that those officers transferring from the Army (Wever,

Kesselring, Stumpff, and General der Flieger Karl Kitzinger) brought certain traditional attitudes with them; even so, service on the Luftwaffe staff was something quite new for all of them, and they had much to learn about flying and aviation in general before they could become fully effective.

It is clear that the fate of the Luftwaffe was inextricably interwoven with the personal qualifications and backgrounds of these men, who were placed in charge of it with little or no preparation at a time when it was not even an independent service, at a time, in fact, when all preparations for an air arm had to be carried out in strictest secrecy. The most immediate concern is with the men in the two highest posts, Goering and his deputy, Milch. Both had retired from military service when the old German Air Force was disbanded at the end of World War I. Then, after fourteen years of bourgeois life, they found themselves suddenly in charge of their old service. Obviously, both lacked the middle phase of military experience, the long years between captain and colonel.

Both of these men retained their roles as "inalterable factors" for the Luftwaffe until almost the very end, and the various facets of their individual personalities had much to do with determining the fate of the new service branch. The degree of authority wielded by the leaders of the Luftwaffe corresponded more closely to the authoritarian concepts of the Third Reich than did that in either of the other two services, and because of this their personal idiosyncrasies could exert a far greater influence than would have been possible within the firmly-defined, more broadly-based, and deeply traditional structure of the Army and its General Staff.

Over and above the rest of the personalities whose influence made itself felt within the Luftwaffe was the figure of Hitler himself, whose personal influence on the top-level air leaders was tremendous. Though enormously important, the role he played does not lend itself to objective definition; yet it must be taken into account as one of the factors contributing to the final defeat of the Luftwaffe in order to understand the full implications of the small, individual turning points which preceded it.

Almost until the last day of the Luftwaffe's existence, Goering was its Commander in Chief. More than any other man, he embodied its fate.

It was Goering's personality—forceful, supremely self-confident, and energetic—which determined the development of the Luftwaffe, partic-

Can there be any doubt but that these personalities alone harbored the seeds of the disaster to come?

What was the connection of these personality factors to the events of the war itself?

In the first place, the Luftwaffe, as the weapons systems destined to bear the brunt of the war without respite from the beginning to the end, was from its founding until its disintegration deprived of the firmly formative spirit of a Commander in Chief sincerely concerned for the welfare of his men. Those pilots who actually got to see and talk with Goering, especially those received by him at Karinhall, went away with a feeling of uneasiness rather than confidence. Goering's hand grew progressively weaker as the demands made upon the Luftwaffe increased. The greater the need for firm leadership, the more conspicuously was it lacking. The weakness of Goering's position was further augmented by his arrogance, which made it impossible for him to cooperate effectively with the leaders of the Army. For example, when the Luftwaffe was ordered to release some of its superfluous ground organization personnel to the Army, Goering made certain that they could not be utilized to fill up the depleted divisions on the Russian front. He was determined at all costs to retain his authority over these men. As a result, they were hurriedly trained for infantry combat in which they had had no experience whatever, and committed by unit in actions which led to their rapid and complete decimation. If they had been integrated into an experienced Army division, they could have learned their trade better and might have avoided total annihilation. As it was, Goering's stubbornness destroyed a chance to increase the striking power of the German Army by reinforcing it with well-trained soldiers who could have replaced the heavy personnel losses in the noncommissioned officer ranks.

Nor can Jeschonnek be absolved of blame. His chief mistake was his stubborn refusal to see, until it was too late, the danger threatening Germany from the air and to recognize the significance of the four-engine bombers being developed by the enemy. The obstinacy which revealed itself in his inflexible faith in the dive-bomber made him insist for far too long on the development of aircraft with good diving performance. In tragic contradiction of his truly excellent military ability and his fine personal qualities, this youthful General Staff Chief precipitated the Luftwaffe into a serious crisis.

It was largely Udet's fault that Germany's air armament program was so inadequate during the fatal first years of the war. In later times the Reichsmarschall, although hardly qualified to express an opinion on the matter, denounced him bitterly for his failure. This tragic error, for which Udet was technically responsible, was largely the result of the helplessness of this really very fine man in the face of a position for which he was not fitted. He was incapable of mastering the intrigues and rivalries which ran riot in the air armament industry; indeed, he seemed incapable of even recognizing them for what they were. A man who shrank from ruthless action, he was simply unable to keep industry in line. In addition, he lacked the ability to evaluate the capacities of his fellowmen and to surround himself with those who would be of most use to him in his work. He was deeply interested in the developmental phase of air armament and displayed unusual insight and practical originality in this field; unfortunately, he never succeeded in acquiring equal interest and understanding for the problems of procurement.

The war was a matter of life or death for Germany. The leaders of the Luftwaffe, however, were anything but a dedicated community; not even the General Staff itself was capable of unity of purpose. And throughout the entire course of the war we find no sign of any attempt to do away with the rivalries and intrigues which were bound, in time, to poison the effectiveness of all concerned in them. Udet's suicide, which might have been avoided if he had been given the chance to function in an atmosphere of comradely loyalty, was a foregone conclusion under the existing circumstances. And his death was soon to be followed by the suicide—just as inevitable—of Jeschonnek.

The effects which these suicides must have had upon the spirit of the Luftwaffe leaders and upon their faith in an ultimate victory must be considered. In both cases every possible step was taken to hush up the manner of death, but in both cases the truth managed to leak out. And the truth could hardly have been very encouraging.

There is no choice but to conclude that the personality factors inherent in the leadership of the Luftwaffe bore the seeds of eventual disaster.

The order for the formation of the Luftwaffe General Staff became effective on 1 August 1936, and the following men became Chiefs of the General Staff.

WEVER

On 15 May 1933, when the Air Defense Office was transferred from the National Defense Ministry to the Reichs Air Ministry, General-major Walther Wever became Chief of the Air Command Office in the new Ministry. Inasmuch as this office was charged with the administration of all questions concerning the command, organization, and training of the new Luftwaffe, it was natural that it should assume the functions of a general staff right from the beginning.

Thus, even though he did not have the official title, Wever, as Chief of the Air Command Office, was really the first Chief of the Luftwaffe General Staff. In this man, the Minister of National Defense had selected one of the very best officers—and probably the best organizer—of the Army General Staff to guide the establishment of the Luftwaffe. Without wishing to belittle Goering's contribution in any way, it must be admitted that all of his plans would have been amateurish piecework without the outstanding assistance of Wever and his immediate staff.

Greeting his new assignment with enthusiasm, Wever devoted his full attention to the new mission with typical zeal. His quick intelligence, his remarkable receptiveness towards the developments of modern technology, and his vast store of military experience soon enabled him to grasp the fundamental concepts of his mission. He worked untiringly to exploit the unusually favorable circumstances provided by the time in order to create a military instrument equal to the other Armed Forces branches for the defense of the nation. He was quick to realize that the chance given him was a unique one, and that he might take advantage of all the available national and economic resources in creating a new and unique force. He himself learned to fly at the age of forty-six and soon became one of the most enthusiastic pilots in the Luftwaffe; in this, as in other fields, he set a challenging example to young and old.

Wever got along extremely well with Goering, his Commander in Chief, since both were imbued with a passionate belief in their mission and with a fiery enthusiasm for the new Luftwaffe. His relations with Milch, to whom he was subordinate, were also good, despite their occasional differences of opinion. By dint of exemplary tact and a willingness to remain in the background on many occasions, Wever was able to avoid serious friction.

An exemplary superior to his immediate staff, he had no difficulty in infecting them with his own enthusiasm and in persuading them unobtrusively of the validity of his own thinking. Whenever he had a free moment, he was off in his airplane to inspect units being formed and those already in existence in all the various branches of his Luftwaffe. He rarely neglected to bring along a huge box of cake when inspecting a remotely-located air base, and over coffee and cake with the young crew members, he discussed their problems with them, listened to their suggestions, and fired them anew with his own enthusiasm and élan. In this way he soon succeeded in inspiring the troop units as well as his own personal staff to extraordinary accomplishments and to ardent devotion to their work.

Wever's death on 3 May 1936 was a tremendous blow to his officers and men alike. With the loss of its first Chief of the General Staff, the Luftwaffe lost the first, and perhaps the most decisive battle of World War II.

KESSELRING

Wever's untimely death left a deep gap which no other officer could fill adequately—not even such an outstandingly capable one as Kesselring. Kesselring, as Chief of the Administration Office, had done an excellent job during the early period of establishment of the Luftwaffe, and now Goering appointed him Chief of the General Staff as Wever's successor.

The close and comradely coordination existing among the top officers of the Reichs Air Ministry, whom Wever had welded together into an effective team, assured that each one was well informed regarding the functions of the others and their common overall goal. This situation can also be regarded as an indication of the effectiveness of service on the General Staff as a factor in creating consistency of concept and action. As a result, the organization functioned like a machine which continues its work automatically, even though a new operator has replaced the old. The growth of the Luftwaffe proceeded without interruption, despite the change in personnel at the top of the General Staff; the new Chief, hardworking and tremendously energetic, devoted himself to the accomplishment of the plans developed by his predecessor.

Like his predecessor, Kesselring made every effort to maintain a close association with the troop units. This was not difficult for him, inasmuch as he had always been an extremely popular superior during his assignment as Chief of the Administration Office. Whenever he appeared on inspection visits in that capacity, piloting his own aircraft, and inquired after the needs and wants of the troops, they could be sure that he would do anything in his power to help them. His relations with his colleagues, his subordinate officers, and the members of the troop units were characterized by the warmth and the heartfelt benevolence typical of him. These qualities assured him of the sincere and undivided devotion of his comrades and subordinates, a devotion which persists to this very day.

Although his activity as Chief of the General Staff bore valuable fruit, and his popularity among his subordinates on the General Staff and among Luftwaffe troop personnel remained undiminished, Kesselring's relations with Milch grew progressively more difficult. Milch employed every means at his disposal to maintain—and, if possible, to increase—his influence over the new General Staff. It was inevitable that Milch's efforts in this direction should incur the opposition of a man with Kesselring's strength of personality, and the latter's personal feelings and attitudes led to adamant refusal to accept Milch's interference. In the long run, however, Kesselring was no match for Milch's smooth dialectic and methods, and on 30 May 1937 Kesselring requested that he be relieved as Chief of the General Staff.

STUMPFF

Prior to his appointment by Goering as Kesselring's successor, Generalmajor Hans Juergen Stumpff (later General der Flieger) had been Chief of the Luftwaffe Personnel Office. In that capacity, he had accomplished wonders and had more than justified his reputation as one of the Armed Forces foremost experts in matters of personnel administration. He had solved the problems connected with his mission in an exemplary fashion, and the importance of his contribution cannot be overestimated. The entire future of the Luftwaffe depended upon the quality of its officer corps; no troop can be better than its officers. When

Stumpff took office as Chief of the Luftwaffe Personnel Office, he had at his disposal only 200 active officers from the 100,000-man Army (Reichswehr) on which to build a Luftwaffe officer corps. During the early years, a certain number of Army replacement officers were detached to the Luftwaffe until the Luftwaffe had built up an adequate reserve of its own. Stumpff had had to recruit the majority of his officers, however, from the ranks of the sporting pilots, the pilots of commercial airlines, World War I fliers, and other inactive officers, and had had to try to fit the special capabilities of each individual recruit into the complicated mosaic of the new force. His success in doing so is all the more remarkable when we consider that Stumpff was unable to pilot an airplane when he was assigned to the Luftwaffe. He had to acquire an understanding for the peculiar requirements of an air force from the ground up, and in addition to this, he even learned to fly himself at a fairly advanced age.

Stumpff's mission as Chief of the Luftwaffe General Staff was a particularly difficult one. To become the follower of two such intense personalities as Wever and Kesselring, at a time when the Luftwaffe was still in its formative stage, was certainly no easy task for a man who had been exclusively occupied with matters of personnel administration up to that time. Stumpff's need to familiarize himself with the fundamental requirements of his new task left him little time to devote to the establishment of a personal relationship with the troop units, as had been the case with both his predecessors. Another source of difficulty was the continual disagreements with Milch, which were becoming increasingly bitter. Moreover, the time had come when the Luftwaffe had expanded to such a degree that a reorganization of the Ministry seemed urgently necessary. Thus, during the period 1937-39 there were a number of reorganizations, some of them coming in very close sequence, within the Reichs Air Ministry, accompanied by shifts in the responsibilities of the State Secretary and the Chief of the General Staff. These frequent organizational upheavals were bound to have a detrimental effect on the work of the General Staff as well as on the performance of the troop units.

After several attempts by Stumpff to find a solution commensurate with the problem at hand, Milch brought forth a contemplated organizational structure which was clearly incapable of meeting the military requirements involved. This continual struggle for authority finally decided Stumpff, in the best interests of the cause, to let his own position as Chief of the General Staff be relegated to the background and to recognize Milch as the permanent representative of the Commander in Chief.

When it became clear that even this concession had failed to improve the relations between the State Secretary and the Chief of the General Staff, Stumpff requested reassignment, to become effective on 30 January 1939. The systematic progress made in the development of the Luftwaffe during Stumpff's period as Chief of the General Staff must be considered all the more praiseworthy in view of the fact that it was accomplished in spite of internal difficulties and their deleterious influence on the conduct of business.

JESCHONNEK

Jeschonnek, Chief of the Operations Staff, was named as Stumpff's successor. Kesselring has the following to say concerning him:

> During the war years, the most impressive personality among the Chiefs of the General Staff was Generaloberst Jeschonnek—an unusually intelligent and energetic person. Even Jeschonnek, however, was not strong enough to oppose Goering successfully (occasionally he did succeed in opposing Hitler) in matters of decisive importance. A very definite lack of harmony brought effective coordination to a standstill.

The following passage by the historian Walter Goerlitz sheds further light on the situation:

> In February 1939, Colonel Hans Jeschonnek, former Commanding Officer of the Luftwaffe Training Wing (Lehrgeschwader) and Chief of the Operations Branch (Operationsabteilung) of the General Staff, became the fourth Chief of the Luftwaffe General Staff. Jeschonnek, the favored protégé of General Wever, was truly a representative of the younger generation, extremely gifted, of quick and dependable intelligence, precise in his thinking, a man of few personal wants, but driven by an all-consuming ambition to achieve recognition for his service branch, the Luftwaffe. He was more of a soldier than a staff man, however. He lacked the ability to handle people, an indispensable quality for anyone who was to maintain himself in the face of Hitler's self-glorification, Goering's moodiness, the tangle of intrigues, and the continual rivalry which were the rule at the Fuehrer's Headquarters.

The brilliant career of Jeschonnek serves as a barometer for the meteoric growth of the German Luftwaffe; at the same time, it is an individual expression of the contribution made by this talented young officer whose tragedy lay in his youth. His contributions to the training of Luftwaffe officers, the equipment of the Luftwaffe along modern technological lines, and the development of the Luftwaffe into an effective striking instrument were undeniably great. The remarkable success of the Luftwaffe, in coordination with the Army, during the early blitz campaigns of World War II was due largely to his work. The preparation and orientation of the bomber and dive-bomber wings for their missions in these campaigns were matters to which he gave his personal attention. He shared Hitler's conviction that, if Germany should go to war, she could attain success only if that war were brought to a rapid conclusion.

Jeschonnek's youth was a decided disadvantage in his relations with Goering. Even though the latter gave full recognition to the character and ability of his Chief of the General Staff, the younger man unconsciously created in Goering a feeling of inferiority which made him hesitate to seek his advice. As a result, Goering often made important decisions lightly without consulting his General Staff Chief in advance regarding their feasibility. This led to frequent serious disagreements between the two men, and the effect upon the performance of the troops was anything but salutary. Since Jeschonnek lacked the personal qualities needed to gain his own way in the face of his superior's often amateurish decisions, there was nothing for him to do but to accept the destructive consequences created by them.

Jeschonnek's difficulties arose from Goering's penchant for taking things into his own hands and from Hitler's unrealistic demands for Luftwaffe support of Army operations, and both of these factors played a role in weakening the Luftwaffe and in hastening its final decline. After the bloody action at Stalingrad, which—according to reports of the Military History Branch, Luftwaffe General Staff—Jeschonnek had not approved, he foresaw clearly the tragic end of coming developments and preferred to end his own part in them by taking his life on 19 August 1943.

KORTEN

Another relatively young officer, General der Flieger Guenther Korten, Commanding General of the First Air Fleet, was named as Jeschonnek's successor. There were not many younger generals available from whom to choose. On the other hand, Goering did not want an older officer as Chief of the General Staff, since his confidence in his own authority was too precarious to enable him to deal with an older, more experienced man, especially one with a strong personality. In Korten, he had a General Staff Chief who was not only an efficient General Staff officer but who also possessed a winning personality, which augured well for his relations with Hitler, the Armed Forces High Command, and other Armed Forces branches, and his subordinate Luftwaffe commanders. And in this respect, Korten certainly lived up to his promise. On 25 August 1943, he took over his difficult assignment.

When it is considered that disorganization and deterioration were already widespread within the Luftwaffe at the time Korten took office, and that it is extremely difficult, under conditions such as these, for anyone to step unexpectedly into an entirely new position, it is no wonder that the new General Staff Chief required a certain amount of time to work into his new job. Then too, the industry and perseverance needed for this task were not his strong point, although he did possess a certain degree of gifted intuition. Today, one cannot be sure whether Korten was consciously aware of the coming catastrophe and its significance for the Luftwaffe. It is certain, however, that he was unable to effect any fundamental changes directed towards a thoroughgoing reform—if, indeed, he had any plans of this sort. From the vantage point of the present, it is impossible to determine whether or not radical action on Korten's part would have been able to avert the catastrophe. In any case, the conspiracy of 20 July 1944 brought his career to a sudden end when he was killed by the bomb intended for Hitler. Thus, the post of Chief of the Luftwaffe General Staff was vacant again, and the feverish search for a new incumbent began.

By this time, it was clear that there were very few officers acceptable to Goering from whom to choose a new General Staff Chief. An additional difficulty, however, was that none of those who came under consideration was willing to accept this unrewarding post under the difficult conditions attached to it.

KREIPE

It is illustrative of the psychological attitude of the Luftwaffe officer corps at that time that Goering encountered such a great difficulty in finding anyone who was interested in the position, which, after all, was one of the highest the Armed Forces offered. Finally, Generalleutnant Werner Kreipe declared his willingness to accept the post. Kreipe was one of the youngest generals in the Luftwaffe and had a varied career, at the front and in General Staff positions, behind him. It seems certain that he could have become an excellent General Staff Chief if he had had the proper support from his Commander in Chief. Without this support, however, he was far too young to have any influence on the ruling clique at the Fuehrer's Headquarters, or to combat effectively the growing influence of the generals in Goering's personal circle. These generals insisted on having their say on anything and everything, but not a single one of them possessed anywhere near the qualifications needed for the General Staff Chief's position.

Kreipe's activity as Chief of the Luftwaffe General Staff came to an end just seven weeks after his appointment on 1 August 1944. His attempt to pit his strength against that of Hitler and Goering, especially in the matter of increased home air defense forces, was a failure. He had overestimated his chances and, after a heated argument with Hitler on 19 September 1944, the latter decided that Kreipe's services as Chief of the Luftwaffe General Staff were no longer wanted, and he was forced to submit his resignation.

KOLLER

It was tragic for the Luftwaffe General Staff—and, indeed, for the entire command organization of the Luftwaffe—that it was not until 12 November 1944 that Goering was able to find an officer, acceptable to himself, who was willing to take over the orphaned position. During the interim period, Generalleutnant Karl Koller, Chief of the Luftwaffe Operations Staff, was placed in provisional charge of the duties of the General Staff Chief, and on 12 November 1944, he was officially assigned to that position, which he was to hold until the end of the War.

Koller was an exemplary General Staff officer, and as the chief assistant of the General Staff Chief (in his capacity as Chief of the Operations Staff), he had rendered invaluable service. He lacked one very important qualification for the Chief's post, however—experience with the troops in the field. Ever since he had left the Air War Academy, where his tremendous zeal enabled him to graduate at the head of his class, he had not had a single day of service in the field. This, of course, was not his fault, but the fact remained that he much preferred service in an office, and he was an acknowledged master of the intricacies of such service. A Bavarian by birth, he did not hesitate to resort to fundamental four-letter words to emphasize a point. However, neither his military ability nor his personality was firm enough to achieve any fundamental reforms in the Luftwaffe, let alone to defend such reforms before Hitler and Goering.

Thus, the fate of the Luftwaffe ran its course; the young force never succeeded in finding a personality of the magnitude of its first General Staff Chief, Wever, to meet the challenge of guiding it through its greatest hour of trial.

4
The Role of Goering

HERMANN GOERING, the first, and for all practical purposes, the only Commander in Chief of the German Air Force, has come to personify the early and almost meteoric rise of the Luftwaffe, and then, almost as abruptly, its sudden decline and ruin.

In November 1922, at a political demonstration in Munich, Goering saw Hitler for the first time. Two days later he attended a meeting of Hitler adherents, and from this time on both he and his wife, Karin, were sworn disciples of this rising political star. Goering called upon the Party leader and placed his services at his disposal. Hitler then fascinated him with an explanation of the quintessence of his program, and Goering, who had recognized no authority but that of the Emperor as the personification of the State, was captivated and became his loyal follower until his death. Hitler entrusted him with the leadership of the *Sturmabteilung* (Storm Troops or SA).

Goering's status as a captain of the old Army and winner of the Pour le Mérite, and the aura which then distinguished any flier, but especially a fighter pilot, his imposing and congenial bearing, the social position he apparently occupied, all made him welcome and useful to Hitler and his young National Socialist Party. The Nazis were only too eager to acquire well-known adherents, and to have been an officer was a factor of considerable importance in Germany after 1918. In his struggle for power, Hitler made frequent and clever use of individuals who were capable of bringing a measure of prestige and influence into the Party. It is therefore likely that in 1922 Hitler may in a sense even have looked up to Goering.

It is difficult to describe the qualities which Goering possessed. His personality was a mixture of benevolence and warmth, slyness and self-assurance, with a touch of arrogance which was just as unconscious as it was accepted by others. All of these qualities together created an aura of superiority which, incredible as it may seem, exerted a powerful attraction upon those with whom he came into contact. As the Nazi Party increased in strength and importance, the figure of Goering (who was hardly the type to remain modestly behind the scenes) emerged into the limelight.

Together with Hitler, who was appointed Reichs Chancellor on the morning of 30 January 1933, his paladin was also carried to the top by the general wave of success. On the same day Goering was named Reichs Minister, Reichs Commissioner of Aviation, and Minister of the Interior for Prussia. He was appointed Minister President of Prussia (Prime Minister) on 11 January.

Soon Goering became the recipient of a veritable plethora of offices. His position of influence in Prussia, where he organized a Provincial Council over which he (naturally) presided, gave him the key to power over all of Germany. Soon he was a fully accredited Minister by virtue of his appointment as Reichs Commissioner of Aviation, an office which was expanded on 1 May 1933 into the Reichs Aviation Ministry. He was also Reichs Minister of Forestry and Reichs Commissioner of Hunting, the only two functions which this overburdened official carried out with any genuine interest and devotion to the very last. On 30 August 1933, the weakening von Hindenburg let himself be persuaded by Goering (whom he already knew from the negotiations of 1930, 1931, and 1932 to have been a main supporter of Hitler) to confer upon him the rank of General der Infanterie. In this way, the holder of the Pour le Mérite, who had been only a captain, and a young captain at that, in 1918, jumped five ranks in one promotion. Having an Army general's rank also gave him standing among the senior officers of the Reichswehr.

As soon as the veil of secrecy could be lifted from the growing Luftwaffe, Goering was styled General der Flieger, and on 1 April 1936 was promoted to Generaloberst. Following the rather shameful overthrow and expulsion of Field Marshal Werner von Blomberg as War Minister, Goering was appointed a Field Marshal of the Luftwaffe on 4 February 1938. This made him the senior Wehrmacht general from a point of rank, a state of affairs which defied all of the traditional axioms of military promotion.

He was considered the number two man in Germany even by representatives of foreign countries. They considered him the most important associate of the Fuehrer and regarded him as a man of compelling power in his own right. Goering understood this and knew how to deal with these envoys. His name, his activity, and his orders were known throughout the country, and Hitler had been well aware of this when he entrusted to him the great task of building up the Luftwaffe.

There is no doubt that Goering approached his new task with genuine interest, especially since it was a task which he had long envisioned as his own project. In the beginning of this venture, just as had been the case when he had become Prime Minister of Prussia, Goering displayed an amazing amount of energy, and as Reichs Minister of Aviation was able to exercise a highly favorable effect upon the young Luftwaffe. "He was always at his best under pressure," recalls Kesselring, "when the rest of us were completely exhausted, and was still able to go on."

This was the happiest period in Goering's life, as he saw his air force growing daily in strength and poise. His success in winning capable persons for the Luftwaffe during 1933 and 1934 was never repeated to the same extent thereafter. During these years he was able to bring his personality to bear in all respects, infusing his colleagues and subordinates with enthusiasm and élan, and the men who had been working for the advancement of German aviation in the Reichswehr Ministry had the satisfaction of seeing the goals for which they had struggled in vain suddenly achieved, apparently with the ease of a flick of the wrist. Most significant was the fact that the Luftwaffe was approved as an independent branch of the Wehrmacht. Goering, through his speeches, had turned Germany into a nation of air enthusiasts.

In his capacity as Reichs Minister of Aviation, Goering was a colleague of the Reichs War Minister and the Reichs Finance Minister, which inevitably served to elevate the status of the Luftwaffe High Command (which was actually subordinate to the Reichs War Ministry). Goering's other governmental offices, and his personality, which refused to recognize any authority but Hitler, created a position of predominance which even von Blomberg's promotion to field marshal was unable to jeopardize. Whenever Goering's staff was unable to find a way to push through Luftwaffe requests for funds, the Commander in Chief of the Luftwaffe would say, "Give that stuff to me!" Soon afterwards he was invariably able to bring Wever the necessary approval from the top, from Hitler himself. "Here it is," Goering would say, "the Fuehrer is surprised that we're so modest. He expected us to ask for a lot more. Incidentally, once and for all, money is no object! Remember that!" How could the Reichs Minister of Finance, no matter how horrified he might have been at the magnitude of such requests, be expected to refuse his signature when Hitler had already given his approval?

Goering, whose forceful personality indisputably made him the creator of the Luftwaffe, was a firm believer in the teachings of Douhet, and insisted upon such a broad demand for equipment and such a rapid expansion of the air forces that his colleagues in the Reichswehr Ministry and in the War Ministry were appalled. Goering was the driving force behind the air arm, and he was the person with whom other military leaders had to contend. Although Stumpff and Kesselring stress Goering's role in devising the ideals of the buildup period, his main contribution to this early period lay in the domineering force of his personality and its impact upon associates and subordinates. The "Iron Man" was clearly an imposing individual with his impressive bearing, portly frame, his startlingly blue eyes, and an array of high decorations resting upon the most splendid of uniforms. His powerful voice had a great effect upon all listeners, and he had learned to make it an instrument of clarity and persuasion. He was inordinately optimistic, and seemed not to know the meaning of the word impossible. One word from him and countless ambitious minds and industrious hands in a number of fields went earnestly to work, each vying with the other to report new successes to the commander. Yet, despite this marvelous and seemingly indestructible leader, was he really so imposing or powerful after all?

As far as the Luftwaffe was concerned, however, there were two aspects of Goering's character which were destined to play a major role in bringing about the collapse of Germany's air forces. The first was his inner compulsion to take everything personally, just as he refused to submit to authority except to that of Hitler, and his refusal to acknowledge any obligation unless it was likely to be useful to him in his desire to dominate or unless it fulfilled a personal need. In such circumstances, Goering did not view the German Luftwaffe as the main mission and vocation of his life. Instead, he regarded it as his personal property. It was *his* air force—one might even say it was his slave organization—and he considered himself to be its absolute master, with control of life or death over it (although he mentioned the latter only for the sake of rhetoric). This attitude explains the most incredible lack of tact displayed by Goering during the war when he threatened to have Udet, his Chief of Supply and Procurement, shot for inefficiency if the British fighters were really "as powerful and as good" as had been reported to him.

He was unable to face sobering or skeptical reports dealing with actual facts and situations. In consequence of his desire to hear only what was favorable, he often refused to face reality, and in the end he really believed that "his" Luftwaffe was an invincible force, whose commitment was alone capable of deciding the outcome of the war. Since he also had a fondness for boasting to the commanders in chief of the other Wehrmacht branches, it is clear that he did not always succeed in winning their sympathies for his service. Moreover, he put the Luftwaffe at a disadvantage from the beginning by exaggerating its performance potential.

The second aspect of Goering's nature which proved so disastrous for the Luftwaffe was his growing tendency to make a distinction between himself and his colleagues by demanding uncompromising devotion to duty from them, while his own zeal in this respect was no more than a pretense. Sometimes, whenever he felt like it, he even abandoned all semblance of industry for long periods of time.

If Goering's intoxication with power and with the achievement of personal goals were genuine, it is then quite likely that his secret awareness of inadequacy would drive him to pretense when he was forced to confront an even stronger personality. Without doubt the qualities which he lacked most of all: a real iron core, a vast body of knowledge acquired by hours of reading and study, cold objectivity, an almost inhuman detachment, an indifference toward the enjoyments of life and external trappings of power, and a primitive naturalness were personified in the character of Adolf Hitler. Since the Fuehrer held Goering's fate in his hands, the Luftwaffe leader was obliged to continue to impress him or, at least, to keep alive in him the favorable impressions about himself and his abilities from an earlier period. Because of his innate cunning, Goering knew that if he failed to impress Hitler he would not only lose his fabulous position of power, but also the sumptuous life of ease to which he had become so accustomed. Probably he instinctively recognized the almost inhuman naturalness which was so characteristic of Hitler's life, yet he submitted to him unconditionally.

But even this explanation is not entirely adequate, because personal advantage was not the only determining factor in Goering's relationship to Hitler. He was really devoted to the Fuehrer, believed in him sincerely, and accepted subordination to him in the fullest sense of the word. Hitler was, in fact, the only authority he had ever recognized except the German Emperor. Thus, even though he might not be able to conceal all of the weaknesses of his character, Goering simply had to appear to be strong, unassailable, and indispensable to Hitler, who embodied power, toughness, and success. Toward this end he played the strong man—and here he was surely acting a part—at the expense of the Luftwaffe and probably at the expense of Germany's future as well. The Fuehrer's Luftwaffe adjutant, Colonel Nicolaus von Below, reports that until late in the war Hitler discussed all matters pertaining to air forces with Goering alone, and that Hitler trusted Goering implicitly. It is therefore hardly likely that Goering, who was often unwilling to listen to reports in his own office concerning the Luftwaffe's lack of readiness, would have informed his Fuehrer of the true situation.

Hjalmar Schacht, the German Finance Minister and a fiscal genius with an exceedingly sharp wit, wrote in his memoirs:

> In the beginning, Goering tried to preserve a certain measure of independence beside Hitler. Goering felt himself to be a dominant personality, and it flattered him to be compared with a figure of the Renaissance. I remember that once, after a session with Hitler, Goering called him a "clever devil." But the more deeply Goering became involved in morally questionable activity, the more abject became his dependence upon Hitler, for the Fuehrer kept a very precise record of the misdeeds of his followers. He did not punish them outright, but used this knowledge to force each one of them into a position of absolute submission.

It is possible that this picture is exaggerated. Goering's supposed description of Hitler as a clever devil does not seem to be clearly consistent with the awesome respect in which Goering held his Fuehrer. Yet, another statement attributed to Goering by Schacht does seem to fit the pattern: "Do you know, Mr. Schacht, I always make up my mind to tell Hitler certain things and then the minute I enter his office my courage invariably desserts me."

The fact that the Commander in Chief of the Luftwaffe was totally incapable of speaking frankly and openly with Hitler, and in spite of the fact that he was the Fuehrer's highest deputy, was unable to make an objective, down-to-earth report without having to impress the listener or to win personal recognition for himself, was one of the major factors responsible for the decline and final collapse of Germany's air arm.

Goering's zeal and energy have been confirmed beyond doubt up to 1933 and even into 1934, but thereafter they diminished rapidly and noticeably. As far as the Reichs Aviation Ministry was concerned, this meant that the conduct of business was pretty much in the hands of Milch, Goering's permanent deputy, a state of affairs which was by no means detrimental to the Ministry. In the long run, however, a situation of this kind was dangerous. A deputy whose authority covers all aspects of activity, and whose office bears all of the work, cannot escape public notice. This was especially true of the Luftwaffe as a newly established branch of service which needed and sought publicity by calling attention to its achievements. It was therefore natural that Milch often acted as the spokesman of the Reichs Aviation Minister on occasions when Goering himself ought to have made an appearance. This situation must have been called to Goering's attention either by the Nazi Party or by someone else. Goering's name was no longer so closely associated with the German Air Force since it was Milch who was accomplishing all of the work.

But Goering had no intention of altering the situation by resuming the industriousness which had been so characteristic of his early work in the Luftwaffe. By this time hard work had completely lost any enticement it may have had for him. Nevertheless, he did put Milch in his place. After Wever's death a conflict had sprung up between Milch and the young General Staff of the Luftwaffe. Kesselring, the Chief of Staff, objected to being subordinated to the State Secretary of Aviation. Goering took advantage of this prevailing dissatisfaction by decreeing that henceforth Milch's office would be on the same level as the General Staff. The General Staff Chief was also granted the right of direct access (*Immediatstellung*) to the Commander in Chief of the Luftwaffe, and the function of the State Secretary as deputy was restricted to the periods when Goering was absent from work by reason of illness or leave. The effect of this action was to destroy the previous inner continuity in the conduct of ministerial affairs, for Goering himself had no intention whatever of stepping into the breach created by the weakening of Milch's position. Actually, in reducing Milch's authority, Goering had prepared the way for the greatest evil of all, lack of leadership, and thus opened the door for internal intrigues and rivalry, which were bound to have a detrimental effect upon the work of the Air Ministry.

Milch declared that he had warned Goering at the time, "You're ruining the air forces this way. Somebody has to be in charge of everything. If I don't do it, then you'll have to . . . but you won't!" Goering then assured him that he would do so, but Milch remained apprehensive. "I don't believe it," he said. "I request that I be relieved of my post." Goering's loud reply was, "Look here, Milch, I'm not demoting you because you've failed, but because you've succeeded too well. The Party keeps telling me that it's Milch who does all the work. And . . . I won't stand for that!"

The question arises, however, why a man like Goering, despite the fact that countless public appearances demanded by his many and varied offices left him little time for his air force, should have sinned against it so gravely by inadequate leadership on one hand and by over-bearing decisions on the other. If it had been simply a matter of his collecting offices alone it would have been one thing, but it was quite another when he began to consume more time and give more attention to furnishing Karinhall with the most superb art treasures, to designing and fitting countless styles of uniforms and clothing, and to indulging in long and undisturbed siestas. When all of these were considered, it is easy to see that there was little time left for serious work.

In the war with France and Great Britain, Germany could have made good use of the energy which had been demonstrated by Goering in 1933 and 1934. At the very least, as Commander in Chief of the Luftwaffe, Goering ought to have taken up permanent residence at the Luftwaffe headquarters in Potsdam-Werder.

The words attributed to Goering by former envoy Paul Schmidt following Britain's declaration of war in September 1939, "If we lose this war, then heaven have mercy on our souls!" indicate that Goering was aware of the far-reaching consequences of that titanic struggle, and had no illusions concerning the effects which a lost war would have upon the Reich, the German people, upon himself and his family. But he did not act accordingly. He had obviously become too addicted to soft living to be able to change, to make a determined effort to abandon his accustomed manner of living for a life of military order and discipline.

Goering was basically an optimist, and it is therefore not surprising that he failed to see any need for determined action or for altering the life he had learned to enjoy so much in peacetime. But, there is still another factor which one is tempted to advance to explain Goering's behavior during World War II. For years he had lived in the sovereign assumption that he was one of the closest intimates of the Fuehrer, that he was, in a sense a godfather to the Fuehrer's feats, and that he was the only person in all Germany who still retained a certain importance in his own right. During the war, however, Hitler's consolidation of absolute powers over the Wehrmacht, Army, and the German populace brought about a change in his relationship to others, including Goering. The gap between the Fuehrer and his staff, including his top-ranking paladin, grew greater and greater. The feeling of being a part of the Supreme Command of the Wehrmacht, which had previously inspired Goering into unusually vigorous activity, gradually lost its basis in fact. Hitler continued to treat his loyal follower with the greatest of consideration, even at a time when he had long since lost confidence in him, but there was no escaping the fact that Goering, like all of Hitler's associates, had become merely a servant.

These possible excuses have been deliberately emphasized. However, in spite of them, Goering's conduct as Commander in Chief of the German Air Force during World War II, when this new branch of service was being put to the most crucial test, remains incomprehensible. It is true that he still took an active part in Luftwaffe affairs during the Polish campaign, and, in fact, personally intervened in many acts of the Luftwaffe High Command. It is also true that the rapid and highly successful French campaign also managed to secure his interest, and he took part in this undertaking with a strong awareness of his own power. He even launched the air offensive against Britain with a rather bombastic speech from his command headquarters.

As soon as it was clear that the air offensive against London was not having the desired effect, Goering rapidly lost interest in directing the operations himself. But there was another factor which went along with the Luftwaffe's failure to down the RAF. With the defeat of France Goering had become intrigued with a new interest, which held sway over him more firmly than any of his well-known peacetime pursuits such as the siestas at his princely estate of Karinhall, his model railway, or hunting in the Rominten heath or in East Prussia. This new passion was the acquisition of property, especially art treasures, for which purpose he traveled to Paris and other French cities in a special railway car.

Even the best informed officers were scarcely able to discern between Goering's periods of official leave and his frequent periods of relaxation. This was precisely the sort of thing that helped to bring about the ruin of the Luftwaffe, for it deprived the service of any leadership at all. The State Secretary ought to have been empowered to fill the breach, but instead, he was quietly deprived of his powers, which (apart from the duty of acting for the Commander in Chief for unimportant matters) were concentrated in his capacity as Inspector General of the Luftwaffe, so that he was gradually "organized out" of the top level command. Moreover, after Udet's death in November 1941, Milch became increasingly burdened down with duties in the area of supply and procurement.

Leadership in the Luftwaffe, such as it was, remained within the purview of Goering, who enjoyed the function of command and who exercised his prerogatives before his colleagues and the Luftwaffe High Command as if he had been appointed to a position of incontrovertible authority similar to that of a cardinal-archbishop of the Church. After the fall of France, no German military commander surrendered as readily or as completely as did Goering to the pursuit of relaxation and the enjoyment of the good life. Very often he summoned his air fleet commanders to Rominten, where the most urgent and difficult Luftwaffe problems were discussed with them between shots during a stag hunt.

In the long run Goering's behavior placed a heavy burden on the shoulders of the Luftwaffe, a burden which became almost intolerable for those in the positions of top responsibility. It is more than mere coincidence that two of Goering's most important subordinates committed suicide. Udet, basically a man of sunny disposition (although sensitive) who was able to laugh at himself and others, and Jeschonnek, the energetic Chief of the Luftwaffe General Staff, both found the situation unbearable and sought their own ways out of the dilemma. Both had been recruited by Goering, and both looked in vain to him for support when the first flush of success gave way to an increasing series of misfortunes.

On 7 February 1940 Goering signed a decree which was to have catastrophic effects upon the Luftwaffe, an order to stop aircraft developmental work. This decision affected work on all equipment which could not be ready for employment at the front within the next year. Without question it was based upon the optimistic assumption that the war would be a short one as Hitler had promised. Because of this decree (which was confirmed again in September of 1941), developmental work had to be discontinued on jet and rocket-propelled aircraft as well as on a number of other vital modern pieces of equipment. Although the air armament firms continued to work secretly on these items on their own initiative, they were unable to assign enough workers to these projects to keep them moving on a reasonable schedule. In any case, the former impetus was gone. The failure to mobilize in 1939 was now aggravated by the failure to take advantage of the period of undisturbed working conditions during 1940 and 1941. The development of the jet aircraft would have created a wide gap between Germany and the Allies, putting the Luftwaffe in a decisive position which the enemy could not overtake. It is not certain whether the development stoppage was Goering's own idea or whether it was issued on Hitler's orders or instigation. Certainly the decree was not issued without Hitler's approval.

Goering's responsibility in the fatal decision to stop the German armored forces before Dunkirk is clear. According to the testimony of Generaloberst Heinz Guderian and Generaloberst Franz Halder, Hitler was nervous and uneasy during the successful advance of the German armored wedge toward the Channel coast (the first phase of the campaign in France). These witnesses assume that he probably subconsciously considered the French forces to be stronger than his conscious deliberations had indicated. He may also have been influenced by the memory of this terrain from his own days as a soldier. In any case, he was obviously worried by the thought that Weygand's army, still intact, might deliver a crippling blow to the rear of the German forces while the panzer units were engaged against the withdrawing British forces along the coast. If an enemy maneuver of this kind had succeeded it could well have cancelled out the remarkable victories won up to that point. The French still had a reputation for courage and stubbornness, and the idea of a blow to the rear of the German armies might also have occurred to the French military staff. On the other hand, if the German armor had advanced deep into the Dunkirk area (or even as far as the critical Halder thought it could advance), Germany would have had a chance to capture the entire British Expeditionary Corps and the remainder of the French Army Group North, which was fighting beside it.

At this moment Goering approached Hitler with a most enticing proposal, one which was so typical of the Reichsmarschall's megalomania. The Luftwaffe, which had already won its laurels in the campaign in the West and which had until then intimidated British fighter pilots so that they hardly dared face the German air might, appeared to its temperamental Commander in Chief (then at the zenith of one of his emotional cycles) as an absolutely invincible force. He saw the Luftwaffe as the instrument chosen by destiny to dive-bomb and batter to destruction the enemy, which was then in full retreat toward the port of Dunkirk. Why bother the German Army with this detail? Quite obviously, Goering's motivations were vanity and an overweening pride in his air forces.

Generalleutnant Josef "Beppo" Schmid, Chief of Luftwaffe Intelligence, was an eyewitness to the entire affair, and described the situation:

> I happened to be present when Goering learned, through normal communications channels, that the German tanks approaching from both east and west had reached the outskirts of Dunkirk. Thereupon, without even stopping to think, he decided that the British Expeditionary Corps had to be conquered from the air. I heard the telephone conversation which he subsequently had with Hitler. Goering described

the situation at Dunkirk in such a way as to suggest that there was no alternative but to destroy by an attack from the air those elements of the British Expeditionary Corps trapped at Dunkirk. He described this mission as being a specialty of the Luftwaffe, and pointed out that the advance elements of the German Army, already battle weary, could hardly expect to succeed in preventing the British withdrawal. He even requested that the German tanks, which had reached the outskirts of the city, be withdrawn a few miles in order to leave the field free for the Luftwaffe.

Hitler, stopping no longer to think than Goering had before making his suggestion, agreed to the proposal.

Goering and his General Staff Chief were firmly convinced that the Luftwaffe would succeed in crushing the British Expeditionary Corps in the Dunkirk area and in preventing its escape to the British Isles. It is now common knowledge that the Luftwaffe did not achieve its goal of destroying the enemy, since it carried out effective attacks only on the city and harbor of Dunkirk, attacks which did nothing to prevent the British from escaping by day and night in small and medium-sized boats from the long, broad, sandy beaches. Those German bombs which landed on the beaches were simply dissipated and buried by the sand, thereby being completely ineffective.

The Luftwaffe also had no opportunity to reassemble for the Dunkirk operation. Thus, participating units were stationed at bases situated relatively far away. One wing of Ju-88 bombers was stationed in Holland, and had to fly along the English Channel to Dunkirk, meanwhile providing easy prey for enemy Spitfires. In the course of the action over Dunkirk the Spitfires even managed for a time to achieve aerial supremacy during daylight hours. Moreover, during the period in question the VIII Air Corps, the unit best trained and equipped for dive-bombing operations, was kept out of action for three days (29-31 May) because of fog over northern France. The result was that the British managed to rescue most of the Expeditionary Corps, altogether a total of 338,226 British and French troops, although they had to abandon 7,000 tons of ammunition, 90,000 guns, 2,300 artillery pieces, 120,000 motor vehicles, 8,000 machine guns, and 400 antitank guns. Goering's intervention enabled the British to free their forces from the deadlock in front of the German armored forces, and allowed the Allies a free hand to withdraw, German Army units not reaching the inner city or harbor of Dunkirk until 4 June, by which time the last British ships had departed.

In this instance Goering had promised much more than he could deliver, at the expense of the Luftwaffe's reputation. This was the first serious loss of prestige suffered by this arm of service. Yet, despite this lesson, the incorrigible Reichsmarschall was no more cautious with respect to the air war against England. The Luftwaffe simply had too many missions to fulfill and Goering overestimated its potential, just as he underestimated the strength and tenacity of British fighter forces. The struggle for air supremacy along the English coast and over southern England, and the shift (before air supremacy had been achieved) to all-out attacks on London and an economic war, were tasks which far exceeded the capability of the German Air Force. The experience at Dunkirk concerning enemy strength and resolve was simply ignored.

During the German air offensive against Britain, which lasted until 10 May 1941, the Luftwaffe for months on end was involved in an endless series of missions which were extremely costly both in materiel and in personnel. Most aerial combat took place over British soil or the Channel, so that those pilots who managed to escape from their damaged aircraft by parachute either drowned in the Channel or were captured by the enemy. In either case they were no longer available to the Luftwaffe, whereas the British pilots in similar situations were soon able to go into the air again in new aircraft. The Luftwaffe's losses were all the more serious because they involved many of its best qualified personnel. Generalleutnant Theo Osterkamp, in his memorandum of October 1943, went so far as to state, "I cannot help thinking that the German Luftwaffe never recovered from this blow, especially in view of the fact that it was forced to curtail training time and to reduce its standards with respect to moral fitness in order to fill the gaps which were thus created."

In Germany, aircraft production was progressing much more slowly than in Great Britain. Even the German pilot training program, which at first had been well ahead of its British counterpart, began to suffer as a result of the continual requisitioning of training planes and instructor personnel for use in airborne operations. Both factors embodied a tacit shift in military superiority for the future, quite apart from the fact that American war materiel shipments to Britain were rapidly becoming a factor with which to be reckoned.

In the aura of glory surrounding Germany's remarkable victory over France, Goering, like his Chief of Staff, Jeschonnek, and like Udet in the Technical Office, failed to realize that fate was beginning to spin its threads into a web of catastrophe for the future. He failed to see that critical evaluation and hard work were even more important after the fall of France than at the beginning of the war. It is true that British air attacks on German cities had not yet reached a point in 1940 where one had to take them seriously, but could such a situation be expected to continue for long?

Clearly the year 1940 was an unproductive year for the Luftwaffe, and one which did little for the future. The situation was aggravated by the fact that five days after Compiègne Hitler placed the Luftwaffe in fifth place on the armament priority list, which made the procurement of raw materials more complicated, and practically impossible for the ineffectual Udet and his staff. There, in the midst of victory, stood factors which were to lead to the defeats of 1944 and 1945, all of them unnoticed by the Commander in Chief of the Luftwaffe.

Hitler felt extremely uneasy about Russia, with which he had concluded a treaty of friendship (albeit with inner reservations and only for reasons of political expediency). He had been thwarted in his hope of securing a peace with England, chiefly because the United Kingdom under the leadership of Winston Churchill had become enraged and was determined, regardless of the costs or the probable end, to see Germany brought to her knees. Thus Germany's leader decided to cut the Gordian knot in the East, and the Wehrmacht's remarkable victory in the West served to increase his self-confidence to an incalculable degree.

The objections which weighed most heavily came from Hitler's intimate circle of associates. Goering, for example, expressed his misgivings about a war against the Soviet Union in the most explicit terms. He realized that if it proved to be unfeasible to crush the British in the air over Britain, the only other possibility would be to strike a blow at the most vulnerable points of British supremacy, Gibraltar and Suez. But Goering was unable to persuade Hitler to accept his views.

This gave Goering the alternative either of going along with the Fuehrer's decision, or of telling him that he wanted no part of the new plans. He could have submitted his resignation, and might have been able to force Hitler over to his way of thinking. In the eyes of the public in Germany and abroad, Goering was the Fuehrer's foremost and most powerful associate, and even a person as stubborn as Hitler might have revised his thinking if the Reichsmarschall had been adamant from the outset.

During one of the sessions in which Goering was questioned by the Nuremberg prosecutor Justice Robert H. Jackson, the question arose as to why Goering had not submitted his resignation. The prisoner replied:

. . . as far as my resignation is concerned, I have no intention of dis-
cussing the matter. During the war I was an officer, a soldier, and
regardless of whether I agreed with a given viewpoint or not, my job
was to serve my country as a soldier.

As Koerner noted, Goering was intensely aware of the implications
of Hitler's decision to attack Russia, but he was also keenly aware of
the possibilities if he had decided to resign. Without doubt he would
have been obliged to relinquish not only the command of the German
Luftwaffe, but also all of his other offices (including the right of succession after Hitler) and the life he enjoyed. He would have been retired
"for reasons of health," which would have removed him from taking
any role in the future of Germany. Even if Hitler had been disposed toward unusual leniency in his case, he would scarcely have wanted to
guarantee to Goering the perpetuation of the title and income of a
Reichsmarschall. Once out of office, the avalanche would also carry
away the income received from the industrial sector.

The situation was complicated by the fact that it was not always possible to separate Goering's private property from state property. Karinhall would have been difficult to maintain, and Rominten would certainly have had to be forfeited, while official inquiries would have made
things trying for a retired Reichsmarschall who owned such costly estates
as Veldenstein and Mauterndorf. An infuriated Chief of State could
suddenly demand the return of certain property, and Goering's almost
pasha-like existence would have come to a sudden end. Besides these
prospects there were other possible dangers. Goering was no longer
popular within Party circles, and his opponent, the indispensable Martin Bormann, was growing in power and prestige, even with Hitler
himself.

By the fateful year 1944, Goering had become no more than a
shadow of his former personality. Among the younger Luftwaffe personnel, who had so admired him before, he was often called the
"Rubber Lion" rather than the "Iron Man." His severest critics, however, came from the Army. Guderian said of him, "He reeked of per-
fume, his face was made up, and his fingers were covered with the
jewels he loved to display."

Guderian remarked that he was present on one occasion (along with
Generaloberst Alfred Jodl) when Hitler bellowed at the man he had
once spoiled with his attentions, "Goering! Your Luftwaffe isn't worth
a damn! It doesn't deserve to be an independent branch of service any
more! And that's your fault! You're lazy!" The candid Army observer

then related how tears ran down the cheeks of the portly Reichsmar-schall who could think of nothing to say in reply. This lack of self-control was also noted on other occasions, and induced Guderian to suggest to Hitler that Goering be relieved of his command. Hitler refused, however, by saying, "That's impossible for reasons of domestic policy. The Party would never understand."

Since Goering had passed up the opportunity in 1941 of exploiting his enormous prestige to prevent the ill-fated campaign in Russia or to retire honorably from public life, in 1944 his position (and possibly even his life) hung on the perilously thin thread of his public prestige and popularity. Guderian noted that the Reichsmarschall, intimidated by Hitler's constant reproaches against the Luftwaffe, began to follow the example introduced by General Adolf Galland on occasions when Goering had been angry with him. Goering began to appear at the military conferences which he could not avoid, "dressed very simply, without his decorations, and with an incredibly unbecoming cap on his head." Jupiter in mourning—sic transit gloria mundi!

During September and October 1944, when the German Reich was beset by a concentrated series of catastrophes, including the collapse of France, the defection of Rumania, and a separate peace in Finland, Goering had narrowly escaped being removed from office. In such circumstances he was bound to be aware that his prestige had fallen in the sight of Hitler, and that there were influential circles waiting to take advantage of his overthrow.

The 20th of April 1945 was Hitler's last birthday. Goering, too, was among those who came to the Fuehrer bunker to congratulate him. During the following military conference, Goering remarked that someone from the Luftwaffe top-level command, either he or the General Staff Chief, ought to move farther south, since the Allied advance was already threatening to cut off northern Germany. Hitler replied: "You go, then. I need Koller here." The two men parted company without any undue emotion.

While Goering, everywhere greeted by his friends, was on his way to the Obersalzberg by way of Bohemia, a decisive event occurred on 22 April. On the afternoon of that day, Hitler collapsed. According to Koller:

> . . . he realizes now that the situation is hopeless. But he refuses to leave Berlin, and insists on staying on in his bunker and defending the city. When the Russians come, he intends to accept the conse-

quences and shoot himself. Keitel, Jodl, Bormann, Doenitz, and Himmler (the last two by telephone) have been trying to change his mind, to persuade him to leave Berlin, since one can't conduct operations from here any more. But it is no use.

Hitler remained firm, telling the others to leave or stay, as they pleased.

Koller left Christian in charge in the north and traveled southward to see Goering, arriving at the Obersalzberg by air on the 23rd. He informed the Reichsmarschall of what had happened and urged him to act, inasmuch as Hitler had "made himself the commander of Berlin and thus automatically excluded himself from the conduct of the affairs of state as well as from the leadership of the Wehrmacht." But Goering was undecided, saying: "Bormann is my deadly enemy. He's just waiting for a chance to get me out of the way. If I act now, I'll be branded a traitor. If I don't act, I'll be accused of letting Germany down in her most difficult hour."

Nevertheless, Goering again checked the text of the law of 29 September 1941 which designated him as Hitler's deputy or successor in all government, Party, and Wehrmacht offices in the event that Hitler's capabilities should become impaired or that he should be eliminated from the scene of action. Upon Koller's urging, the Reichsmarschall decided (with the help of the General Staff Chief) to direct an inquiry to Hitler by radiogram:

> My Fuehrer, in view of your decision to remain in Berlin to defend the city, do you agree to my now assuming command of the Reich with full authority in domestic and foreign policy, on the basis of the law of 29 September 1941? If I have not received a reply from you by 2200, I shall assume that you have been deprived of your freedom of action and shall act in accordance with my own best judgment. I cannot express my feelings in this hour of my life. May God protect you. I hope that you will decide to leave Berlin after all and come down here.

The radiogram was sent at 1500 hours on 23 April 1945. Goering also issued orders to Keitel and Ribbentrop to report to him the following day unless they should receive counter-instructions from him or from Hitler in the meantime. The Reichsmarschall, now full of determination, ordered his General Staff Chief to undertake certain preliminary measures. Immediately upon the receipt of Hitler's reply he planned to fly to see Eisenhower, Commander in Chief of the Western

Allies, with whom he hoped to reach an early compromise in person-to-person negotiations. Koller writes:

> Once the decision had been taken, Goering was energetic and eager for action, as if some heavy weight had been lifted from his shoulders. He was looking forward to contacting the Americans and kept reiterating his confidence that he could work out a satisfactory agreement with the Americans and the British. In former days, I had often called him "his master's voice" (after the famous trademark of the dog sitting in front of a phonograph loudspeaker) because of the many occasions when he was unsuccessful in pushing through his protests against some matter to Hitler and then afterwards, in his awe of the Fuehrer, would present the words and decisions of the Fuehrer with the true ring of conviction as though they were his own. Now he seemed to be a different person somehow. During dinner he beamed and was clearly looking forward to the new task confronting him.

But his joy was premature. Hitler interpreted his radiogram as an ultimatum and as evidence of betrayal. He did not even need to be goaded by Bormann. The Reichsmarschall was finished, as far as Hitler was concerned. Hitler, enraged, turned completely against the man who he believed to have betrayed him. Goering was summarily stripped of all his offices. As reported to Koller on 29 April by Colonel Hans Wolter, who witnessed the events on the Obersalzberg, the news reached Goering in the form of a telegram from Bormann's office with the following text:

> What you have done warrants the death penalty. In view of your valuable past services, I shall not institute proceedings, provided you renounce all your offices and titles. Otherwise, appropriate steps will have to be taken. Adolf Hitler.

Hitler had summoned von Greim to his bunker in embattled Berlin. On 26 April (largely due to the skillful flying of the German aviatrix Hanna Reitsch) von Greim managed to reach Berlin in his Fieseler Storch aircraft. The city was then surrounded by the enemy and was the scene of heavy fighting. Von Greim did not arrive unscathed, however, having sustained a wound in his leg. Koller had also been ordered to report, but was unable to reach the capital. He telephoned von Greim, the newly appointed field marshal and Commander in Chief of the Luftwaffe, from the Wehrmacht High Command Headquarters in the woods near Fuerstenberg. Von Greim was still optimistic, although it was obvious that Germany was heading toward the ultimate collapse with frightening rapidity. Despite the lateness of the hour, he had succumbed to the enchantment of Hitler's personality. Koller reported von Greim's incredible words as follows:

> Just don't lose hope! Everything will still turn out all right. My contact with the Fuehrer and his strength has strengthened me like a dip in the fountain of youth. The Fuehrer sat at my bedside for quite a while and discussed everything with me. He retracted all of his accusations against the Luftwaffe. He is aware of what our service branch has accomplished. His reproaches are directed solely at Goering. He had the highest praise for our forces! It made me exceedingly happy.

At last the implications of Hitler's remarks, which began while Jeschonnek was still in office, began to emerge. It was not the Luftwaffe that was to blame, it was Goering. Von Greim was deeply embittered toward the former Reichsmarschall, and most of his associates held their former chief in contempt. Goering's imprisonment might well have resulted in an execution, especially after 30 April 1945, when a radiogram came to Goering's guards from Bormann. According to Koller, the radiogram read as follows:

> If Berlin falls, and we are killed, you are responsible by your honor, your lives, and your families for seeing that the traitors of 23 April are liquidated without exception. Men, do your duty!

By this time Goering had already been transferred from the Obersalzberg to Mauterndorf Castle, the scene of his happy childhood. An SS Brigade Leader, on his own initiative, relieved the SD of its guard duties and entrusted them entirely to the Waffen SS. Goering, now desperate, continued to demand help from Koller, whom he accused of "selling him out" in his report concerning activities on 23 April. He even had Koller's secretary called to pass on the message that, "If Koller is anything but a swine, and if he has a spark of decency in him, he'll be here tomorrow morning."

But all these are merely the last throes. Reality had already progressed beyond them. Goering's liberation had become a fact. On the day of Hitler's death, the leader of the SS unit guarding the former Reichsmarschall called Kesselring to ask whether he "should carry out the death sentence against Goering and his family . . ." Kesselring, hearing about this for the first time, forbade "execution of the sentence and ordered the SS to withdraw and permit Goering, his family, and his staff to move about freely in Mauterndorf." According to Koller, that must have been on 5 May, since it was on that day that Kesselring informed him of the end of Goering's arrest.

Koller arranged for Goering's move to Fischhorn on the southern shore of Lake Zell, since he feared that Russian troops might occupy Mauterndorf. On 8 May the Goerings left the castle. On the previous day he had sent von Brauchitsch to Koller with a letter to Eisenhower (again the thought of face-to-face negotiations) and one to the nearest American divisional commander. On the way to Fischhorn Goering met the American Brigadier General Robert Stack, who—obviously on the basis of the letter delivered by von Brauchitsch—was prepared to take the former Reichsmarschall under his protection.

Goering's resplendent past was now irrevocably gone, and this was the beginning of the somber last act of his destiny before his accusers at the International Military Tribunal at Nuremberg, an act which was to decide whether he would go down in history as the symbol of a defeated Germany or whether the world's picture of him could be endowed with more favorable characteristics. There did not seem to be much hope of the latter when one considers his lethargy of the last years and the thoroughgoing change in his status. The night surrounding him was black and starless.

5

The Deputy: Milch

WITH THE SINGLE EXCEPTION of Goering, no member of the German Air Force High Command exercised such a lengthy and continuous period of influence as Field Marshal Erhard Milch. As State Secretary of Aviation he shared with Goering very heavy responsibility for both the rise and the fall of the Luftwaffe.

On 3 February 1933, only four days after the establishment of the Reichs Commissariat of Aviation, Milch had already become Deputy Reichs Commissioner of Aviation, and on 22 February 1933 was named by Goering (with the full approbation of Hitler) as State Secretary of Aviation, and given simultaneously equal rank within the Reichs Air Ministry. Milch advanced rapidly. On 24 March 1934 he was promoted to the rank of Generalmajor, on 28 March 1935 to Generalleutnant, and on 20 April 1936 to General der Flieger. His strength within the governmental aviation circles could be seen in the fact that thereafter his military advancement kept pace immediately behind the Commander in Chief of the Luftwaffe, Goering. When Milch's chief became a field marshal on 1 November 1938, the State Secretary was promoted to Generaloberst, and on 19 July 1940, when Goering was elevated to the rank of Reichsmarschall, Milch (along with Sperrle and Kesselring of the Luftwaffe and several Army generals) received the coveted field marshal's baton. In citing the State Secretary for promotion, Goering credited him with "outstanding merit in the buildup of the German Air Force."

Milch, despite his generally practical outlooks and his normally logical approach to matters, especially in the handling of personnel, had an inordinate sensitivity to the personal attitudes of his colleagues, possibly because he could not help being aware of the whispers so frequently bantered about within the Ministry about his Jewish background. It was fairly well known in higher German aviation circles that Milch was at least partially of non-Aryan descent on his father's side, and that official documents had been altered to make him fully acceptable to the Nazi regime. It is thus probably safe to assume that he could not entirely overlook everything that he heard, particularly at a time when he still needed strong backing from the Party and from Goering.

Although he faced a number of bureaucratic hurdles in gaining acceptance for his ideas during his first years in office as State Secretary of Aviation, Milch's greatest power struggle came after the untimely death of Wever, the first Chief of the Luftwaffe General Staff, on 3 June 1936. Still somewhat uncertain of his own position and strength, and noting Goering's flagging interest in Air Ministry matters, Milch began to fill offices with men of his own choice and to take other steps calculated to strengthen his hold upon the Ministry. These measures did not go unnoticed by Kesselring, the successor to Wever and head of the first officially designated Luftwaffe General Staff. Kesselring's position as Chief of the Luftwaffe General Staff was not a pleasant thing to Milch, who was quite content with the arrangement as it had existed under Wever. Now, being an official entity, the psychological impact of the Luftwaffe General Staff was something with which to be concerned. Was it not possible that this body might attempt to encroach upon the domain of the State Secretary's office?

But, in order to comprehend the singular position of Milch, it is necessary, even at the risk of being repetitious, to present certain facts and points of consideration. Within three months after the death of Wever the Reichs Aviation Ministry brought together three powers whose relationships with each other were not always harmonious and were often sharp and bitter. The most important of these was the position of Goering, who wore two hats as Commander in Chief of the Luftwaffe and Reichsminister of Aviation. The other two were the office of State Secretary of Aviation (Milch) and the Luftwaffe General Staff (headed by Kesselring).

The Commander in Chief of the Luftwaffe was no soldier, or at least he had not been one for a long time. As Reichsminister of Aviation he had become a general officer overnight, and soon afterward had been raised to the very apex of the newly formed Luftwaffe hierarchy. The very possession of so much rank, without the broader knowledge and skill which is so essential to it, and which can be acquired only through years of service and experience, must arouse in its bearer a certain inner sense of insecurity. This was surely aggravated by the fact that Goering was not a worker and did not devote himself faithfully or thoroughly to the tasks of the Aviation Ministry.

Clearly, a man who demands supreme power for himself, without having the ability to work steadily or accurately, and who even lacks a desire to work, requires the assistance of an energetic and competent deputy who will accomplish the work for him. Milch thus became more and more an absolute necessity for the Reichsmarschall. The State Secretary, in fact, shouldered the lion's share of Goering's responsibilities. In a totalitarian state suspicions are much more apt to arise than in either a monarchy or a democracy. This being the case, is there not a danger that a deputy whose work is so successful that it brings him increasingly into the foreground will one day step into the place of a superior who, being a drone, holds a position of power but does not exercise it? In the Third Reich all government power became more and more concentrated in the person of the Fuehrer, and the last remaining spheres of power and influence were imperceptibly drained of their authority until they were mere recipients of Hitler's orders. Because of this development, one could assume that the Fuehrer might one day raise the true worker to the position of leadership, placing Milch in Goering's ministerial post.

In such circumstances it behooved Goering to proceed with some caution. It is said that trees should always be lopped off in good time. Therefore it seemed desirable to the Reichsmarschall to discover whether his deputy, Milch, had an Achilles' heel whereby, in case of danger, he might be removed. Milch had such a heel in that he was no more a professional soldier than Goering, despite his service prior to and during World War I. There were two aspects of this which made him especially vulnerable. Not only was he the deputy of a ministry which was becoming increasingly military in character, but after 1935 he was also the deputy of the Commander in Chief of the Luftwaffe. Such a man might therefore quickly arouse the suspicions of the command apparatus of the Luftwaffe, the General Staff. This vulnerability of Milch made him more acceptable to Goering, who thus felt that he always had an ace in the hole. Of course, once his suspicions were aroused the Reichsmarschall did not want to leave the State Secretary with too much power, at least not more than necessary for the accomplishment of his duties.

Like Goering, Milch wanted very much to be considered as a soldier, and he coveted high military rank. Yet, in contrast to Goering, he did not want rank for appearances alone, or even for the feeling of power it might impart; he wanted it because he knew that he needed it in order to achieve his desired reforms and programs within the Luftwaffe. Thus a chasm continued to exist between Milch as a general (and later as a field marshal) and other officers of his rank. Milch, it must be recalled, had simply skipped nearly thirteen years of Army service, yet he was still several years younger than the two most important Army officers acquired by the Luftwaffe, Wever (born in 1884), and Kesselring (born in 1885). Owing to his rapid successions of promotions, Milch had gained an advantage of not merely thirteen years, but of nearly twenty. Furthermore, he was no General Staff officer, and his past experience with troops was relatively meager. Having never done any General Staff work himself, and faced with the eagerness to learn on the part of newly acquired Army personnel, Milch's tremendous advantage in aviation experience was bound to decrease as time went on. By serious application, the Army personnel soon demonstrated their talents (which had brought them to the fore within the Army) and were successfully transformed into excellent Luftwaffe officers. It must be borne in mind that civil aviation, the area in which Milch's experiences were formed, was being continually converted into military aviation from the late 1920's on, and especially after 1933. This was a field in which the regular military men were more at home than Milch, even though his superiority in technical matters and in questions pertaining to aircraft production remained undiminished.

Milch had an advantage, however, in that his connections with Hitler and the Nazi Party were materially better than his connections with Goering. Thus, Goering was obliged to keep in the back of his mind the possibility of having to rely upon the Luftwaffe General Staff to help him in curtailing the scope of the State Secretary's influence. But, Goering also feared an overly powerful Luftwaffe General Staff, especially one filled with officers who were, from a point of experience and date of rank as general officers, his superiors.

The State Secretary of Aviation, although he had been a captain at the close of World War I and had been a soldier and officer longer than Goering, was connected with reconnaissance and pilot replacement units, and lacked the dash and color of a highly decorated fighter pilot. He was regarded by the military as a civilian, even though he held the rank of field marshal (a promotion which was granted to him after the pretense of a few days in command of a regular air unit). Goering's dizzy rise had to be accepted as fate, since he was, after all, something like a supreme war lord for the Luftwaffe. But, many of the higher air force leaders felt that it was unbearable to have a second Goering around their necks. This second "civilian" was even more unpleasant and inconvenient because he worked so hard and knew so much about his business, and thus never hesitated to have his say about the conduct of affairs. Was this "working-Goering" to command the Luftwaffe? Neither the General Staff nor its Chief wanted to accept this possibility as an irrevocable fact, and from the time of the organization of the official General Staff, they rebelled against any sort of subordination to the State Secretary and against his constant and all-embracing deputyship. Basically, the General Staff wanted to see its own chief above Milch in the chain of command, thereby leaving only one non-soldier in the Luftwaffe command structure, Goering, who would then find himself facing a united military front. The General Staff felt that, because of his natural indolence, Goering would presumably allow the work of the military to run its course undisturbed in a purely military manner through regular military channels. Everything could then be brought under the control of the Chief of the Luftwaffe General Staff, who would actually function as Commander in Chief of the Luftwaffe.

Milch was a superb organizer and could handle large organizations well. He knew that Goering did little work, and being overloaded with offices and titles, actually would be unable to devote much time to the German Air Force, even if he were inspired by a greater desire for achievement. The State Secretary therefore compensated for Goering's lack of industry. In so doing, however, he was not of a disposition to remain in the shadows. He was, to put it mildly, no Gray Eminence. Neither was it possible for Milch to play such a part had he been so inclined, for his chief was not in the building and seldom close at hand. He was, instead, enthroned in a palace in which, according to his fancy, he would receive the heads of his ministries. Because of Goering's frequent absences, the next in command had to spring into the breach and handle affairs in the Ministry and make the necessary public appearances. Milch became the customary voice of the Luftwaffe before the eyes of the public, acting with full willingness as Goering's right-hand man. Despite the fact that he allowed this, the Reichsmarschall often felt injured because Milch took the laurels, and worried that he might usurp his position. Moreover, there were always plenty of informers in the Third Reich, and it must have embittered Goering to learn that, in the inner circles, Milch occasionally referred to himself as the Minister.

Milch had no intention of yielding even to the Luftwaffe General Staff, when it attempted to subject him to pressures. From his point of view as State Secretary and permanent deputy of the Reichsminister of Aviation, it only stood to reason that he could not relinquish any of his several offices in the establishment, and any influence he could get over the General Staff was all to the good. Milch believed that a deputy had to be a deputy in all things, and he was well aware of many difficulties which were coming to a head. For this reason, he caused the several individual offices in the Ministry to be made immediately subordinate to him, a contradiction to the role of a mere deputy of the Chief.

Goering suspected most of Milch's motives until the very day when Milch left the Luftwaffe, while the Luftwaffe General Staff was anxious to shake off any influence which Milch exerted over it. Hitler's old Party favorite, Goering, never came up with a solution to the problems between the Luftwaffe General Staff and his deputy, the State Secretary. There were three possible courses of action: the first was to allow the State Secretary to exercise his old powers and bid the General Staff to obey his directions; the second, of which Milch may have had ambitious visions, was to make the State Secretary also Chief of the Luftwaffe General Staff, and thus enable him to intercept all opposition (this, of course, would have been a solution with the most serious question marks for the future); the third could have been the dismissal of Milch from the Ministry.

The Reichsmarschall did not satisfy Milch's ambitions for the office of Chief of the General Staff. That would have made Goering's silent rival far too powerful. But, neither did Goering clearly adopt either of the other two possibilities. Milch remained as State Secretary of Aviation and deputy to the Reichsmarschall, and was not sacrificed to the General Staff of the Luftwaffe, despite the Luftwaffe Commander in Chief's anxieties over his hard-working, but ambitious assistant. Nevertheless, Milch's feathers were painfully plucked.

On 2 June 1937, the Reichs Minister of Aviation made the Luftwaffe General Staff directly responsible to himself. He did likewise with all other significant positions within the German Air Force. This arrangement was not effected in a permanent way, so that matters within the Reichs Aviation Ministry, precisely the most decisive and sensitive organization of the entire command, remained in a continuous state of uncertainty and disharmony. This situation persisted until 20 June 1944, when Milch turned over most of his duties and responsibilities to the Speer Ministry, remaining Inspector General of the Luftwaffe for the time being and thus keeping one foot in the establishment. Goering's failure to act decisively and in a farsighted manner in 1937 opened the door to widespread insecurity in the German Air Force, which tended to plague the organization until the very end.

Any effort to evaluate Milch's impact upon the Luftwaffe must begin with the founding of the German Air Ministry. No one will deny that the State Secretary had earned considerable merit in helping to found the Reichs Aviation Ministry, and subsequently, the Luftwaffe.

"Milch," according to Kesselring, "was, next to Goering, the decisive personality, and despite his youth, proved to be extraordinarily useful in the establishment of the Luftwaffe." Generalleutnant Klaus Uebe stated that Milch "taken in the right way and assigned to the right position was a motor without equal."

During his early years with the Ministry, this great aviation specialist was a highly skilled and tactful mentor for the newly arrived Army colonels who were to play such a major role in the German Air Force, and it was he, along with Wever, who converted Goering's great impulses into constructive activity.

In the spring of 1937 Goering ordered a halt on all work concerned with the four-engine bomber, a decision which was to prove disastrous for the Luftwaffe. This order was issued despite the fact that a four-engine bomber program had been in progress since the autumn of 1932, and that on 26 April 1937 the Technical Office of the Luftwaffe listed the Ju-89 and the Do-19 as models ready for testing. Now, however, attention and energies were turned toward the enticing, but overrated, twin-engine bomber, the Ju-88. After the war Milch outlined the importance of the stoppage decision, and lamented that, "The great four-engine bombers of Junkers [Ju-89] and Dornier [Do-19] were not included in the construction series despite excellent performance of test models. Thus we had no really adequate aircraft for strategic operations."

To what extent did Milch himself share in the formulation of this truly disastrous decision? At Nuremberg he commented that on 29 April 1937 the Reichsmarschall had halted construction on the long-range bombers upon the suggestion of the Chief of the General Staff, Kesselring. In the light of this statement, particularly if one considers the tension then existing between the State Secretary and Kesselring, there would seem to be grounds for the assumption that Milch did have a role in making the decision. Yet, Deichmann, who in 1937 was Chief of Branch I of the General Staff, declared that in that same year he had requested an audience with Goering and had expressed (in the presence of the State Secretary) his great concern because he surmised that the Reichsmarschall was going to abandon the four-engine bomber project. Deichmann implored Goering, "in any case to allow the continuation of development of this aircraft." Milch, however, claimed that the advantages ascribed to the four-engine bomber by Deichmann were "pure fantasy," and that the "Ju-88 program left no industrial capacity for the production of four-engine bombers." Milch argued against the supposed advantages such aircraft would have for use at home or abroad, declaring that such claims were in any case irrelevant since the German aircraft industry could produce a bomber fleet of only about 1,000 four-engine aircraft, whereas it could turn out many times that number of twin-engine bombers. He feared, moreover, that the development of even a few large bombers might adversely affect the Ju-88 production program. Deichmann's final pleas that the matter be put to a test rather than decided at once fell on deaf ears, and Goering accepted Milch's view that nothing should be done which could possibly exert a negative influence upon the Ju-88 program.

During the early campaigns of the war, Milch, who had become a field marshal in the great promotion surge of 19 July 1940, was a veritable storehouse of energy. He was untiring in his visits to the front, both as Goering's deputy and (after Udet's death in November 1941) as *Generalluftzeugmeister* (Chief of Special Supply and Procurement). One of the most farsighted actions taken by Milch was the order to supply winter clothing to the Luftwaffe as soon as he heard the plans for an imminent campaign against the Soviet Union. Because of this, and because of the tireless efforts of the Quartermaster General of the Luftwaffe, von Seidel, the German Air Force (unlike the German Army) was quite adequately equipped with proper clothing when the untimely blasts set in late in 1941.

In the summer of 1941, while Germany's fortunes on the Eastern Front were still riding high, Milch found himself forced to assume a most difficult task under problematical circumstances. It had become imperative to intervene in the province of the Chief of Luftwaffe Supply and Procurement, Udet. Udet was directly subordinate to Goering, but was obliged to inform Milch of all important and decisive matters. As Goering's deputy, Milch was able to keep himself informed quite well anyway. Both Milch and Udet were in relatively close contact with one another, and appeared together in various aircraft plants for the testing of new models. But Udet was by nature overly sensitive and tended to build suspicions out of nothing. He disliked the fact that Milch often peered into the workings of his office, especially the huge C-Amt or Technical Office. Udet suspected Milch of secretly coveting his position and of trying to undermine his position in order to enlarge his own sphere of control. There was little doubt that Milch often acted like an imperialist with ruthless elbows, and every failure on Udet's part made Udet more apprehensive of the State Secretary. Because of this situation and the well-known sensitivity of Udet, Goering allowed the Chief of Supply and Procurement to confer directly with

Goering, often without Milch. Udet, in all probability did not relay all of the results of these discussions to the State Secretary.

It still remains unclear why the State Secretary did not take timely action and call attention to the threatening danger that the German aircraft production program might fail, and it is difficult to understand why he did not use his influence as Goering's deputy to make serious remonstrances about the situation to his superior. Of course, the Luftwaffe General Staff did no better in this respect. Both the General Staff and the State Secretary urged an increase in aircraft production, but Udet protested that he was not issued enough raw material from the Wehrmacht High Command to make any progress. The war was clearly becoming a long-drawn-out affair, one which was bound to require increasing amounts of raw materials and which would require increased production in every area.

Milch's failure to alter the situation or to make serious efforts in this direction (despite his hasty temperament) was probably due to his continuous interest in handling Goering with care. Yet, Udet was in some ways closer to the Reichsmarschall than the State Secretary, a fact which may have embittered Milch and made him secretly hostile toward Udet. Furthermore, Milch may have harbored strong feelings about Udet having control over the vast complexes of the Office of Luftwaffe Supply and Procurement, an organization for which the State Secretary was by training and experience much more suited than Udet. According to General der Flieger (Ret.) Karl Bodenschatz, chief of Goering's Ministerial Office, the appointment of Udet as Chief of Luftwaffe Supply and Procurement meant the "sudden exclusion" of Milch from all matters pertaining to defense production. Bodenschatz believed that the State Secretary may have been so embittered by this situation that he was quite willing to let Udet "fend for himself" and, if things took a turn for the worse, "take the full brunt of the consequences." This point of view is understandable from the side of human nature, which manifests itself among the learned as well as among the unenlightened, yet failure to take timely action and thus ward off disaster cannot be condoned in any circumstances.

When Udet's health began to fail, and with Goering's anxieties for the future of the Luftwaffe and of Germany increasing, Milch was finally given a free hand in reorganizing Udet's disarrayed offices. Outwardly Udet was allowed to retain his office, but Milch had the authority to put things in order. With complete disregard for personal considerations, Milch energetically set to work making key changes in Udet's organization. Unable to bear this humiliation and finding himself out of step with the ruthlessness of the Third Reich, and deserted by Goering, Udet chose to take his own life on 17 November 1941.

Milch then had to spring into the breach with full responsibility. He assumed Udet's post, managed to bring aircraft production back into line, and to give the aircraft industry a new impetus. The number of new constructions rose rapidly. Under Udet the monthly fighter production exceeded 400 only in March, April, and May of 1941, and then only because of the dangers arising from the planned offensive against the Soviet Union. In only three other months was Udet able to produce more than 300 fighters. Altogether only 2,992 fighter aircraft were turned out in 1941. But, in 1942, under Milch, the German aircraft industry produced 4,583 fighters, and in 1943, when production began to open up, 9,601 Fw-190's and Me-109's were brought off the assembly lines. The story was much the same for German bombers. In 1941 only 4,007 bombers (Ju-88's, He-111's, and Do-217's) were built, but in 1942 this was increased to 5,228, and in 1943 to 6,601.

The State Secretary of Aviation was much more effective and consistent than his predecessor. He was certainly more energetic, harder, more ruthless, and doggedly tenacious in pursuing his objectives. Yet, he was unable to secure a significant increase in the allocation of raw materials for the Luftwaffe.

The State Secretary of Aviation did save the Luftwaffe from a fatal standstill in the field of aircraft production and air armament, but he cannot be spared the reproach that he gave too little support to new developments in the Luftwaffe while there was still time to effect a turning point in Germany's air war. The Me-163, for example, a creation of the Messerschmitt engineer Professor Alexander Lippisch, had been completed in several models as early as 1939, and on 10 May 1941 had flown at a speed of 621.138 miles per hour. This plane could have protected Germany's vital production centers had Milch expedited its completion. He likewise failed to put his shoulder squarely behind the wheel in promoting the Me-262 jet fighter (and probably also the Arado Ar-234 jet), whose development was cautiously continued by Willi Messerschmitt despite an order in 1940 to halt new developments. In this entirely new area of jet propulsion Milch turned out to be the epitome of timidity, fearing that any failure in the program could bring about his dismissal.

The post which had been held by Udet and which was taken over after his demise by Milch was not an enviable one. More and more as Hitler began to express his annoyance with Goering and the progressive weakening of the German air forces, the embittered Reichsmarschall felt compelled to resist with all his might the curtailment of his own powers and influence. Hence, he began to exert pressures downward, and the State Secretary-Chief of Supply and Procurement was the first person to feel the impact of these attacks. Goering, in the discussion of 3 October 1943 (during which time he condemned his former best friend, Udet), became coarse and blustering, shouting:

> What does the Field Marshal [Milch] think he's doing anyway? . . . Six months ago he told me not to worry, that by this time everything would be in order. What kind of a pig-sty is this? . . . Things have become worse than they were under Udet! Where is the increased production? There is none, except for the fighter planes! If the construction of bombers is stopped, then it's no trick to produce more fighters!

As Goering's influence over Hitler diminished to the point of a tensely camouflaged crisis, the relationship between Goering and Milch deteriorated correspondingly. Comments carelessly made by the State Secretary came to the ears of the Reichsmarschall, making him (who knew only too well how insecure was his seat in the saddle) still more furious and suspicious. One day Goering revealed to his old comrade and Chief of Luftwaffe Personnel, Generaloberst Bruno Loerzer, that he wanted to make him head of a new office, Chief of Personnel Armament, which was to be directly subordinate to the Reichsmarschall, and in which all personnel offices would be united. Then, according to Loerzer:

> Goering took from Milch all jurisdiction over legal matters, which Milch had held until then, as well as the right to grant pardons. Practically nothing was left to Milch. His position as State Secretary had been completely undermined. I asked Goering, "What is Milch to say to that?" He answered me, "I want to have these things close to me. Milch is always working against me."

In February 1944 the Luftwaffe suffered the most dire distress from American and British air attacks. On 1 March, with the authoritative cooperation of Milch, a Fighter Staff (*Jaegerstab*) was formed, an organization established to protect the defense plants and to expedite fighter aircraft production. Speer and Milch were its leaders. Saur, at the request of Milch, became his chief of staff. For the tremendous defense work which then got under way, the Chief of Supply and Procurement (Milch) could not claim the sole credit. In fact, Milch's

THE REORGANIZATION OF I FEBRUARY 1939 *

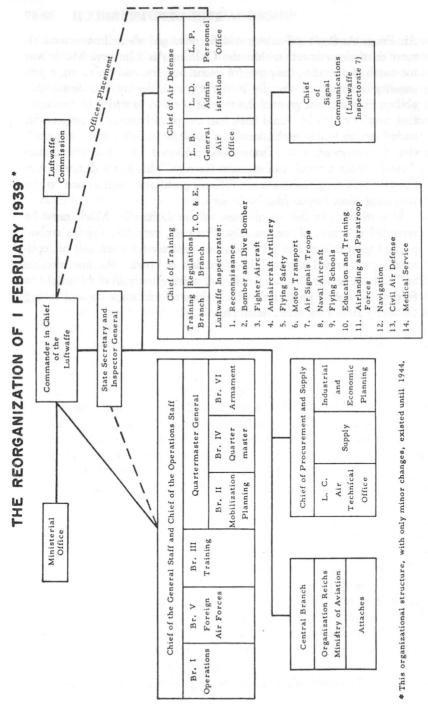

FIGURE 3

* This organizational structure, with only minor changes, existed until 1944.

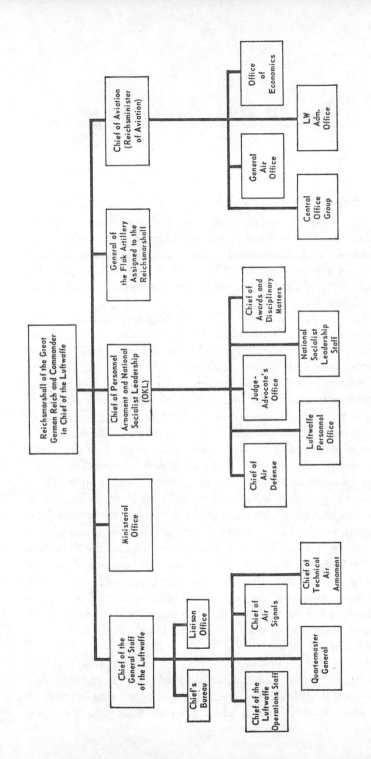

FIGURE 4

6
The Artist: Udet

ONE OF THE MOST COLORFUL and best known of the five personalities who held the highest positions of responsibility in giving form to the German Air Force was Ernst Udet, a man with cosmopolitan outlooks and numerous friends among the artists and intellectuals. His appointment in 1936 to a high post in the Luftwaffe undoubtedly invested the German air arm with some of the magic surrounding his famous name.

Udet, who served as Luftwaffe Chief of Supply and Procurement until his death, was the first German Air Force leader to surrender to despair concerning Germany's chances for an ultimate victory, and to see no further purpose in life or possibility for his continued existence in a high military post. Strangely enough, Udet was the most cheerful serene leader in the Luftwaffe and a man who seemed, at least outwardly, to be the most confident officer of them all. When he later took his own life, the particulars of his suicide were withheld from the public for fear of the possible interpretation which might have been put upon it by enemy military leaders and foreign powers as well as by the German people. His death was officially attributed to an air accident, which helped to produce a legend about this famous personality. It was broadly hinted that Hitler, Goering, and even Milch might well have had a hand in his demise. In reality, Udet's suicide was the inevitable and final aspect of a breakdown in his personality and the disastrous events which he had so irrevocably set in motion. The death of this unusual man was the culmination of a life which, although apparently composed and settled, was intensely linked with a series of errors and signal failures in Luftwaffe planning, development, and production. All of these were, in short, cardinal failures in Udet's leadership of the Luftwaffe Technical Office.

Udet, the son of a businessman, was born on 26 April 1896 and was a flying enthusiast even in his earliest school days. Everything that went up seemed to enthrall him, whether it was lighter-than-air craft or airplanes. During World War I, while still little more than a boy, he became one of the most famous combat pilots in the Imperial German Army, and, with sixty-two aerial victories, achieved a record which stands second only to that of the legendary Captain Manfred Freiherr von Richthofen, the "Red Knight of Germany." Udet's victory score stood three times higher than that achieved by Goering, Richthofen's second successor to the command of his famous Fighter Wing No. 1. Among a host of high decorations and honors Udet received the coveted order of Pour le Mérite.

One by one, Goering selected nearly all of his old Pour le Mérite comrades of World War I for the new German Air Force. Most of them were only too glad to answer his call, and the gap between their lowly World War I ranks and their service ages was generously closed by means of rapid promotions. Udet was naturally on Goering's list, for a service branch starting from scratch could hardly afford to ignore a personality who had already become a legendary figure.

On 1 June 1935 he entered the German Air Force with the rank of colonel, and on 10 February 1936 was appointed to succeed Ritter von Greim as Inspector of Fighter and Dive-Bomber Forces. In this capacity, Udet, a connoisseur of small aircraft, was right in his element, and was finally in a position to influence aviation matters to a great extent. Thus, one of Germany's most talented pilots had come to a point where he had a force of enthusiastic and youthful workers and the opportunity to advance his own wishes in developmental work.

It was unfortunate for Udet and for the Luftwaffe that he did not hold this position (for which he was so ideally suited) for a longer time. On 9 June 1936 he was named Chief of the Technical Office, a far more comprehensive area of responsibility and a completely different kind of job.

With his appointment as Chief of the Technical Office, the wheels of destiny were set in motion for Udet as a person. At the same time, the appointment entailed the grave risk that in the long run his appointment might turn out to be detrimental for the fields of development and procurement in the Luftwaffe. No one had been more free than Udet for the previous seventeen years, and the only responsibilities he had accepted in all that time were those which just happened to coincide with his own desires, none of which involved long-term responsibility. Above all, no one had ever tied him down to a desk or committed him to a definite routine. The plain fact was that actual professional military service was something entirely new to him, especially the constant awareness, even in the highest ranks, of the need to be a shining example of order and self-discipline.

When Udet took over the Technical Office, its organization structure was horizontal—in other words, testing and manufacturing were on an equal level, and each of these departments dealt with all the various types of aircraft and with the models of each type. In the quiet efficiency which had characterized his activity as Chief of the Technical Office, Wimmer had managed to provide his successor with an enviable legacy of developmental work which gave promise of bearing tangible fruit in the near future in the form of aircraft much superior to those produced by Germany's neighbors. These aircraft were the bombers, the Ju-86 (which, of course, later proved to be unsatisfactory), the capable He-111 and Do-17, whose flying characteristics in initial tests had aroused the enthusiasm of Wever.

There were also two four-engine bombers, the Do-19 and the Ju-89, which were being tested by two aircraft firms. During 1935-36 there were three dive-bomber models being tested, the Ju-87 A, the Ar-81, and the He-118. With a perfectly clear conscience, Udet was able to decide on the more capable and robust Ju-87. As a matter of fact, this aircraft later proved to be valuable during the war, first in support of the successful offensives of the Wehrmacht, and later (until almost the very end of the war) in support of German infantry forces in their unequal struggle against the Red Army.

As far as fighters were concerned, the Arado, Heinkel, and Messerschmitt companies had all been commissioned to design an up-to-date model, and all of them had possible aircraft ready for testing. Soon after taking over office from Wimmer, Udet flew all three models in a comparative performance test and decided in favor of the Me-109, a choice which was fully justified in view of its subsequent highly satis-factory service.

The first serious problem encountered by Udet in his new office was the critical state of the raw material situation, a problem which became apparent at the beginning of 1937. Primarily, it took the form of short-ages in iron, steel, and aluminum and had a catastrophic impact upon the Luftwaffe's program. Not only did it greatly delay the fulfillment of program goals, but it also prevented an urgently needed expansion of the armaments industry. The Heinkel and Messerschmitt companies were even forced to lay off valuable personnel as a result of the curtail-ment of their production orders. Needless to say, when the war began the lack of these trained workers made itself painfully felt. Luftwaffe leaders made no effort to avoid, or even to mitigate, the effects of the curtailed allotments by means of a drastic cut in their own program, in particular by a modification of the Luftwaffe's construction program.

But this situation had little to do with the sins of commission or omission perpetrated by Udet and his staff.

Udet had a valuable legacy which was just beginning to bear fruit, and he had access to the counsel of a man of wide experience in precisely the field in which he needed help. This man was Milch. One must weigh the human aspects of all these things in order to judge with any degree of fairness. There is no doubt that the former director of Lufthansa was flattered to be asked for his opinions, and it was both necessary and personally satisfying to him, as the permanent deputy of the Reichs Aviation Minister, to keep the important sector of air armament under constant surveillance to prevent what he considered to be steps in the wrong direction. There could be no denying that air armament was one of the most vital fields in the Aviation Ministry.

These circumstances took on even greater significance after the death of Wever, when Milch and Kesselring (Wever's successor as Chief of the General Staff) came into conflict concerning the leadership of the Ministry. Kesselring sought to strip the State Secretary (who had hitherto kept an eye on all of the Ministry offices) of every vestige of power, and had little concern about Udet. The Technical Office was subordinate to the State Secretary (in his capacity to act as permanent deputy for the Reichs Minister of Aviation), and because of this, was not one of the offices being contested between Kesselring and Milch. The Technical Office was in direct subordination (with Milch's guidance and supervision) to Goering, who alone could decide what its status was to be. On 18 January 1938, when the Chief of the General Staff-State Secretary conflict was interrupted (although never finally resolved) by a top-level reorganization, Goering was obliged to intervene more directly than before in Ministry matters, while Milch was deprived of considerable power. Udet and the rest of the office chiefs were directly subordinated under the Reichs Minister of Aviation.

This reorganization of the top-level of the Reichs Aviation Ministry is recognized as the beginning in that body of a lack of cohesion and leadership. The changes wrought by this reorganization deprived the State Secretary of his authority to keep an eye on the technical Office, but in effect provided no alternative supervision. Goering had no intention of stepping into the breach, although this was the logical and consistent thing for him to have done.

The new organizational arrangement was extremely significant to Udet. Goering's relationship to him (a former comrade-in-arms) became more intimate than to the other men directly under his command, even Milch. Consequently, it was clear that the right of direct access to the

Reichsminister could have a more profound effect upon Udet than anyone else, except the Chief of the Luftwaffe General Staff.

All this, of course, was bound to strain the association between Udet and Milch. The State Secretary was keenly aware that the reorganization had been primarily directed at his office, and he could not help but interpret Udet's direct subordination to Goering as a loss of another important area of influence, and may even have wondered if it did not come about, in part, by Udet's urging.

When Udet first assumed direction of his new office the relationship between the two men was harmonious, and the "Milchians" were always ready to assist the "Udetians" in any way they could. Ploch states that the relationship between the two men was like that of father to son. After the reorganization, however, Milch became more reserved, and it appeared to many that Udet, whose self-confidence had been immediately boosted by the change, was drawing away from his former friend. After all, the Luftwaffe, with all of its new aircraft models, was well on the way to becoming the best in the world, and on 1 April 1937 Udet was promoted to Generalmajor and on 1 November 1938 to Generalleutnant.

In these circumstances, Udet, who was approaching the climax of his career, was not inclined to keep Milch too well informed about his conferences with Goering and the activities of the Technical Office. He had no desire for a guardian, and now that he had been granted the right of direct access to Goering, he defended this privilege jealously and suspiciously. Udet's inclination toward suspicion was one of his more unfortunate qualities, especially so since he often held this attitude when it was wholly unnecessary.

With the deterioration of his relationship with Milch, Udet lost a pillar of support which he badly needed, especially on the shifting ground on which he stood in the labyrinth of complex air armament functions. He therefore continued on without an experienced and level-headed advisor, being forced to rely more and more upon his own subordinates. This brought to an end the possibility for fruitful work in the armament sector of the Ministry. His chief of staff, Ploch, was not particularly helpful, since he too found it difficult to maintain a comprehensive view of all that was transpiring. Udet's adjutant, Colonel Max Pendele, was a willing assistant as far as his own area of responsibility was concerned, but was not a highly competent advisor nor a solid supporting pillar. Udet therefore had no alternative but to place himself in the hands of his top engineers, whom he had made the most important people in the Technical Office.

When a supervisor who is not entirely sure in his field falls under the influence of his subordinates, it probably lies in the nature of things that these subordinates then do their utmost to keep their chief isolated from other, outside, influences. Can it be doubted then that Udet's subordinates did nothing to mitigate the growing estrangement between their chief and the State Secretary?

The estrangement between Udet and Milch was unfortunate to begin with. Later on, however, when the first real difficulties and genuine disappointments began to crop up following the successful early years, it became positively detrimental. The old huntsman Udet had stumbled into a pitfall which was to be as disastrous to himself as it was to the Luftwaffe. This trap concerned the two aircraft models, Ju-88 and He-177. In each of these two cases the aircraft represented a thoroughly feasible aeronautical idea. Great hopes were placed in both of them, and in the case of the Ju-88 an all-out effort was ordered and full authority granted to insure its timely production in quantities to impress the world. This was designed as a high-speed bomber with a long penetration range. If the aircraft was able to meet the range objectives (620 miles) of its designers, it would then be able to cover all of Great Britain and the waters surrounding it. According to Major Helmuth Pohle, in the spring of 1938 the General Staff intended to requisition only 200 test models of the Ju-88 (all equipped for diving performance) as a basis for further development. However, these planes were suddenly released for mass production in the autumn of 1938, mainly because of the Czechoslovakian crisis. Owing to the speed of the Ju-88, the Technical Office calculated that its armaments could be reduced as well as the overall weight of the aircraft.

This estimation was shattered by the demand of the Luftwaffe General Staff for diving performance. This requirement was fostered and advanced by a group of young engineers, although Udet liked the idea as well. For a twin-engine aircraft to be capable of dive performance, it required a much more solid and robust construction as well as the installation of dive brakes; this, in turn, meant decreasing the speed because of a considerable increase in weight. As if this were not enough, the decreased speed then made it mandatory to install additional airborne armament. According to the original plans the plane was to have a flying weight of about six tons, which would have allowed its development into a really high-speed bomber, but by the time the plans had been altered for the last time, the weight had increased from six to nearly thirteen tons. Milch describes the final result as a "flying barn door which was capable of becoming a bird again" only after it had dropped its load of bombs. In connection with the increase in weight of the Ju-88, Dr. Heinrich Koppenberg, Member of the Board of Directors of the Junkers firm, mentioned the "horrendous number of changes, some 25,000 in all," which contributed to the problem.

Goering's hopes, which were certainly shared by Hitler, became pressing obligations for Udet. He therefore breathed a sigh of relief on 15 October 1939 when he was able to unload these responsibilities on the robust shoulders of Koppenberg. On this day Goering gave Koppenberg general, overall authority to requisition any other aircraft plants outside of the Junkers complex which might be required for the manufacture of the Ju-88. The industry was thus forced to give top priority to the Ju-88 program.

The conferences and planning for the production of the Ju-88 occurred under the pressure of a potential conflict with Great Britain, a possibility which Luftwaffe leaders had not previously foreseen. Koppenberg's crucial failure—by the beginning of World War II there was only one group of Ju-88's complete with aircrews and ready for action—understandably resulted in a general feeling of anxiety. As a matter of fact, on the occasion of a joint trip through the Midland Canal (*Mittellandkanal*) in the spring of 1939, Lieutenant Colonel Josef Schmid heard Goering remark to Jeschonnek, "What can we do about Udet? He can't possibly accomplish what we need!"

Pendele's chronology of Udet records a visit on 15 August 1939 by Udet to Hitler, with the notation, "Difficulties in the mass production of the Ju-88." The worry about the postponement of the production deadline for the Ju-88, which put it nearly a year behind schedule, was augmented by worry about its diving performance. The latest requirement demanding full diving capability cost the life of Captain Freiherr von Moreau, a capable and highly-experienced officer. A few expert pilots like Pohle were able to achieve a dive at 80°, but Pohle's hope that average pilots could be trained to accomplish this feat was never realized. Pohle, Technical Officer on the Luftwaffe Operations Staff, had been too optimistic in judging others on the basis of his own flying ability. During the war, as it turned out, the Ju-88's were used in diving attacks only over water, while the gliding approach was preferred over land targets. Thus, in the final analysis, the aircraft had been increased in weight and encumbered unnecessarily.

Udet was in his element during visits to the aircraft plants, especially when he was able to guide foreign visitors over the premises to show them the available facilities. In his memoirs, Heinkel gives us a rather ill-humored report of the masterful aplomb with which Udet guided the French Air Marshal Joseph Vuillemin around the Heinkel plant in August 1938 and, in fact, even led him around by the nose a bit by representing the German air armament program to be considerably more extensive than it was in reality. As we know now, guided tours of this sort played their part in maintaining the peace.

In a situation like this, Udet was an actor and his performance was highly effective. After all, he was used to enthusing a world audience with his aerial acrobatics. However, while it was all very well to deceive foreign visitors on the grounds that such deception served the cause of peace, Udet had no right to deceive the commander in chief of his service branch or the chief of government of his nation by giving them overoptimistic information during their extensive tours, so that they were bound to draw erroneous conclusions as to the real strength of the Luftwaffe and the deadline dates by which they might expect new, highly significant developments on a mass-production scale. Yet, this is precisely what Udet did during a highly critical period for Germany's foreign policy.

On 3 July 1939 Hitler and Goering visited the testing center at Rechlin. Pohle, who took part in the inspection visit as a representative of the Luftwaffe General Staff, commented:

> The day before a dress rehearsal of the visit was held. During the rehearsal, Udet gave a speech in which he mentioned each individual model and made a number of very incautious predictions as to how soon each would be ready for testing at unit level. I immediately mentioned my reservations to Jeschonnek, and as a result Udet was more careful the next day. Any tour of this kind has a certain fascination for the participants. Goering simply let himself be carried along by this fascination, but Hitler was not taken in to the same degree. Nevertheless, this visit to Rechlin was poison, for Hitler as well as for Goering.

On 13 September 1942 Goering gave vent to his reproaches with these words: "I witnessed demonstrations at Rechlin before the war, and I can only say, what bunglers all our alleged magicians are! The things which I, and the Fuehrer as well, were shown there have never come true!" At this time his anger was directed chiefly against the industry. In March 1942, however (again during a visit to Rechlin), Goering remarked, "Actually I had made up my mind not to set foot again inside the testing station at Rechlin after the way its engineers deceived the Fuehrer and me during an inspection visit in the summer of 1939, when they really sold us a bill of goods. As a result of what he had seen during this visit, the Fuehrer made a number of highly important decisions. We have only our good fortune to thank that things turned out as well as they have and that the consequences were not more serious."

Goering's comments were a reproach against the engineer personnel of the Luftwaffe, but especially those associated with Rechlin. Generalingenieur Huebner replied to this attack by saying, "It is clear enough that the full responsibility for the 1939 inspection visit must be borne by the Chief of Luftwaffe Supply and Procurement, Generaloberst Udet."

Hitler also mentioned the Rechlin visit as one of the reasons for the ultimate failure of the German air arm. Milch claims that he warned Hitler at that time, "My Fuehrer, the things which you are seeing here are things which will not be ready for use in front-line units for another five years."

Although the development of the He-177 had been carried on with the utmost nonchalance up to that time, from then on no time was lost in rushing it into production (without even providing for adequate testing). All of the requirements and instructions from Berlin to the Heinkel firm reflected the nervousness of people who had lost their footing where they once assumed they were standing on solid ground. The plants at Oranienburg and the Weser Flying Works were to assume the manufacture of the aircraft, and by mid-1940 were scheduled to be turning out 120 per month. During an encounter in late March in Berlin, Heinkel found Udet in a highly restless state and smoking nervously. Udet remarks, "I hope there won't be any trouble with the He-177. The Ju-88 has caused enough difficulty for my taste. The He-177 has got to get into operation. We don't have any other large bomber that we can use against England. The He-177 has got to fly! . . . It must!"

This mood of depression and anxiety was dispelled briefly by the storm of rejoicing over the triumphant campaign in France. Generalrichter Dr. Kraell remembered that Udet was exultant about this and repeated again and again that the "war is over. Our plans [the aircraft program] are not worth a damn! . . . We don't need them any longer!"

The Chief of Supply and Procurement, like Goering and most of Germany's top-level military leaders in World War II, who never really thought through the terrible dangers inherent in such a conflict, had

Ju 87: The famous "Stuka" dive-bomber used with terrifying effectiveness against Poland and France. It proved to be less useful later on against seasoned troops. (Army Air Force Photo National Archives)

Ju 87: In flight the "Stuka," a relatively slow-speed plane, was vulnerable to steady antiaircraft fire when it pulled out of its screaming dive. (Official U.S. Air Force Photo)

Ju 52: The workhorse of the Luftwaffe; the three-engine transport that was the equivalent of our DC 3. Sturdy and versatile, it could carry between 22 and 30 men. (Official U.S. Air Force Photo)

Me 109: A single-engine fighter; one of the mainstays of the Luftwaffe. Its range was 440 miles. (Army Air Force Photo National Archives)

Me 109: Despite Allied bombing, the Germans produced increasing numbers of fighters, including the Me 109, during the later years of the war. In 1943, for example, more than 9,000 fighters rolled off the production lines in Germany. (Official U.S. Air Force Photo)

Me 110: A twin-engine night fighter; one of the major defensive weapons against Allied bombers with a range of 1,300 miles. (Official U.S. Air Force Photo)

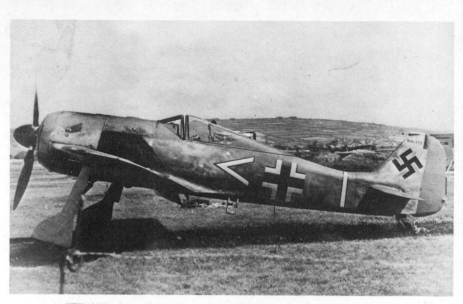

FW 190: One of the few new planes developed and produced by Germans during the War; a single engine fighter designed to replace the older Me 109. (Army Air Force Photo, National Archives)

FW 109: Had a range of 525 miles; used mainly for defense over Germany against daylight bombing attacks by American B 17 Flying Fortresses. (Official U.S. Air Force Photo)

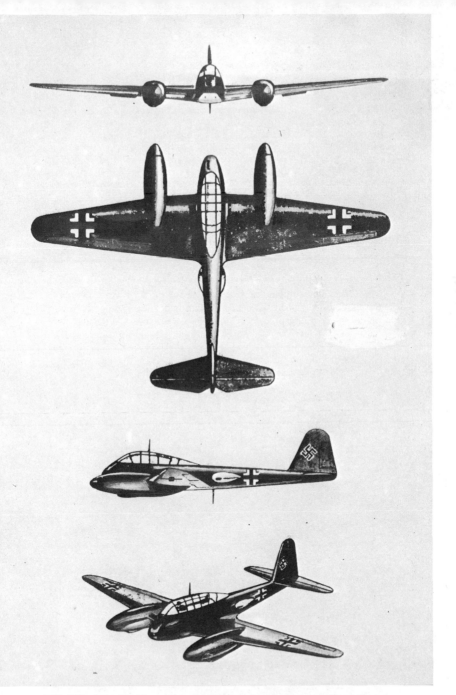

ME 210: Developed as a new model of the Me 110; a twin-engine long-range fighter. Its production was held up by the requirement that it include a dive-bombing capability. (Navy Department, National Archives)

Me 210: The dive-bombing requirement for the new Me 210 caused tremendous waste in labor and manufacturing. Although some planes were finally produced, the delays made them useless as new weapons. (Official U.S. Air Force Photo)

Me 262: Germany's new jet fighter, developed in 1941, could have been ready for production after test fliers expressed delight with its performance. It could have made a major difference in Germany's defense against Allied bombing attacks. (Official U.S. Air Force Photo)

Me 262: Hitler's demand that the Me 262 be equipped for bombing missions in addition to its fighter capability delayed production until it was too late for the jet to go into action in any effective way. (Army Air Force Photo, National Archives)

He 111: A twin-engine bomber that could carry four-550 pound bombs. It was one of the major attack weapons of the Luftwaffe. (Army Air Force Photo, National Archives)

Do 17: One of Germany's older twin-engine planes; another one of the Luftwaffe's major attack bombers. (Official U.S. Air Force Photo)

Do 17: A light bomber; used extensively in all major German campaigns in missions over the Low Countries and over England and Russia.

succumbed to the intoxication of victory. At the same time, Udet's fantastic optimism helped to buoy him up in the face of the nagging worry over low aircraft production, the unforeseen delays in the Ju-88 program, and its failure to measure up to the prescribed standards, especially in terms of range. Udet was further encouraged by being promoted to the rank of General der Flieger on 1 April 1940, and to Generaloberst on 19 July 1940.

But this enjoyment was short-lived for Udet, a bon vivant and a courageous man who had the misfortune to be completely misplaced in his job assignment, a man who would much have preferred an airman's life, engaged in untrammeled combat for victory or death. The failure of the offensive against Great Britain, the mounting aircraft losses resulting from this seemingly endless struggle, and the disappointments connected with the long-range fighter model, the Me-110, were becoming increasingly painful. All of these worries affected his health and his ability to cope with problems.

In June he allowed himself to be persuaded by Koppenberg (who wanted to make his Ju-88 the standard bomber of the Luftwaffe) to postpone the production deadline for the He-177 by three months and to limit production to three aircraft per month for the time being. Udet's share in the development stoppage of 7 February 1940 (when his carefree days ended) has still not been established beyond doubt. Even the concept of the development stoppage and Udet's first reaction to the overall affair require further investigation. In any case, the first rude awakening came when, in consequence of Hitler's contemplated action against the Soviet Union, air armament was placed fifth on the list for the allocation of raw materials. As a result, the Luftwaffe had to cancel all of its plans for expansion.

According to Pendele, this extremely unfavorable priority allocation came right after the armistice agreement with France. Germany's leaders, however, still under the spell of victory, allowed themselves to be comforted in the hope of an early peace. It seemed to matter little that the Luftwaffe fared badly in the allotment of raw materials, and neither the General Staff nor the Chief of Supply and Procurement tended to think seriously of their plans in terms of accumulated wartime experience or within the framework of the impending war against Russia. After all, the latter project must have occupied the minds of top Luftwaffe leaders from a fairly early date, and those who were most concerned ought to have made every effort to find a way in which urgently needed aircraft (especially those best suited for the coming action), and those which were cheapest to manufacture in terms of raw materials, could still have been turned out despite restrictions and un-favorable priority ratings. Past experience pointed in the direction of es-tablishing strong tactical air forces from which a strategic air fleet should have been created. Production of the single-engine bomber should have been increased considerably, while that of the twin-engine machine could well have been reduced, since single-engine bombers could have been utilized with greater economy in the coming conflict with the Soviet Union against relatively weak air defenses.

With the opening of the campaign against the Soviet Union all of the factors which had sown their seeds of disaster beneath the surface began to come out into the open: the lack of internal leadership within the huge agency, Udet's inability to cope with an industry which was neither innocuous nor reliable, and the isolation of a man who was more and more drifting along with events. Udet did not have a single strong personality to stand beside him as a loyal subordinate, and lacked any significantly strong personalities in the various subsections of his organization. The edifice had forfeited whatever solid founda-tions it had, and there seemed to be no way to stop the swaying so that armament activity could function smoothly and even speed up its tempo.

A firm hand had been conspicuously lacking with respect to the se-lective reduction of aircraft models then being produced and develop-ment programs which seemed unpromising. The fact remains that at the time things were building up toward Udet's downfall, the sixteenth major aircraft program since the beginning of the war had just been launched. The constant need for modifications which is reflected by this figure clearly indicates the degree of uncertainty present in the pro-duction program. However, it must be admitted that many of these modifications were the result of Goering's indiscriminate approval of every change suggested by his pampered young coterie of Luftwaffe stars and of the fact that Udet, in order to obviate any possibility of confusion, ordered a separate program designation even in the case of relatively insignificant changes.

Heinkel reported that he received a message early in February 1941 from his business agent in Berlin (a private air attaché such as those kept by all of the German aircraft firms) to the effect that the "confu-sion in the Technical Office and in the aircraft industry as a whole was beyond belief."

That month, Goering started an argument with his old friend, Udet. The Reichsmarschall himself had been sharply criticized by Hitler, who demanded an explanation of why the German Air Force was so far behind. Goering realized by that time that he had made a mistake in supporting Udet for the task of Chief of Supply and Procurement and the Technical Office. The unfavorable production figures in the aircraft industry—these were ultimately traceable to the failure to order all-out industrial mobilization in 1939—had become intolerable to the Luftwaffe's Commander in Chief, just as they had to Hitler. Goering then told Udet, "If I were not in trouble, I wouldn't need you!"

On the other hand, Udet—tormented by worry—was simply ignored when his concern over the increasing number of British flights over German territory led him to issue warnings such as the following: "If we cannot considerably increase the fighter forces and cannot go off the defensive by 1942, the war is lost."

Udet was also concerned about the possibility of America's entry into the war. At about this same time, he also discussed the need for strengthening the fighter arm with Fritz Siebel, Luftwaffe entrepreneur and an old friend of his. Siebel reports that the former dashing fighter pilot was "gravely ill, apathetic, plagued once again by serious hemorrhage headaches, and an intolerable buzzing in the ears for which no doctor seemed to be able to find a cure."

Just before the beginning of the campaign in Russia, Goering had made a decision which was to have tragic consequences for Udet, and which was bound to wound him deeply, for this decision brought to the fore a man whom Udet had feared ever since their friendship had come to an end, Milch. Yet Goering's decision was not a sword blow, intended to sever the Gordian knot, but only a half measure, pointing in the direction of his growing determination to deprive the Chief of Supply and Procurement of his power.

On 20 June 1941, the Reichsmarschall issued orders to Milch to the effect that a "quadrupling of the present level of production in all sectors of armament" was to be achieved "within the shortest possible time." In order to permit the fastest possible accomplishment of this production increase ordered by the Fuehrer, Milch was given full authority to take whatever steps he deemed necessary.

The Chief of Supply and Procurement was reduced to a nonentity. In short, Udet's huge agency could no longer function without close (and eventually subordinate) coordination with Milch. Milch was selected to bring about a quadrupling of air armament production, a feat which was impossible without a clearly defined program, which in turn implied a careful selection of the models to be produced. Milch's intervention could no longer be resisted on the grounds that it represented intrigue, since it became his duty to intervene if he was to carry out his orders. This naturally led to tremendous friction and produced conflicts which would have been extremely difficult for Udet, even if he had a firmer hand on the reins, and even if Milch was a man of less efficiency and ruthlessness in doing a businesslike job.

Goering's half measure was his refusal to call a spade a spade by failing to cut clear to the heart of the matters by subordinating the entire office of the Chief of Supply and Procurement to the State Secretary. It was a typical case of attempting to put out the fire without getting anything wet! Milch was to be in charge, but at the same time, Udet, Goering's old comrade, was to be spared any embarrassment. Udet knew that he had forfeited his freedom of action and no longer had a voice in matters, even though this had not actually been put into writing. Half measures, even when motivated by the best of intentions, invariably do more harm than harsher measures which are more in keeping with the realities of the situation. A direct replacement of Udet by the harder-nerved Milch, and the assignment of Udet to a suitable important post might have saved Germany one of her most famous pilots. It is, of course, possible that Udet, by this time bruised and exhausted, might have followed the path of desperation in spite of such a solution.

There was now no clear delineation of areas of authority between Milch and Udet. The two of them still went on inspection tours together, and there were many joint conferences which both had to attend. But none of these enforced associations were able to resurrect the old friendship. Udet felt his own power slipping with each encounter, while Milch could hardly help being annoyed by Udet's passive resistance.

Udet's first open and bitter disagreement with Milch came on 9 August 1941. Pendele and Ploch were in Milch's office and Milch asked them, "What's the status of aircraft program 17-a?" Ploch replied, "Udet has gone to see the Reichsmarschall about it." Milch, who felt that Udet had gone over his head, banged on the desk and declared that the program had been assigned a scope ten times greater than was actually necessary. Milch picked up the telephone and ordered Udet's return, whereupon Goering sent the State Secretary a blistering cable. The Reichsmarschall, however, still refused to make a clear delineation of the command problem. On 17 July he summoned both Milch and Udet before him and reprimanded them for their inability to get along with one another.

Milch brought up the question of a reorganization of the office of the

Chief of Supply and Procurement. Udet was reluctant, but finally agreed that the twenty-two section chiefs should be replaced by four office chiefs. His colleagues, the engineers who were mentioned earlier and Ploch, all bitter enemies of Milch, did what they could to sabotage the reorganization idea, while Goering continued to refrain from taking firm action.

Goering advised Udet to take a vacation. His attitude was still a friendly one, and he even invited Udet to spend some time in the peace and quiet of the Rominten Heath. But Udet had lost his interest in hunting, and soon returned to a sanatorium.

While Udet was convalescing, Milch paid a visit to him and once more brought up the matter of a proposed reorganization of the Office of Supply and Procurement. Milch's visit was hardly conducive to the successful continuation of Udet's cure, especially since Udet had, meanwhile, withdrawn his approval of the reorganization idea. However, on 7 September 1941 Goering gave Milch the necessary approval for organizational changes within the Technical Office and the Office of the Chief of Supply and Procurement. The axe soon began to fall. The most important members of Udet's staff were dropped, one after the other.

On the morning of 17 November, Udet telephoned Mrs. Inge Bleyle, the woman who shared his life, and said hurriedly, "Inge, I can't stand it any longer. I'm going to shoot myself. I wanted to say goodbye to you. They're after me."

Mrs. Bleyle said afterwards: "In vain I pleaded with him, and begged him to wait. I told him that I would be right there. I heard the shot over the telephone. When I got there, he was dead. His bed was covered with notes, brief letters of farewell."

7
A Child of His Times: Jeschonnek

HANS JESCHONNEK, the fourth Chief of the Luftwaffe General Staff, was merely a boy in 1914 when he was infected by the enthusiasm of that year, and as a very young volunteer fought in many of the great battles of the German Army. Like many other German military men, he was deeply depressed by the collapse in 1918, which he found almost incomprehensible after having witnessed so many victories.

The outcome of World War I was such that it influenced the intellectual development of Germany's soldiers in two main directions, or extremes. One group viewed any future involvement of Germany with great anxiety, fearing that even local engagements would result immediately in a gigantic coalition of enemies against them and thus lead to a multi-front war.

On the other side there were those, generally the younger men (many of whom had held junior positions at the front), who recalled mainly the great accomplishments of German arms in the war, and especially those achieved against heavy odds. They tended to equate the final defeat with the failure of the political and military leadership. The real causes of Germany's defeat were in their eyes of scant consequence, and they often expressed the idea that the German Army was "unconquered in the field," a phrase which also became the theme of a three-volume work by General von Dickhut-Harrach.

This belief in the invincibility of the German Army became a deep conviction of German youth, and the idea was expanded to include the concept that a German Army could never be conquered as long as the homeland, in time of war, was not the victim of a stab in the back. Out of this grew an incredible pride, and leaders who shared this conviction were filled with an almost childlike optimism concerning the strength of their people. They had no difficulty in finding faithful followers. The strongest believer of all was Hitler, who continued almost to the end to think that Germany's fortunes would change.

Jeschonnek also belonged to the circle which believed in a great and victorious future. His feelings were intensified by his personal devotion to Hitler, whom he saw as a genius of first rank. But in Jeschonnek there was nothing of the demonic which might have made him impervious to the vicissitudes of war or reason. Instead, he had an alert, acute mind which eventually led him to recognize the real truth beneath events, and to see that Hitler, and he along with Hitler, had been wrong. Victory was no longer to be achieved and defeat was certain. With this realization the strength of his personality was shattered. Moreover, there were the threats which menaced his position, and the problem of Goering. Patriotic, sensitive, ambitious, and naturally optimistic, Jeschonnek finally anticipated the approaching calamity. Suicide for him was the only proper way to preserve the hard and unshakable mask of the soldier. Far more lonely than hundreds of thousands of his comrades-in-arms, he died as he had lived, a child of his times.

Jeschonnek, son of an assistant secondary school master, was born in Hohensala, then part of Prussia, on 9 April 1899. He volunteered for war service at the age of fifteen and a half years and attended the Cadet School at Berlin-Lichterfeld, thereby qualifying for service in World War I. By 1915, he had received his commission as a lieutenant and two years later made his way to the ranks of Fighter Squadron 40. When the end of the war came, he had two aerial victories to his credit.

He served in the Army Ordnance Department from 1923 to 1928, when he completed his General Staff training as the best officer in his class, and then served in the Inspectorate of the Reichswehr Ministry. In 1934, he attained the rank of captain in Bomber Wing 152 and in 1935 he was promoted to major. The following year on 1 October he assumed command of Training Group III of Air Administrative Area I in Greifswald. This assignment was one of the happiest of his career and he was able to take an active part in the testing and experimentation of aircraft, which helped bring the Luftwaffe rapidly to the forefront among the world's air forces.

Jeschonnek was a colonel at the young age of thirty-nine years. This was indeed unusual in a deeply-rooted, professional, peacetime army, although in the special situation of the rapid buildup of a new service (offering rapid promotional opportunities) it was quite understandable. But to become a forty-year-old Generalmajor, a forty-one-year-old General der Flieger, and a forty-three-year-old Generaloberst was quite another thing. Despite his fine mind, what would compensate for his lack of experience in high command positions and for the refinement of thought that could not be conferred along with his high ranks and positions?

Now he was charged with the command of a body that had grown to be so enormous and its organization so complex that only an experienced old hand could have grasped the idea of how to control it. Even when one considers his brief span of life, Jeschonnek was, after all, a Generaloberst for only seventeen and a half months, and had occupied a key post as colonel for only nine and a half months. None of these high posts were associated with experience at the front. From the colonelcy on, his advancement was precipitous and unsound. Facing heavy responsibilities to which he was unequal became his fate or kismet!

To be sure, history records many cases of extremely youthful men (quite aside from monarchs) who held the highest ranks and commands, men whose destinies had decreed them to become the supreme commanders of their nations; for example, Alexander the Great, Charles XII of Sweden, and Frederick the Great. Hannibal was about twenty-six years old when he assumed command of the Carthaginian Army in Spain and led it through its historic campaigns, in which his greatest successes, those of Lake Trasimeno (217 A.D.) and Cannae (216 A.D.) occurred in the first quarter of his career. Prince Eugene of Savoy was not yet thirty-four years old when, as Imperial Generalissimo, he won his famous victory over the Turks at Senta. In his early twenties, Archduke Karl Philipp zu Schwarzenburg of Austria won at Wuerzburg the greatest victory of his career as commander in chief. In the same year the thirty-one-year-old Napoleon Bonaparte won his finest campaign as commander of the French Army in Italy.

However, in the case of Alexander, Hannibal, Frederick II, Eugene, and Napoleon, it is a matter of genius of the first order. Too, in Archduke Karl there is the example of a militarily gifted son and brother of an emperor; in the case of Eugene, a Turkish war had already been raging for fourteen years and had taken a heavy toll of the first and second ranks of leaders; and Bonaparte had inherited from the French Revolution a number of young and enthusiastic generals to replace the older generation of commanders who were viewed as unreliable by the young leader.

But, in addition, the conduct of war in every century prior to the introduction of compulsory military service and the rise of massive armies (along with the technical means for the transmission of orders) gave vigorous and ambitious youth far greater opportunities for success. In former times it was a matter of personal observation, of instantaneous initiative, of quick decision, of inspiring and courageous personal action, and of direct influence to the combatants by fervid words, often in the midst of a crisis, that counted. All of this was done on a battlefield over which one could command a view.

By World War II (in fact, in World War I), however, the opportunity to distinguish one's self by personal commitment, the item so decisive in deciding issues in the past, had vanished, and it was this situation into which Jeschonnek found himself thrust. Because of the gigantic theaters of action and the huge massed forces, all dependent upon factors such as tremendous logistical support, the specific vigor of youth could not bring into play those values which were once so prized and significant in warfare.

But, it should also be noted that the great captains mentioned above held the highest command positions, while Jeschonnek, although Chief of Staff, held no direct personal command. Even in World War 1 the Chief of the General Staff was no longer seen on the field of battle, such as had been the case with the elder Helmuth von Moltke in 1866, who went into combat beside his emperor. Both world wars meant painstaking and unrelenting desk and map work for the General Staff Chiefs.

Considering again the element of age, the classic example of the General Staff Chief was Field Marshal Count Helmuth von Moltke, who attained that position at the age of fifty-eight, and led the victorious campaign against Austria in 1866 at age sixty-six, and against France in 1870 at the age of seventy. Count Alfred von Schlieffen and the younger Moltke also reached that office at the age of fifty-eight. Paul von Hindenburg became Chief of the General Staff at the age of sixty-nine, and Conrad von Hoetzendorf became Chief of the Austro-Hungarian Army General Staff for the first time in 1906 when he was fifty-three, and for the second time in 1912 when he was past fifty-eight.

Of the Army Chiefs of the General Staff in World War II, Halder held that position at age fifty-four, Kurt Zeitzler at forty-seven, and Heinz Guderian at fifty-six. Only in the Luftwaffe did youth figure so prominently in the higher positions. Wever became Chief of Staff at forty-six, Kesselring at forty-eight, Stumpff at forty-eight, Guenther Korten at forty-five, and Karl Koller at forty-seven. None of them, however, approached the youthful level of Jeschonnek, who had arrived at this point before his fortieth birthday.

Schmid, Chief of Luftwaffe Intelligence, points out that youthfulness was an advantage in the eyes of Goering, who was happy that he had such a young Chief of the Luftwaffe General Staff. Even Hitler was pleased to have a vigorous young man in the post, a man with such excellent military bearing. Goering believed that he could work more easily with this young man than with older officers, many of them his seniors, who had definite high command views. He remembered the great prestige and personal stature held by Wever and Kesselring. It was perhaps inevitable, considering Goering's self-interests, that he chose Jeschonnek, so that when the Luftwaffe's failures began to appear, he could easily shift the blame to the promising young officer. Goering's unrestrained reproaches against Jeschonnek hampered the latter's work in the General Staff, and even though the Chief of Staff sought to stand on his own and defend his own policies, he found himself forced by Goering more and more into the role of an operations aide.

It was likewise difficult for Jeschonnek to prevail with his views before generals senior to him in age, rank, and length of service. With all due regard being given for saving face, he was often obliged to make concessions, especially among the senior officers of the numbered air fleets. Kesselring, for instance, certainly demanded nothing unreasonable of the Chief of the General Staff, but he did have the power at the beginning of the campaign in the East to wangle two more air forces for his Second Air Fleet than Jeschonnek had originally authorized. There was also Field Marshal Hugo Sperrle, Commander of the Third Air Fleet, a strong-willed man who was difficult to handle. And there was the ruthless Wolfram Freiherr von Richthofen, a man as demanding as a prima donna; Jeschonnek would hardly have acquiesced to so many of his demands if Richthofen had not been like a "favorite brother Benjamin" among the generals.

One fact ought also to be pointed out in this discussion, namely, that there was a very influential circle of friends around Goering, who were bound to him (and willingly acted as his vassals) through close association in Fighter Wing "Richthofen," or from common experiences during the difficult years after World War I. They were richly rewarded for their loyalty by meteoric promotions and other benefits. They had Goering's ear and could appear at his quarters at any time, even if they did not remain (as happened toward the end of the war) permanently with his Karinhall entourage.

This inner circle included Generaloberst Bruno Loerzer, Commander in Chief of the 2nd Air Corps and later Chief of Personnel; State Secretary Paul Koerner; and General der Flieger Karl Bodenschatz, who acted first as Chief of the Ministerial Office (Reichs Air Ministry) and later as Goering's liaison official at Hitler's headquarters. These were personal associations against whose influence the Chief of the General Staff was powerless. None of these men had much appreciation for Jeschonnek, who had so soon become Chief of the Luftwaffe General Staff.

Perhaps even more galling was the fact that during the war Goering (who absented himself from his headquarters for such long periods of time) would go to Karinhall, to his hunting lodge in Rominten, or to picturesque Veldenstein in Upper Franconia, and would issue orders through his adjutants. The latter (Colonel Bernd von Brauchitsch and Lieutenant Colonel Werner Teske), and Goering's personal physician, Dr. Ramon von Ondarza, formed a kind of collateral government, the "Little General Staff" as it was derisively called, which harassed and confused the man who had to perform the real General Staff work.

Jeschonnek's youth was undoubtedly also the reason for his inability to win over subordinates who were of his own age or slightly younger. With them he was brusque and reserved, often carried to excess his innate tendency toward sarcasm, and could reject in a most dictatorial manner any dissenting opinions. He was not endowed with the great gift possessed by Wever and Kesselring of a radiant personality that shone on all alike, firing them with enthusiasm and winning their cheerful cooperation.

However, the young Chief of the General Staff did open his heart to his younger comrades. He prized youth, overrating it just as did his master, the Commander in Chief of the Luftwaffe, and as the Third Reich in general tended to do. Youth, that was the age for aviation! One might hazard the reflection that the comparatively youthful Jeschonnek felt drawn to younger personnel because he himself was somewhat drawn away from them.

During the war the rising number of great fliers, like Adolf Galland, Werner Baumbach, and Werner Moelders, always found him to be understanding and helpful. That had its advantages, since the Chief of the General Staff was thus kept informed about morale at the front, and the result was a regular rejuvenation of commands. This also had certain rather important disadvantages. Jeschonnek had a weakness for forthright, energetic people, and he was too trusting. Because of this it was no wonder that these pampered youths grew too cocky. They were still basically immature people who had not yet measured up to their elevated rank.

With his appointment as Chief of Branch I (Operations Staff) of the Luftwaffe General Staff on 1 February 1938, Jeschonnek entered the

German Air Ministry as one who was ready or proficient in his own person. One year later he became Chief of the Luftwaffe General Staff.

There were two things that motivated the young lieutenant colonel in 1937 and which remained as dogma for him for a long time. One was his military, and the other his political, conviction. Both were to become ominously enmeshed, although not until the war began. These two factors influenced both the rise and the fall of Jeschonnek. That in the end both convictions were violently shaken in him is evidenced by the inner void, indeed the despair, which caused him in 1943 to take the revolver into his hand.

Jeschonnek entered the Air Ministry as a firm advocate of the dive-bomber. The high-altitude bombing scores at Greifswald had been exceedingly poor. Since the scores, even in low-level bombing, showed no significant improvement, Jeschonnek thought that only the steep dive could effect a change. The possibility of carpet bombing had not been envisioned at that time. By its beguiling successes, the Ju-87, which had just come into the Luftwaffe's inventory, had won considerable favor. One group of the Training Wing was already equipped with Ju-87's.

Jeschonnek was quite receptive to the new German political leadership. Molded in his cadet training by the traditional ethos of the Prussian officer, strict discipline and austere self-denial in the performance of duty and in subordination to the military hierarchy, Jeschonnek strove to personify this ideal and dedicated himself to his career in an almost romantic, outdated way in the midst of a changed world. Hitler (who after the death of von Hindenburg bore the title of Fuehrer und Reichs Chancellor) referred time and again in his speeches and proclamations to Prussianism and its virtues, repeatedly invoking the figure of Frederick the Great, a man with whom he really had little in common, as the epitome of this Prussianism.

Hitler further satisfied the military tradition in Germany by immediately launching a great rearmament program to build up a strong Armed Forces establishment (Wehrmacht). Wever had already gone cheerfully along with Hitler and the new era.

Jeschonnek's confidence in Hitler led him to believe that the Fuehrer would be able to secure a revision of the Treaty of Versailles in such a way that Germany's desires could be achieved without embroiling Europe in a war. Hitler claimed that these desired objectives consisted solely of Danzig and the Polish Corridor, and not even east Upper Silesia. Moreover, Hitler had sacrificed the German-speaking South Tyrol for the sake of friendship with Italy, and had declared that the matter of the former German colonies should not be a casus belli for the Reich.

Jeschonnek believed almost as an article of faith that he was face to face with a great political genius who was increasingly assuming the role of a genius in the military sphere as well. He undoubtedly turned to Hitler as a leader, without assuming a simultaneous allegiance to the Nazi Party. With respect to this aspect of his life, Student held the view—this would seem to be the correct one—that Jeschonnek entered into the "orbit of National Socialism willy-nilly," through his professional military career. Hitler's uncanny power to sway people had succeeded in turning the apparently cool-headed young Chief of Staff away from his sober evaluation of matters to an unconditional belief in the rightness and certainty of success of Hitler's measures. Thus Hitler became the irresistible power that determined his destiny and advanced him at his relatively young age to an elevated position.

A concomitant cause was undoubtedly Jeschonnek's willing submission to Hitler's chief paladin, Goering. One might say without exaggeration that in Jeschonnek's ideology two convictions had become crystallized into a single firm concept. His first conviction was that of the decisive significance of precision bombing (hence the dive-bomber) and the concept of the blitzkrieg, which was to be initiated by annihilating blows from the Luftwaffe, and the second (capping the climax) was that he believed Hitler was an infallible genius. The consistency with which Jeschonnek defended his first conviction and which oriented him toward the second portended tragedy for both himself and the Luftwaffe.

It must now be examined whether the Chief of Staff, in his blitzkrieg orientation, followed a specific political directive or objective issued by Hitler. If so, then Jeschonnek would have been curbed in his purely military evaluation of affairs. Did he no longer actually have any other consideration open?

That possibility must be categorically rejected. Even if the political leadership had given a directive or reassurance that involvement in a major war was not to be expected, the Chief of the General Staff would still not have been absolved from his responsibility to prepare for all conceivable contingencies. In 1939 Hitler assured Goering that war with Britain was unthinkable. Hitler certainly did not want such a war, because he considered the continuance of the British Empire a necessity, and because he greatly desired a friendly relationship between Germany and Great Britain. But there was always the possibility that England might act on her own volition and declare war on Germany just as it had done on the night of 4 August 1914.

Certainly, a war with Britain could not be carried out by blitzkrieg, and Jeschonnek ought to have considered the possibility of such an encounter. On 18 February 1938, Jeschonnek's own Operations Staff (Branch I of the General Staff) informed General der Flieger Hellmuth Felmy, Commanding General and Commander of the Second Air Fleet, of Goering's intentions concerning "preparations for the conduct of battle in the West," and on 23 August of that year Felmy received the order to clarify targets and operational and command possibilities in case of an air war against Great Britain. In his report of 22 September 1938, Felmy expressed his own point of view in the following terms:

> With our present available resources, only a harassing effect can be counted upon. Whether this can lead to the attrition of the British will to fight depends in part upon imponderable and, in any case, unforeseeable factors. . . . A war of annihilation against England appears to be out of the question with the resources thus far available.

After Felmy again had a discussion (2 May 1939) in the office of the Chief of the General Staff and had been charged with the plan for the conduct of the air war in case of a conflict with Britain, the experiences gained in war games during the previous autumn were tested in a war game of the Second Air Fleet at Braunschweig, 10-13 May 1939. The final critique was held on 13 May. In this critique, the year 1942 was taken as the basis for mission planning in case of trouble with Britain. On 22 May 1939 conclusions had already been drawn from this critique by Branch I of the General Staff, which had obtained a good picture of the situation from a Branch V report of 25 August 1938, and even more so from the intelligence reports coming in after January of 1939.

The extraordinarily incisive staff study, entitled "Designation of Strategic Targets for the Luftwaffe in Case of a War Against England in the Year 1939," began by stating emphatically:

> The armament, state of training, and strength of the Second Air Fleet cannot bring about a decision in a war against England within a short time in the year 1939.

Six days before, the staff of Generalleutnant Hans Geissler was established by order of the Chief of the General Staff of the Second Air

Fleet to test all questions regarding the preparation and conduct of air attack on and over the seas as well as along the coast.

Hitler had plainly expressed himself on the possibility of a prolonged war. This was done in his speech of 23 May 1939 to the Commanders in Chief of the Armed Forces branches and their chiefs of staff. Jeschonnek was present and he was undoubtedly impressed. Hitler's words have been preserved in the notes taken down by his Chief Adjutant for the Wehrmacht, Lieutenant Colonel Rudolf Schmundt. With the exception of the imminent case of Poland, it appears that Hitler did not count upon a blitzkrieg in every situation. Although Schmundt's minutes contain contradictions, it is clear that Hitler wanted to direct a series of quick, annihilating blows in the West, but questioned whether success could be quickly achieved. Because of this, he ordered preparations "for the long war in addition to the surprise attack in order to destroy English capabilities on the Continent." Hitler conceded that the destruction of the British fleet (presumably by the Luftwaffe) could force the immediate capitulation of Great Britain.

It appears quite certain that Hitler did not want a war with Britain, but according to Schmundt, he did have doubts concerning the possibility of a peaceful settlement with that nation and thought that Germany had to prepare for such a contingency. In this connection he stressed the necessity (if Britain intervened in Poland) of "attacking Holland with lightning speed." He said that every country's armed forces must "strive for the short war, but must, on the other hand, also be prepared for a war of ten to fifteen years' duration." This, of course, included the military as well as the head of state. Even if Hitler had occasionally spoken to Goering with greater optimism, and even if Goering had appeared overly optimistic of the prospects of success in war to his General Staff, still it might be an exaggeration to say that Jeschonnek had merely gone along with the intentions of the political leadership. Hitler's speech of 23 May 1939 might have strengthened Jeschonnek's conviction about the correctness of a blitzkrieg type of operation and encouraged him to prepare for a short war, but his preparation was preconceived, and he had not even adjusted to the prevailing political views of the government.

From Felmy's staff study it appears that Jeschonnek knew that the blitzkrieg was impossible in the case of an adversary like Great Britain, and his own operations staff had accepted this view. Because of the inadequacy of German air armaments, the Chief of Staff henceforth should have examined with extreme care the deterioration—which was evident to nearly everyone—of relations between the Reich and Great

Britain. Surely it was then imperative to accept Plocher's viewpoint of armament in depth rather than armament in breadth.

Although there is no clear insight into the inner self of Jeschonnek, one can assume that he had confidence in Hitler's genius, confidence that it would be possible for the Fuehrer to conduct the war against Poland without the intervention of either France or Great Britain. However, as matters then stood, this was tantamount to trusting in a miracle.

When Jeschonnek became Chief of the Luftwaffe Operations Staff in 1937, Wever had only been dead for a little more than a year, but nothing had changed in that year (in fact, from 1936 to 1939) that could have increased public optimism. On the contrary, the situation had become increasingly critical.

In connection with the above-mentioned Felmy staff study arises the question of whether Hitler was informed about the none-too-optimistic finding that the Luftwaffe was incapable of more than a harassing action against Great Britain. In the spring of 1939 Hitler was faced with the serious problem of whether he should or should not advance his claims against Poland, which had been sharply rebuffed by Polish officials (backed by Great Britain, France, and the United States). In the few years just prior to 1939 Hitler had successfully bluffed the world with respect to the strength of his air forces, and succeeded in worrying enemy experts whom he had "taken in."

Hitler, and with him Goering, believed in the overwhelming strength of the German air arm, and he undoubtedly took this into account in his military and political calculations. If Hitler had heeded the facts of the case, namely, that it was impossible to rain annihilating blows from the air against England because the strength of the new air arm was unequal to the task, he would have had to water down his enthusiasm in dealing with the Poles and would have made stronger efforts to reach a genuine understanding with Neville Chamberlain.

It was of the greatest importance to inform the Fuehrer immediately concerning the actual state of military preparedness. This task was primarily Goering's, a man who then had direct access to Hitler. According to von Below, Hitler's Luftwaffe Adjutant, all air problems, until far into the war, were handled tête-à-tête between Hitler and Goering. As Chief of Staff, Jeschonnek could only strongly urge his chief to inform the Fuehrer of the true nature of the situation. Jeschonnek's subordinates of those days (including Schmid in particular) doubt whether the Chief of Staff would have done so, considering the personality and attitudes of Goering.

How meager historical research becomes when the lips of the most significant witnesses, Jeschonnek, Goering, and Hitler, remain forever sealed, and when so few written records are extant from these three to illuminate the problem!

At this point another question crops up concerning an event which occurred early in 1939. The Munich Pact turned out to be less than a genuine appeasement, since Great Britain then took steps to strengthen her armaments. At the same time Hitler reinforced his arms and services in anticipation of his planned political operations, especially against Poland. On 6 December 1938, Goering disclosed this to his departmental chiefs in Karinhall. The Fuehrer was to be notified by January 1939 that the program necessary for the accomplishment of his plans had been completed.

The detailed calculation of Hitler's demand amounted to a requirement of sixty billion Reichsmarks and a huge quantity of metals which were in short supply. The several Luftwaffe office chiefs concerned declared the fulfillment of this demand to be impossible. However, in order to meet the demand to some extent, Kammhuber, Chief of the Organization Staff, worked out an emergency program (which still called for the expenditure of twenty billion Reichsmarks). Thereupon a meeting took place (8 January 1939) in the conference room of the Reichs Air Ministry under the chairmanship of Milch, with Stumpff, Chief of Staff, in attendance. All office chiefs were consulted about Hitler's demand and all declared that Hitler's plan, as well as that of Kammhuber, was impractical, even in the area of training. Only Stumpff concurred with either of the reports and demands, and this was with that of Kammhuber. Milch finally attempted to conclude the meeting with the comment:

> Kammhuber, pack up your stuff! We're going to the Field Marshal! The Fuehrer's program is the objective, but at least the Kammhuber program must be carried out. Have any of you gentlemen anything more to say?

At this juncture, the Chief of the Luftwaffe Operations Staff, Jeschonnek, arose and said, "I object! In my opinion it is our duty not to stab the Fuehrer in the back. If the Fuehrer has ordered this program, he knows by what means it can be carried out." At this the State Secretary said, "Jeschonnek, *you* come along with me to the Field Marshal." After a while they both returned, and Milch told the group that Goering had decided that the Fuehrer's program could be carried out, and that he had complete confidence that each office chief would do his utmost to see to its accomplishment. Kammhuber, who as an organization expert figured with firm concepts, declared that he was unable to work within the framework of "as much as possible," which was no program at all, and submitted his request for troop duty. On 1 February 1939 Jeschonnek replaced the office-weary Stumpff as Chief of Staff, which brought the believer in the Fuehrer program into one of the top positions.

Despite optimistic predictions, no mountains were subsequently moved in the Air Ministry by such faith. Instead, the work went on in the old beaten track and at essentially the same old pace. There was no talk of an all-out effort to come as close as possible to fulfilling Hitler's mammoth program. The "utmost," as Kammhuber had foreseen, was little more than lip service. "Thereafter," said Kammhuber, "the German Air Force drifted!"

As has already been mentioned, Jeschonnek was keen and capable of managing situations, but lacked imagination and an ability to foresee possible events. He failed to recognize the warning signals that British air power was growing. He still thought in terms of an offensive Luftwaffe and wanted bombers, as his refusal to accept Milch's offer to increase fighter production revealed. He could not see that two fighter wings and a number of far too weak groups—these were subsequently incorporated into the Night-Fighter Forces—in the homeland would eventually be unable to repulse British air penetrations over the Reich. He was not conscious of the fact that failure to defeat the Soviet Union quickly would then mean an unusually hard and long campaign, a consequence of which would be the critical need to defend the homeland.

He continued to hold fast to his stubborn views, which had made him an enemy of the four-motored bomber project, and which caused him to underestimate the dangers to Germany from an Anglo-American four-engine bomber force. In July of 1942 Colonel Dietrich Schwenke, who was then giving a lecture in Kalinovka in the presence of Jeschonnek and his Chief of Intelligence, Schmid, reported on the tremendous armament and armament capability of the Western Allies, and the American four-engine bomber force in particular. In the middle of his lecture, Jeschonnek broke in with the comment, "Every four-engine bomber the Western Allies build makes me happy, for we will bring these four-engine bombers down just like we brought down the two-engine ones, and the destruction of a four-engine bomber constitutes a much greater loss for the enemy."

What dangerous and incorrigible optimism! And this at a time when the RAF was stepping up its attacks on Germany itself! First came the raids on Luebeck (28-29 March 1942), on Rostock (24-27 April), and then (and much more impressive) the great raid on Cologne (30-31 May), which caused 12,000 fires, 1,700 of major proportions. Attacks by 1,000 bombers on Essen and Bremen were quick to follow. Germany's affliction from the West had begun, and the attacker's losses were not high enough to frighten him off, primarily because of the weakness of the German fighter arm. On 19 September 1942 the Allies struck Munich, and then turned to Krefeld, Hanover, and Stuttgart. These were just a few of the many terrible raids. The homeland was ablaze.

While German troops pushed ahead over the broad plains of Russia or through the deserts of Cyrenaica and Egypt, thousands of civilians in Germany lost their lives from British air raids, and the great cathedrals, town halls, and architectural masterpieces, which for centuries had been the glory of Europe, sank in smoke and ashes. The German defense was unable to commit its trifling strength by day so as to destroy an entire bomber formation, let alone inflict heavy enough losses upon the enemy to cause him to desist because of the risks involved. German night-fighter strength was also inadequate and neither Jeschonnek nor Goering had any great sympathy for this arm. Jeschonnek's faulty decision concerning fighter production was beginning to have frightening consequences.

Goering and Jeschonnek were more interested in launching reprisal attacks against Britain, just as was Hitler who believed that "terror could only be broken by terror." Although this idea was correct in principle, because in war it is only when both protagonists endure great suffering that the desire for settlement and humanity can predominate, in this particular instance it was completely erroneous. The German bomber forces available were far too weak to accomplish such an objective, and after suffering heavy losses in the best units, the Luftwaffe was too weak to even match the British attacks. In addition, Luftwaffe bombing raids were marked by severe losses.

Except for a few small raids, the Americans had not yet taken part in the attacks on Germany. The large-scale commitment of the "Flying Fortresses" (B-17's), however, was expected to begin in early 1943. No matter how much Milch tried to push German production, it was impossible to keep abreast of the massive American production figures, to which were added the considerable British figures.

Jeschonnek, according to Schmid, worked most "unwillingly on air defense." It is possible to understand the youthful general's train of thought. Attack and the offensive is the way of battle for the vital and the strong, and it requires great self-control to admit that one is no longer strong, and even more to face the fact that the nation is gravely threatened, requiring a defense that would conserve all of the available military power. The German soldier generally prefers attack to defense, a characteristic which was emphasized in the General Staff training prior to the First World War. Hannibal's Cannae, the classic battle of extermination, was the great German objective in warfare, and this was virtually realized at Tannenberg. Hannibal's other side as a master of defense, in which he achieved results equally as great, if not greater than in his offensives, seemed to be of less interest to the former German General Staff. The later General Staff training between 1919 and 1933 (of which Jeschonnek was a product), because of the numerical weakness of the Reichswehr, paid more attention to defense than before. In the Luftwaffe, Douhet was the ideal and Douhet taught attack.

However, Jeschonnek, as the Chief of the General Staff of his branch of the Wehrmacht, should have been able to rise above the most rigid aspects of tradition and his own rather narrow intellectual orientation. Unfortunately, he was not flexible enough to do so. His management of air defense was dragging and improvised in character, and suggestions for modernizing and streamlining air defenses "remained a mystery to him." Kesselring acknowledged this, but added that, "the combining of national air defenses into a single air fleet is to his credit." But, this was not due to Jeschonnek's farsightedness, but rather to the pressure of events which compelled the creation of this organization.

The Luftwaffe General Staff Chief had not been close to Udet, and his relationship to Milch was extremely poor. Such matters were of prime importance as Germany's air position began to deteriorate. The once exalted Luftwaffe was being consumed in an increasingly hopeless battle over the Reich, and faced the fury of Hitler who knew as did the German people that Goering's arm of service was utterly unable to thwart Allied plans to destroy Germany. In such circumstances, the three men who had the most to say about leadership in the air defense effort ought to have become more closely united. However, this did not occur.

At one time Jeschonnek had been an aide to Milch. This association began well enough, but they parted on poor terms, and during the Greifswald period Jeschonnek had frequent arguments because of Milch's policies. A sort of deadly enmity developed in which the young

General Staff Chief refused to have anything to do with Milch. Thus Milch could neither serve as a prop nor as an advisor. Milch declared, "The only time during the war when I represented Goering was during the winter of 1940-41, when he was on leave. For about two months I was stationed at his headquarters near Beauvais. On the same day that I arrived, Jeschonnek left for Karinhall. He relayed his orders to von Waldau by telephone." One should not lose sight of this.

Jeschonnek should have made some effort to soften this situation, especially since he was the younger of the two, and junior in rank. It would have been beneficial to both men to have established a new sort of relationship, and would have given a powerful boost to German air strategy.

The relationship of the General Staff Chief to Goering was somewhat different, and toward the end assumed threatening proportions. Schmid mentioned Goering's enthusiasm for Jeschonnek, an enthusiasm which lasted into the war as long as German arms were successful. But, when the failures began to appear and become obvious to all, there was no real human contact between them. Goering sat too high in the saddle. It was not that the Chief of the General Staff had an aversion to Goering. In fact, according to Frau Kersten, "Jeschonnek was often an enthusiastic admirer of Goering. He liked him and was happy when he could convince him of something."

But, Jeschonnek, a proper Prussian, abrupt and soldierly in his manner, could never find the right or lasting approach to the informality-loving Goering, who remained a Bavarian at heart. Bodenschatz once advised Jeschonnek to "tone down his Prussian ways in the presence of Goering." Bodenschatz even offered to intercede for him on occasions, but Jeschonnek always turned him down.

On the other hand, Goering often acted imperiously with his General Staff Chief, giving, as Kesselring related, "either directives which could not be fulfilled or none at all." If Jeschonnek did not handle things to suit Goering, the Reichsmarschall "blew up." Yet, even under Goering's screaming, Jeschonnek remained "a gentleman." This happened more and more frequently, since Hitler began to shut Goering out of his confidence and to deal directly with Jeschonnek, a fact which infuriated the Reichsmarschall.

Problems were compounded by the fact that Diesing took great pains to poison Goering's mind about Jeschonnek. Schmid has described the "second General Staff" organized by Colonel von Brauchitsch as one of the reasons for Jeschonnek's suicide. Schmid noted that, "Brauchitsch had four or five General Staff officers in his office, with whose collaboration, and without informing or consulting Jeschonnek, he issued Reichsmarschall orders directly to the commands." It is not difficult to imagine how depressing this must have been for the lonely, withdrawn man to see himself undermined, with his chief's approval, in his own headquarters. Often he was unable to secure an appointment with Goering, while the Little General Staff walked in and out of the Reichsmarschall's office with impunity. Deichmann wrote about the relationship between Goering and Jeschonnek, noting that:

> If Goering appeared before his troops in the company of his General Staff Chief, one could observe how the latter played the role of a recipient of orders. "Write this down! . . . See to that!" Such was the usual tone used by the Reichsmarschall with his General Staff Chief.
>
> The Chief of the General Staff, who had much work to do, found his time taken up with social affairs and waiting around in outer offices in a way which was disrespectful to his rank. If Goering was with Hitler, the Chief of the General Staff would have to wait for hours on end in a room at Fuehrer Headquarters on the possibility that information concerning some matter might be needed.

Because of his jealousy of Jeschonnek's popularity with the troops, and because he desired to keep his General Staff Chief close at hand, Goering refused to allow him to visit the front.

One cannot dismiss the idea that after the Stalingrad catastrophe the time had come to change the leadership of the Luftwaffe. Kesselring mentioned this in his memoirs. The situation demanded, however, the removal of both Goering and Jeschonnek. Goering had heavily damaged the Luftwaffe's position and Jeschonnek was already worn out by 1943 as a General Staff Chief. Perhaps with the leadership of a resolute and fanatically dedicated person, such as Freiherr von Richthofen, the German Air Force might still have been saved. Surely Richthofen was the best choice to succeed Goering for he could have been forceful and firm with Hitler. Jeschonnek could have been given command of the Fourth Air Fleet (Richthofen's old unit), which would have provided a useful post for him and would have saved the young Generaloberst. Of course, a separation of Goering from Hitler as a military collaborator could not even be mentioned. Such a change in the Luftwaffe High Command would have made too powerful an impression upon neutral and enemy nations, especially inasmuch as Goering was Hitler's legally appointed successor. In Hitler one could see that he became increasingly sharp, critical, and insulting toward Goering, but at the same time, he tolerated so much in Goering's weaknesses, probably because of the memory of the old days and the early Party struggles. Hitler held on to his Luftwaffe Commander in Chief just as he did to his unconditionally loyal Jeschonnek. Thus the practical solution for 1943 and the future of the war never took place.

Tortured with worries, the General Staff Chief saw one difficulty after another stretched out before him, and it was not only the air forces which troubled him, although the discrepancy between the Luftwaffe's strength and that of the Anglo-American air forces continued to increase, and although the He-177 could not be put into mass production, nor even the Me-262 jet, which by 1943 was progressing well enough despite the loss of time due to the development stoppage. For Jeschonnek, the decisive factor was his relationship to Hitler. And the way things stood, the fates of Hitler and Germany had become inseparable. The Fuehrer affected the young General Staff Chief like a secret magnet. Without question Jeschonnek's Spartan way of life must have impressed Hitler, who was perhaps overly impressed by good military bearing and behavior. Hitler was attracted by Jeschonnek's Prussian abruptness and manner, characteristics which had just the opposite effect upon Goering, whose personality was so different. Kesselring thought that Jeschonnek's impact upon Hitler "worked to the advantage of the Luftwaffe."

After the Cologne raid, and even more so after Stalingrad, Hitler's relationship with Goering changed. With his acuteness, the Fuehrer began to recognize the shortcomings of the Reichsmarschall. Colonel Eckhard Christian, Chief of the Luftwaffe Operations Staff, who by 1943 had won considerable influence with Hitler, was then instrumental in bringing Jeschonnek into closer relationship with the dictator. Hitler, who had been accustomed to holding private meetings with Goering, began to invite Jeschonnek. The General Staff Chief was then able to experience all of Hitler's bitterness toward the Luftwaffe for its breakdown and failures. He was also able to see himself equated with the paralysis and decline of the air forces. Every Anglo-American raid on a German city filled the Fuehrer with new wrath, and occasionally he reacted with furious outbursts of temper. Jeschonnek, chalk-white, found himself in the position of bearing the brunt of these violent displays of anger. On one occasion, however, as the participants left a briefing, Hitler held Jeschonnek back, put his arm around him and clapped him on the shoulder saying, "Of course, I didn't mean you at all!"

What a difficult position for the young Generaloberst! He had indeed found himself ground down between two millstones, the strong personalities of Hitler and Goering. He had to take everything they served up to him. Hitler blamed Goering for the Luftwaffe's failures, and Goering, in turn, vented his wrath on Jeschonnek. Undecided as to which way to turn, Jeschonnek found himself in an increasingly helpless position. Kesselring has stated that, "Opposite Hitler he was alone, since Hitler no longer trusted Goering. But, unlike Goering, he was also opposed from below."

It is clear that Goering, feeling even more insecure, was angered by his General Staff Chief, who still seemed to have some standing with the Fuehrer. This prevented any close working relationship within the Luftwaffe High Command. It is less clear just when, or even if, Hitler actually lost faith in Jeschonnek. Dr. Karl Bartz in his *Als der Himmel brannte* ("As the Heavens Burned") claimed that Hitler was only biding his time for the right opportunity to rid himself of Jeschonnek, but this idea finds no support elsewhere. Hitler's feelings about the destruction of the cities are easy to imagine when one recalls that he had great interest in architecture and in the preservation of the ancient cities. It is, of course, possible that Jeschonnek felt he had lost his Fuehrer's trust, for the Generaloberst was perceptive in many areas.

By the spring of 1943 he surely realized that events had taken a turn for the worse, that the Anglo-American air forces were capable of dealing much heavier damage than he had thought and that Germany had lost air superiority in Africa. German and Italian troops were steadily losing ground in the Tunisian bridgehead and capitulated on 12 May 1943. The Allies, possessing air superiority over the weakened Second Air Fleet, landed on 9 July 1943 in Sicily where Italian betrayal and collapse assisted the enemy to rapidly win ground.

The Luftwaffe, bled nearly white, struggling to defend the homeland, and to prevent collapses on a number of far-flung fronts, needed to be strengthened. The first prerequisite was a different example at the top but Goering had no interest in such ideas, nor was he willing to change his way of life. Moreover, he was quite happy to let his Chief of Staff bear the blame alone. In such a situation what could Jeschonnek have done? Hitler's fits of passion against the Luftwaffe continued to increase with each daily transmission of bad news, and even if it was directed mainly at Goering, Jeschonnek was the one who had to bear it. It is not difficult to imagine that one day the outbursts would be turned upon him.

Two ways were open to Jeschonnek. The first would have been a frank report to the Fuehrer as Supreme Commander of the Wehrmacht, stating that the Luftwaffe was sick at the top, that it required workers and raw materials for a decisive rearmament, that its schools had to be allowed to continue undisturbed, and that every effort had to be made to get the Me-262 jet into mass production, or the German Air Force would be helpless and impotent. The men who surrounded Jeschonnek begged him to take this step. To them, however, the cause of all of the difficulties was incorporated in the person of Goering. Leuchtenberg said "He [Jeschonnek] often spoke to me concerning his difficulties with the Reichsmarschall. I asked him if he didn't want to report it to the Fuehrer, but he replied, 'I can't do it. Perhaps you could, but I can't.'"

Frau Kersten also mentioned the necessity of making a report to Hitler about Goering and the problems in the Luftwaffe High Command, but he invariably said, "I can't go against Goering. I am a soldier!"

The second possibility was to resign his post as Chief of the General Staff, a decision which could have been made on the ground of health alone, since Jeschonnek had been suffering for some time from stomach pains and cramps. To the Generaloberst, however, no forty-year-old dared to make such a claim, since for the soldier the mention of ill health would have been a humiliation. Jeschonnek might have assumed the command of an air fleet, and feeling the pressure of his job, once implored Goering to give him such a position and to replace him with Richthofen or Kammhuber. He would have enjoyed such an assignment and could have rendered excellent service, but he was unsure whether he dared to leave his post at that time. Leuchtenberg recalled his comment at the time, "I can still master this difficult situation." According to von Below, Goering consulted with Hitler about Jeschonnek's request to take over an air fleet and the Fuehrer declared it was absolutely out of the question. Hitler, in fact, demanded that the two top Luftwaffe leaders effect a reconciliation and start working together. For fourteen days this worked out satisfactorily.

The question could be raised whether it is possible for a youthful officer, energetic and tough, a soldier through and through, to deteriorate to the point where he saw no other course of action than to take his pistol in hand. He had been portrayed as a cool, sober, and often perceptive officer, yet one who could be short with his comrades, and even be unapproachable in discussions. He never allowed lower ranking colleagues to give a real expression of opinion. He issued orders and developed his own point of view. To the public he thus seemed to be solid, steady, and able to handle whatever might come. But, was he really this sort?

It is known that he surrounded himself with officers of equivalent or inferior rank, especially younger officers, on whom he could never look as equals. It was not his strength which made him unapproachable and even solitary, it was his inner nature, which instinctively kept him from situations where arguments could arise in which his convictions might be questioned, where senior officers (who had no hesitation in speaking out) might be present. His hardened exterior concealed an extremely vulnerable inner person.

Certain aspects of his character, his periods of depression and even emotional breakdowns, allow one to conclude that these were manic-depressive characteristics, even though other evidence seems to contradict this. Certainly he found himself in an ever greater inner conflict concerning the possibility of winning the war and of trusting in Hitler's leadership. General der Flieger von Seidel recalled that in the winter of 1941-42 Jeschonnek reacted almost violently when criticisms were leveled at the Army's conduct of the war, and shouted, "You must believe in a successful outcome!" Schmid recalled that the summer of 1942 was the turning point in Jeschonnek's true belief in a successful outcome of the war, yet he refused to allow any discussion of this. It was during this period that von Seidel had lunch with him at the *Wolfsschanze* (Wolf's Lair) in East Prussia, and the General Staff Chief loosened up and admitted the terrible mistakes that had been and were still being made.

As early as 12 April 1943 Guderian visited Jeschonnek and noted that he was "tired, resigned," and unwilling to come to an open discussion on any factors affecting both the Luftwaffe and the armored forces. Guderian, a sharp observer, believed that Jeschonnek had lost his inner strength, and one can safely say that from this time on he was emotionally burned out.

Jeschonnek had to reckon with being relieved of his post, an unbearable disgrace, and knew also that the failures were going to be more and more laid at his feet. It was impossible to ascribe all of the mistakes and shortcomings of the German Air Force to Goering. Jeschonnek knew only too well how deeply he was involved in the overestimation of the Ju-88; in the failure of the He-177; in creating an air force with no reserve strength, an air force designed for blitzkriegs; in insisting upon fulfillment of Hitler's program, only to modify it to mean "produce what you can"; in failing to impress his superior with the fact that the Luftwaffe could not fight a protracted war; in agreeing to stop aircraft development and to leave fighter production at a low figure, and in failing to properly mobilize his armament program; in underestimating the Anglo-American air menace; in agreeing to the air logistical operations at Kholm, Demyansk, and worst of all, at Stalingrad; in allowing the Luftwaffe to become a fire-fighting brigade for the Army; in failing to develop a strategic air arm and an air transport command; in recognizing too late the need for adequate air defense forces; and in overemphasizing medium bombers to the disadvantage of fighters.

Since Jeschonnek had no well-developed religious convictions and his family life held little meaning for him, he was bound to his duty, and when this rock began to crumble he had no force which could stabilize him. In this situation he thought of suicide. On one occasion (just before the overthrow of Mussolini) his Adjutant, Leuchtenberg, had to take a revolver out of his hand. Leuchtenberg then told Kesselring that he feared Jeschonnek might try it again.

The Kursk offensive in the East had failed, and the planned strategic withdrawal to the Dnieper River (the Hagen Line) had to be accelerated because of the overthrow and imprisonment of Mussolini on 25 July, which suggested that Italy would withdraw from the Axis and would therefore have to be occupied by larger German troop units. The Russians, powerful on the ground, were becoming increasingly strong in the air. At the same time (25 July 1943) came the terrible Anglo-American raids on Hamburg, killing 40,000 civilians among which were 5,586 children, attacks which were not terminated until the night of 3 August. Then, on 17 August, came the American daylight attack on the ball-bearing works at Schweinfurt and a raid on the aircraft plants in Regensburg. Although the Luftwaffe seemed to win a great defensive victory on this occasion, highly important war industries were seriously damaged, and the enemy showed his capability to penetrate to the innermost points of the Reich.

Frau Kersten mentioned a telephone conversation between Goering and Jeschonnek on the afternoon of 17 August, during which the General Staff Chief was treated in a gross manner. General Meister also recalled a conversation between the two men concerning the coordination of night fighters and flak forces. Goering created a terrible scene because Jeschonnek, for technical reasons, had held back an order. He shouted to Jeschonnek, "You stand in front of Hitler like a lieutenant with your hands on your trouser seams!"

During the night of 17-18 August, Germany received another heavy blow. Over 500 RAF bombers attacked the research and construction sites at Peenemuende, where, in utmost secrecy, the V-weapons were being made. The damage incurred was at first overestimated. Meister related, "I learned about the attack about seven or seven-thirty in the morning and presented my report to Jeschonnek around eight. He received it quietly. I then went to a situation conference. Jeschonnek did not appear."

Leuchtenberg said, "I was holding breakfast for him. A major wanted to report to him about something. The secretary, Frau Kersten, then called him on the telephone. He said, 'I'm coming immediately.' But, he didn't come. He then called up Frau Kersten and said, 'Leuchtenberg should go ahead over [to the conference].'"

Secretary Kersten described the tragic events which followed:

> . . . I phoned Jeschonnek several times, without being able to reach him. Then I knocked, entered, and saw him lying dead. I hadn't heard a shot, which is even more unbelievable, since I wasn't more than thirty feet from him, and we were separated only by the wall. A note lay by the dead man: "I can no longer work together with the Reichsmarschall. Long live the Fuehrer!"

It is now time to clear away the legends surrounding Jeschonnek's death. It is untrue, as Milch has claimed, that Jeschonnek had had a heated discussion with Hitler on the afternoon preceding his suicide during which Hitler had told him that the failures were his responsibility and that he "ought to know now what was expected of him." This account is denied by those who were best informed about the situation. Von Below states that Hitler again and again tried to make life easier for Jeschonnek, especially with Goering.

The slip of paper found by Jeschonnek's body pointed to the fact that the despairing General Staff Chief must have seen in Goering the man responsible for the Luftwaffe's decline. There are numerous witnesses who knew of a thorough altercation between Jeschonnek and Goering prior to the former's death. According to Leuchtenberg, there were other notes which mentioned military events, decisions, and the relationships between Hitler and Goering. Frau Kersten said these consisted of about ten pages.

Were these notes in the nature of a memorandum? And, if they were, to whom was the memorandum directed? Unfortunately, little is known about this except that it aimed at Goering. The Reichsmarschall mentioned this himself before witnesses so that there was no doubt he knew of it. Meister, arriving at Jeschonnek's command post, was ordered by Goering to open the safe. Meister continued:

> He personally studied Jeschonnek's reference files and found among them a study, the only other copy of which belonged to Below. He didn't give it to me to read, but I believe it recommended that Goering have a deputy, something which had first been planned with Pflugbeil in mind, later Greim. Goering said to me, "You see, the man was working against me!" . . . Goering read both of the slips of paper which had been found by Jeschonnek, then gave them back to me, keeping the study for himself.

Kesselring, who appeared at Jeschonnek's burial despite an order forbidding it, said, "As I approached Goering, he said to me, 'Jeschonnek didn't die. He shot himself.'" Goering then mentioned a memorandum which Jeschonnek had directed to Hitler, asking for a change of command for the air war and added that it was "directed against me."

From the remarks of Schmid, Goering, and Milch it appears that the General Staff Chief did draft a study for Hitler. Leuchtenberg commented that Jeschonnek had said, "My death should be a beacon light." However, he had no time to see that it became a beacon. With the rapid onset of bad news, he obviously saw no possibility of finishing his draft. He was at the limit of his strength and rushed forward to his death. His suicide makes it clear that he was not hard enough, nor well enough adjusted, to bear the burdens imposed on his high office.

8

The Role of Hitler

NONE OF THE personality factors significant to the history of the German Luftwaffe, however, played such an important role as those of a single man, Adolf Hitler, who held Germany under the fateful sway of his personal forcefulness from 1933 until 1945.

Coming from a simple background, the product of a joyless childhood and the unhappy conditions of the Vienna of his youth, the World War I private utilized the confusion resulting from the collapse of 1918 and the general dissatisfaction at the provisions of the Versailles Treaty in order to become the founder and leader of the strongest political party Germany had ever had.

In 1933 he became Reichs Chancellor and a year and a half later, at von Hindenburg's death, he assumed the title of Fuehrer and Reichs Chancellor. His personal struggle for political power had become the nemesis of the Weimar Republic. After von Hindenburg's death he embodied the fate of seventy million, then eighty million, Germans and finally that of Europe and the world. The collapse of his regime in 1945 did not restore the world to its prewar status.

From the very beginning, Hitler's unswerving self-confidence inspired his listeners, even those of higher social background than his own, first with a feeling of fascination and then with an unwilling conviction of his superiority. Even during the early days of his career he was accustomed to do most of the talking himself, and his conferences were usually monologues with the other members listening to Hitler. An uncanny power seemed to emanate from him, an almost eerie personal magnetism and this—coupled with his truly amazing powers of memory in an era when most of his contemporaries made no attempt at all to train and develop this faculty—made it very difficult for anyone hearing his speeches and pronouncements to remain free of his influence. Only confirmed skeptics managed to escape his sway, and then only so long as they stayed well out of his sphere of influence.

For all those, however, who had followed his political activity from the beginning, he was truly the "leader." People relied implicitly on his faculty for making the right decision in any situaton and believed him to be politically infallible. The conviction that he was destined to succeed in everything he undertook was deeply rooted among his followers. The antipathy felt by most of the Party leaders for the two Christian churches led to a kind of Hitler-worship reminiscent of the days of the Roman emperors. More and more rarely were opinions expressed which might in any way cast doubt upon this cult. Most opposition subsided with the overthrow, in 1932, of Gregor Strasser, who represented quite a different direction of thought as regarded domestic policy, and the last vestige of a certain independence of spirit disappeared when Ernst Roehm and his SA leaders went down in the Blood Bath of 30 June 1934.

As far as its relationship to Hitler was concerned, the Party went through all the various stages from loyalty to the Fuehrer, with the emotional element of faith and devotion as its guiding principle in the political struggle, through faith in the Fuehrer, embodying the conviction that Hitler was the savior sent by God (Providence or Fate) to assuage Germany's economic and social ills and to liberate her from foreign domination, and finally to absolute obedience to the Fuehrer, with its concomitant suppression of all independent thought and personal doubt. The motto "Fuehrer, command and we shall follow!" repeated again and again by organized choruses at political rallies, on placards, and on banners acted as hypnotic suggestion on Germany's masses as they went into action with all the inexorableness of a religious movement.

Goering was one of Hitler's earliest followers. We know the later Reichsmarschall best as an arrogant egotist whose vanity concealed ruthless ambition and a good deal of disdain for his fellowmen. Even so, in contradiction to the opinion held by Grossadmiral Raeder, one of Goering's severest critics, there would seem to be no doubt concerning Goering's loyalty to Hitler. We may also be certain that he had a great deal of faith in the Fuehrer and that he considered him to be the chosen savior of the German nation. His first wife was devoted to Hitler with an almost adolescent adoration. Then, too, Goering was fully aware of his indebtedness to his Fuehrer for the power, prestige, and income which he enjoyed. This probably became even more painfully clear to him later on, when his influence with Hitler was on the wane.

In the beginning, however, there was no thought of abject obedience to the Fuehrer as far as Goering was concerned. Hitler often turned to him for advice, and he was easily the first in line after him. It was Goering's intervention, for example, which moved Hitler, in March

1938, to more rapid action than he had planned in the question of Austria. In March 1939, Goering tried to dissuade his chief from establishing the Protectorate of Bohemia-Moravia, and prior to the outbreak of the war he took it upon himself to utilize the offices of a Swedish go-between, Birger Dahlerus, to preserve peace at all costs. In other words, Goering still had a mind of his own and a certain amount of initiative as a private citizen.

It was not until after the war began, as the problems faced by the Luftwaffe became more and more critical, and as it began to be obvious that the Luftwaffe could not possibly master the tasks heaped upon it— approximately in June of 1942—that Goering joined the ranks of those whose obedience to the Fuehrer was automatic and indiscriminating. His motives in doing so were not very idealistic. Above all, he wanted to regain Hitler's confidence, which had cooled noticeably since the Luftwaffe had begun to suffer defeat, and in order to do so he gave up all pretense of independence. Soon, however, he was motivated by fear —fear for his own skin, fear of being deposed, fear of being pushed into the background during his conferences at the Fuehrer's headquarters by Martin Bormann, head of the Nazi Party, who was growing more and more powerful. His fear expressed itself in a fierce jealousy of Jeschonnek, long a favorite of Hitler's.

The motives leading to Jeschonnek's faith in Hitler and his frequently unreasoning obedience to him were far more idealistic. His experience as a youthful volunteer during World War I and later as an officer deeply depressed by the conditions in his fatherland made him unhesitatingly ready to pledge his loyalty to Hitler, the Messiah of a new and better order. His faith in Hitler's genius was genuine. He was sure that if Hitler could prevent a war in 1938, he would be capable of doing so in 1939. At the time the war broke out, his faith was still unshaken. His attitude was one of inflexible confidence in the inevitability of a German victory, and as late as the winter of 1941, he still refused to listen to the "almost traitorous" doubts which von Seidel began to put before him. Not until Stalingrad did he begin to doubt that the outcome of the war would be favorable for Germany, but once he opened his mind to these doubts they rapidly developed into certainties. From this point on, he was no longer indiscriminating in his obedience to Hitler. His veneration of Hitler as a person presumably remained unchanged; by this time he had long since lost any respect he may have had for Goering. It is quite possible that his suicide, which may really have been a last, desperate gesture of protest against Goering and his tragically incompetent leadership, was also an expression of the despair, loneliness, and hopelessness which Hitler was no longer able to dispel.

In the case of Milch, we can hardly speak of uncritical obedience to Hitler; Milch was not the sort of man to give unquestioning obedience to anyone. Even so, von Seidel speaks of him as "personally deeply loyal to Hitler." The enthusiasm and energy with which Milch, who was on excellent terms with the Party and its leaders, worked to realize Hitler's goal of a strong German air force could only serve to strengthen the faith of his co-workers in their Supreme Commander.

One thing must be clear. The Luftwaffe, a newly created service with a far higher percentage of younger men than the other two branches, was inevitably more receptive to Hitler and National Socialism than the Army. The Luftwaffe was not bound by tradition; there was no leader caste of Prussian nobility, insistent on its right to rule. During the period of the Weimar Republic, the Army had established a little-publicized but very real position of power and felt itself to be above the machinations of a political party. The newly created Luftwaffe, on the other hand, was commanded by Hitler's closest associate who had no scruples about using his personal prestige to increase the funds, recognition, and degree of loyalty accorded to his service branch by the new state. There is no point in denying the fact that Goering—whose energy and effectiveness during the early years of the Luftwaffe's existence are still recognized and appreciated today, even by Luftwaffe men who never fell under his personal sway—had a great deal of influence, particularly on people who were so casually associated with him that they could afford to be indulgent as regards his weaknesses. Of those staff officers transferred from the Army, the most significant was Wever. Wever, to put it mildly, was receptive to Hitler and his ideas, although there is only one source for the statement attributed to him (shortly before his promotion to the rank of General) to the effect that the Luftwaffe officer corps would either be National Socialist or it wouldn't be at all!

The second of the officers taken over from the Army, Colonel—and soon thereafter General—Kesselring, was a thoroughly idealistic person, an inveterate optimist willing to fight for his convictions. Kesselring took over his new position with all the enthusiasm of his temperamental nature and soon gave evidence of his gift for winning over his colleagues and of his untiring perseverance, qualities which characterized his military career. Promoted to Generalfeldmarschall by Hitler during World War II, Kesselring never permitted his faith in the Fuehrer to waver, and retained Hitler's full confidence until the end.

The third Army officer to achieve a position of prominence in the

Luftwaffe was Stumpff, a man of docile temperament, glad to be able to follow the strong voice of authority. Even Stumpff, however, was caught up by the vitality emanating from the new government and from his immediate chief, Goering.

These, then were the older staff officers who transferred to the Luftwaffe from the Reichswehr. A second group comprised Reichswehr officers who had been active in the former German air force or had subsequently received flight training at Lipetsk. On the average, this group was about ten years younger than the aforementioned, and brought with it a certain youthful eagerness and optimism which was easily attracted to a government dedicated to action and progress. All the others, the older Pour le Mérite wearers from Keller to Osterkamp were also fired by the enthusiastic activity of the early days. Ritter von Greim, the most serious-minded of the latter group and easily the most significant personality among them, was the victim of a positively abject devotion to Hitler until the very end. On 20 May 1945, the Fuehrer and his empire having finally succumbed to the long-threatening shadow of death and destruction, von Greim, unable to face the future, took his own life.

The course of events since 1933 clearly lends credence to the hypothesis that the Luftwaffe, augmenting its members year by year with especially selected younger men eager for action, felt its existence to be closely tied to Hitler and his political fate.

And how many successes Hitler had to his credit!—the suppression of all active opposition at home; the revitalization of German industry and the abolishment of unemployment, which had haunted the Weimar Republic since its inception; the confirmation of Germany's freedom of action by walking out on the League of Nations (14 October 1933); the nonaggression pact with Poland (26 January 1934); the halting of the encircling Stresa Front; the naval agreement with England (June 1935); the return of the Saar (January 1935); the introduction of conscription and the revelation of German rearmament (March 1935); and the deployment of troops to the Rhineland (March 1936), although the Versailles Treaty had clearly specified that no German troops might be stationed there. And Hitler's greatest coups in foreign policy, the annexation of Austria (13 March 1938) and the absorption of the Sudetenland, succeeded in spite of the serious reservations held by the Chief of the Army General Staff, General Ludwig Beck. Despite the memorandums warning against action in the Sudetenland which he issued under dates of 5 and 29 May, 3 June, 16 and 29 July 1938, Beck was unable to disguise completely his inner adherence to Hitler's views, which were bound to lead, sooner or later, to the dissolution of Czecho-slovakia, and thereby, to war.

The Conference at Munich (September 1938) showed Hitler at the most powerful moment of his entire career, at a point at which he had violated both the letter and the spirit of the Versailles Treaty and had succeeded in obtaining not only Italian, but also English and French consent for his action. In March 1939, the reincorporation of the Memel Land and the dissolution of Czechoslovakia (establishment of the Protectorate Bohemia-Moravia and assumption of protective sover-eignty over Slovakia) cost him little more than a flick of the wrist. This first step in the direction of German self-determination, at the same time a step in the direction of final disaster, seemed to the world to be further evidence of Hitler's innate talent for success. Even during the early days of the war, Hitler's prophecy of the military weakness of France seemed destined to triumph over Beck s cautiously high estimate of the fighting effectiveness and strength of the French Army, as Ger-many easily conquered France in a rapid and brilliant campaign. It was at this time that the phrase "the greatest military leader of all times" was minted, and it soon found its way into common usage.

Thus far Hitler's intuition, his appraisal of the enemy, and his stub-born will seemed to have been right. Adulation of this sort for a single individual, however, was to prove a source of serious danger.

"No man may be said to have been happy until his death." These words of the Athenian sage, Solon, reported by Herodotus, have sounded their warning throughout the history of the world. Their meaning can be extended, too; before his death, no man may be said to have been invincible, to have been intuitively right all of the time, in short, to have been destined to succeed in everything to which he turned his hand.

Let us see what effects this boundless faith in one man, this irra-tional belief in his divine power, had on the top-level leaders of the Luftwaffe. We cannot deny that it served as a source of inspiration and enthusiasm in the beginning. Both Goering and Jeschonnek, whom the wave of Hitler's success carried to the peaks of their respective careers (Goering to the unique rank of Reichsmarschall and Jeschonnek, in 1939 still a lieutenant colonel, to the ranks of General der Flieger and finally, in 1943, of Generaloberst), felt themselves to be the architects of Germany's liberation, the chosen instruments of the greatest military leader of all times, as they thought. They were highly gratified to be able to contribute with their Luftwaffe to the final victory, and they were ready to prove themselves worthy of their chief by committing

Luftwaffe strength to the limit, with a growing disregard for sound military planning. Doubts, arguments of logic, and difficulties were simply beside the point in view of the magnitude of their mission.

Neither one, however (and this was true to a greater or lesser degree of all those under Hitler's sway—the degree depending upon the extent to which they believed in him), was a free man any longer. Neither was capable of using his mind dispassionately. They were no longer the guiding spirits of their service branch, able to evaluate its position in the light of the overall situation and to make the appropriate decisions coolly and objectively. Not true of an established monarchy, basing its existence on inherited tradition or parliamentary law, it is the curse of the totalitarian state that critical thinking is interpreted as heresy, doubt, and defeatism. This is inevitable because the head of a totalitarian state must base his strength on general acceptance of his program —even if this acceptance must be forced—in order to maintain and increase his power. Goering, with his growing inclination towards a pasha-like manner of living—not necessarily an evil in itself—and Jeschonnek, with his unswerving confidence in victory and his isolation from his colleagues, were both slaves, balancing themselves between Fuehrer and Fatherland on a narrow and perilous tightrope.

Both had already been the victims of a number of delusions. Was the Hitler of 1940-41 the same as the Hitler of 1938-39, when all of his prophecies came true? Had not the British declared war—in spite of Hitler's prophecy to the contrary? And had not they persuaded the French to help them? Had Hitler succeeded in making peace with England, as he intended to do after the campaign in Poland, or at the latest, after the German victory in France? And—assuming that he had no other choice in the matter but to march against Russia—was the Soviet campaign really turning out to be the fast one he had expected, and indeed prophesied?

There is no such thing as infallibility in military or political life, and those who are spared the ignominy of defeat are rare favorites of fate. Anyone who pledges himself wholly to a leader in the assumption that the latter has always been right and will always continue to be right automatically takes leave of his own freedom of judgment and becomes nothing more than an instrument of another's will, regardless of how high his position may be.

Constant subordination to a superior personality, no matter how admirable a one, must lead sooner or later to atrophy of the individual's ability to think for himself. And one of the basic premises for the successful leadership of a military service during wartime must surely remain the ability of its commander in chief and general staff chief to think independently and to draw the appropriate conclusions from their thinking.

This is not only indispensable for the service branch concerned but also for the commander in chief and general staff chief themselves. In the case of the Luftwaffe, the primary mission—primary to the exclusion of all else—of both of these personalities was to carry out the will of the Fuehrer they thought to be infallible. And therein lay the greatest danger for the future.

In summary, it is clear that, from the very beginning, Hitler relied implicitly on Goering and his all-encompassing promises in all matters pertaining to the Luftwaffe. For this reason, he refrained from interfering in the work of the Luftwaffe General Staff—at least as long as things were going well. Moreover, the excellent work done by the Luftwaffe General Staff in organizing and building up the new force was so apparent to everyone that there was really no basis for criticism. The performance of the young Luftwaffe during the early campaigns of the war was also above reproach, although here the credit did not go so much to the General Staff Chief and his colleagues as to Goering, whom Hitler overwhelmed with praise and honors during this period. Hitler and Goering firmly believed that they alone were responsible for these early military successes and this conviction naturally led to their depending less and less on the General Staff. This attitude led to greater and greater difficulties as the war went on. Hitler arbitrarily considered himself responsible for the victories and blamed the incompetence of the General Staff for the defeats. Inevitably, Hitler's direct intervention in the command function often had a catastrophic influence on the events of the war and also did much to undermine the mutual confidence between the troops and the General Staff.

As far as the Luftwaffe was concerned, the following instances of Hitler's interference proved to have especially serious consequences:

1. Hitler's demand on 6 December 1938 for the establishment of a so-called Fuehrer-program, which called for an expansion of the Luftwaffe completely beyond the available means. The result, of course, was a shift in emphasis from vertical to horizontal growth which made it impossible later on to compensate adequately for wartime losses resulting from the greatly increased scope of activity. The ultimate consequence was the rapid exhaustion of Luftwaffe striking power because of a lack of adequately trained replacement personnel.

2. Hitler's demand that the Luftwaffe expend every effort to destroy the British army at Dunkirk, although such action was not at all neces-

sary from the standpoint of military efficiency. As a result, the Luftwaffe sustained serious losses without attaining the hoped-for degree of success.

3. The stubborn continuation of the Battle of Britain even after it had become apparent that further efforts were pointless. The result was a further weakening of Luftwaffe strength through losses of materiel and—more important—of experienced personnel, losses which had not yet been made up by the time the war ended.

4. Hitler's order of 11 September 1941 to cease all developmental work which could not be completed within one year. This order put an immediate stop to research and developmental activity on aircraft models and engines and, as the war progressed, resulted in the Luftwaffe's hopeless inferiority to the enemy in these respects. It was particularly catastrophic in that it precluded any further work on the Me-262, a jet fighter aircraft which, if its development and production had been speeded up in time, would have given Germany a considerable advantage over the Allies and might have effected a revolutionary change in the air situation.

5. Hitler's order to supply Stalingrad by air. This resulted in a further weakening of Luftwaffe units which were, in any case, already occupied beyond capacity with air supply operations elsewhere.

6. Hitler's order of 1944 that tank production be given priority over air armament despite the fact that the situation of the Luftwaffe was clearly desperate.

7. Hitler's stubborn insistence on utilizing the jet fighter (on which developmental work had continued despite the order of September 1941) as a fighter-bomber. In the end not a single one of the types developed was ever used as a fighter-bomber at the front. By the time the aircraft finally did make its debut as a jet fighter, it was too late for it to do very much good; it was not until nearly the end of the war that a few were ready for employment at the front. Through his stubbornness and his conviction that he knew better than anyone else, Hitler lightly threw away Germany's chance to gain an advantage over the enemy.

The above instances of interference by Hitler in the fields of air armament planning and the employment of the Luftwaffe are certainly not the only ones; however, they were the most decisive in effect and were clearly factors which helped to bring about the final collapse of this new and very promising branch of the Armed Forces. To be fair, on the other hand, we must realize that such interference would probably have been impossible—at least in the form in which it occurred—if the Luftwaffe had had as chief a man capable of convincing his Supreme Commander, by well-founded and reasonable arguments—based on ability and experience—of the realistic potentialities and requirements of his branch and of the most rewarding fields for its employment.

⑨
Problems of Command

HITLER AND THE LUFTWAFFE
TAKE OVER GENERAL STAFF

HITLER'S ATTITUDE towards the Luftwaffe General Staff was colored by the same factors which motivated his distrust of general staff service as such. His antipathy, which could develop into intense hatred on occasion, was largely due to the subconscious feeling of inferiority which characterized this man who had risen from the bottom, and who always wore the Iron Cross, First Class, awarded in World War I, as his only decoration—apart from his Party emblem—to convince himself and others that he was a military expert of the first water.

Even so, Hitler was too shrewd to neglect using the Reichswehr as the nucleus of the armed force he planned to create. This force was to be the primary instrument of his power politics and was to be groomed and trained for this role from its very inception.

Instinctively he felt that the General Staff, the intellectual elite of this instrument, represented the most serious threat to his plans. And the frank and open battle waged by Beck (the first chief of the Army General Staff) did nothing to dispel this feeling.

Although Hitler's distrust of the Army General Staff dated from the very beginning, it was quite a while before the Luftwaffe General Staff became aware of any disparaging remarks directed against itself. Whereas the Army General Staff had to fight to maintain its position of leadership within the Armed Forces, and thus was bound to come into ideological conflict with the dictates of National Socialism and with its leader, the comparatively new Luftwaffe General Staff had neither the inclination nor the time to worry about such matters as prestige within the Armed Forces. While the leading personalities of the Army and its General Staff frequently gave public expression, by word and deed, to their mistrust of National Socialism, the top-ranking Luftwaffe officers were so fully occupied by their immediate missions that they had neither the time nor the interest for intervention in political matters. A certain feeling of gratitude that Hitler was making it possible for them to tackle a new and fascinating military project may also have played some part; the decisive factor, though, was probably Goering's ability to divert political criticism away from the General Staff and the officer corps of the Luftwaffe. In any case, the Luftwaffe was spared the almost daily friction faced by the Army and its General Staff, and the tension between Hitler and his Armed Forces leaders had far less effect on the Luftwaffe General Staff than on the Army.

This relationship between Hitler and the Luftwaffe General Staff, which may be termed a neutral one, lasted through the early war years, possibly because Hitler's instinctive distrust of anyone wearing the General Staff uniform was lulled to passivity in regard to the Luftwaffe General Staff by the extraordinary success enjoyed by the Luftwaffe during this period. In any case, Hitler was definitely amenable to suggestions regarding air armament and the employment of the Luftwaffe forces until 1940. Thus, any mistakes made up to this point in armament planning, organization, or commitment of forces must be laid squarely on the shoulders of Goering and his General Staff chiefs.

Hitler's attitude, however, changed rapidly as soon as the Luftwaffe began to run into difficulty. That these difficulties were due in great part, first, to the fact that he had trusted Goering implicitly and had taken little personal interest in the affairs of the Luftwaffe, and, second to his own decisions in the field of armament planning for the Armed Forces, was something he refused to recognize. He simply placed the blame for everything on Goering and the Luftwaffe General Staff.

There is little point in trying to absolve Goering and his General Staff Chief of all blame for the wrong decisions which were made—on the contrary, both were largely responsible for what happened. The decisive point, however, is the fact that in a dictatorship all decisions are ultimately taken by the head of state—either by direct order, by exploitation on the part of the dictator of the fear felt by subordinate agencies, or by the influence he wields over blindly trusting followers. The dictator's word is law; he is infallible, regardless of whether he belongs to the right or left wing. Ultimately a mass psychosis is created which threatens to paralyze the entire nation. It could never have occurred to Goering, as one of Hitler's first converts and as his helper during the early days of his struggle for power, to doubt the rightness of any of Hitler's opinions or decisions, even when Goering's own professional ability (which, to be sure, was not great) ought to have convinced him to the contrary. There's no better illustration of the relationship between Hitler and Goering than the following scene.

During the summer of 1937 Hitler faced certain difficult political decisions. Accordingly he called upon the Commanders in Chief of the various Armed Forces branches (including Goering, of course) to brief him on the status of the armament program. With great enthusiasm Goering elaborated on the virtues of the various types of aircraft in use, stating that his bombers were capable of almost anything imaginable. Understandably Hitler was left with the impression that Germany's bomber fleet was unbeatable. There is no way of telling whether Goering deliberately set out to deceive Hitler or whether he was merely carried away by his own eloquence. In any case, Goering was clearly astonished when one of his officers dryly pointed out that, at the moment, Germany did not possess a single up-to-date bomb. Hitler, who had let himself be fired by Goering's enthusiasm, was shocked. It was only with difficulty that he was able to keep his temper.

After the conference was over, Goering turned on his officers with bitter reproaches. He brushed aside their argument that it was absolutely necessary to keep the chief of state accurately informed as to the actual strength or weakness of his armed forces.

Several days later, Hitler—still smarting under the embarrassment created by the recent conference—sent for Goering and several of the top-ranking Luftwaffe leaders. He explained that he had been thinking over the problem of the bomber fleet and had discovered a solution, ". . . Germany has more than enough of those metal cylinders used for oxygen, acetylene, etc. We can fill them with explosives and use them as bombs!"

One of the officers present dared to point out cautiously that they couldn't be aimed properly, that they would flip over in the air, and so forth. Hitler was obviously annoyed—these General Staff people always thought they knew better! Goering, however, seeing a chance to make good his slip at the last conference, was quick to seize it, and replied:

"My Fuehrer, may I express my thanks for this wonderful solution! I must admit that none of us could have thought of such an ingenious idea! You, and you alone, have saved the situation. Good Lord, to think that we're all such dumbbells! I shall never be able to forgive myself!"

Whereupon Goering's dumbbells, deeply impressed by the perspicacity of their Commander in Chief, went home to discover, upon close study of the technical data involved, that this brilliant solution was no solution at all!

But Goering was not the only one—his General Staff chiefs, too, were more or less fascinated by Hitler's daring flights of fancy. Wever, for example, was a devoted believer in National Socialism and was firmly convinced that Hitler was destined to raise Germany from her status as a second-rate nation. He did not live long enough to recognize the evils inherent in the system. Kesselring and Stumpff were believers, too, although with serious reservations. As older officers in the General Staff chief's post, they could not remain unaware of Hitler's insufficiencies as a military expert, while the younger officers had had no opportunity to judge for themselves during the years before the war.

In the case of the fourth General Staff Chief Jeschonnek, who took office on 1 February 1939, the situation was quite different. The historian Richard Suchenwirth has the following to say in this regard:

> . . . Politically speaking, the newly appointed General Staff Chief, who had been active in various key posts in the Reichs Air Ministry since the beginning, was personally receptive to the doctrines of the new regime. After all, he was a product of the old Prussian school and did his best to exemplify its ideals (strict discipline, devotion to duty to the exclusion of all personal considerations, subordination of self to a higher purpose, and the tendency to devote oneself to military service with an almost romantic ardor somewhat out of place in a changing world).
>
> Jeschonnek was fully convinced, and he accepted Hitler's genius, not only in the political sphere but in the military field as well, as an article of faith. In his case, one must speak of personal devotion to Hitler as a leader rather than of adherence to the doctrines of the National Socialist Party.

It is difficult to estimate the degree to which Jeschonnek's faith in the infallibility of his Fuehrer diminished during the course of the war; he was a man of few words, and apparently he never gave expression to his feelings in this regard. It seems clear, however, that his suicide was motivated not by doubts in regard to Hitler but rather by the unbearable situation which had developed between him and his Commander in Chief, Goering, the eternal intrigues of the clique with which the latter surrounded himself, and finally the nagging fear that he himself might in some way have been responsible for the collapse of the Luftwaffe. An indication of his unswerving faith in Hitler is a memorandum justifying his actions as Chief of the Luftwaffe General Staff and presenting various recommendations for the future development of the Luftwaffe, which he prepared for Hitler shortly before his death.

Korten, Jeschonnek's successor, was also able to win Hitler's confidence. Here again, the difficulties which Korten faced stemmed less from the Fuehrer's Headquarters than from his Commander in Chief and the latter's immediate circle.

Kreipe, however, who succeeded Korten when the latter was killed in the unsuccessful attempt on Hitler's life in July 1944, was to witness a complete break between Hitler and the Luftwaffe General Staff. Kreipe's earnest efforts to persuade Hitler to reorganize his armament program with greater emphasis on home air defense (particularly to authorize production of the jet fighter which Hitler wanted to use as a fast fighter-bomber) met with immediate and adamant resistance. It was at this time that Hitler demanded that von Greim be appointed to the Fuehrer's Headquarters as Luftwaffe general and that he be given full authority to act for the Luftwaffe. This meant, of course, that both the Commander in Chief, Luftwaffe, and the Chief of the Luftwaffe General Staff were to be ignored—in short, it was a vote of no-confidence against Goering as well as a categorical refusal to deal with the General Staff. Von Greim, however, an officer and a gentleman, soon asked to be relieved from his position at the Fuehrer's Headquarters and, with his resignation, the situation reverted to what it had been.

Now Hitler began to depend upon his personal pilot, a former Lufthansa captain named Bauer, for competent advice in questions concerning the Luftwaffe. Although he held the rank of an SS-Gruppenfuehrer and was a Generalleutnant in the police force, Bauer was no more than a layman in military affairs in general and Luftwaffe affairs in particular. His knowledge was limited to the things which any older experienced pilot had to know about his trade. His gems of wisdom, however—typical of these was his comment that he could fly a Ju-52 to London and back without the slightest difficulty—found a willing and interested listener in Hitler, and had much to do with the latter's tendency to term any objections brought up by the General Staff to his fantastic demands as pessimism, defeatism, and sabotage. Without any doubt it was partly due to Bauer that Hitler's antipathy towards the General Staff gradually turned into intense hatred.

Hitler's attitude towards the General Staff was bound to lead to the conspiracy of Army General Staff leaders on 20 July 1944. They saw in Hitler not only the General Staff's most implacable enemy but also the ultimate ruin of the German people, and felt that it was their duty towards the nation to put a stop to his activity. That no one from the Luftwaffe General Staff participated in this conspiracy was not due to the fact that none of them would have been willing to act against Hitler, but simply that no attempt was made to take anyone from the Luftwaffe into confidence regarding the plot. This, in turn, was proba-

bly due to the traditional feeling on the part of the Army General Staff
that the Luftwaffe was National Socialist, both in tendency and sympathy, and was not to be trusted with the undertaking at hand.

In general, the opinions prevailed that the Armed Forces High Command and its chief were little more than yes-men. It is no wonder that
they enjoyed as little prestige with the Luftwaffe General Staff as with
the General Staffs of the other Armed Forces branches. As a result, the
Armed Forces High Command was felt to be a parallel rather than a
superior agency whose chief duty was to straighten out family quarrels
within the services. Its effectiveness as an instrument of military command becomes conspicuous by its absence when we think of the great
authority enjoyed by the top-level command of the Army during World
War I.

At the beginning of World War II there was, to be sure, a certain
uniformity in the views of the three Armed Forces branches concerning
the conduct of operations. But as the war progressed and the military
difficulties faced by the German Reich grew more and more critical, the
importance of the Armed Forces High Command as an authoritative
military instrument dwindled in direct proportion to the growing need
for just such an instrument.

The Armed Forces High Command failed completely to supply the
effective support which the Luftwaffe General Staff needed so badly.
There was a certain reluctance to interfere in any way with Luftwaffe
affairs, because no one in the Armed Forces High Command was willing to risk the danger of a clash with Goering—at least not so long as he
enjoyed Hitler's favor.

This feeling of reluctance diminished gradually during the course of
the war, however, as is evidenced by the fact that the Army High Command had no compunctions about pushing through its plan to speed up
the tank procurement program at the expense of the Luftwaffe armament program—and this without even consulting Luftwaffe leaders.

The comments of Koller, the last Chief of the Luftwaffe General
Staff, are of interest in connection with the relationship between the
Armed Forces High Command and the Luftwaffe High Command dur-
ing the last phase of the war.

> In June 1944, in order to counter the many recent attacks on Luftwaffe
> policy, I took advantage of a small conference at the Obersalzberg to
> point out the weakness of Luftwaffe armament resources, and voiced
> my feeling that the Armed Forces High Command, which ought to
> have supported the Luftwaffe armament program in the interests of

the Armed Forces and the nation as a whole, had limited itself to negative criticism. I stated frankly that our top military leaders had simply neglected their duty in this connection.

And with this I had stumbled into a wasps' nest! They refused to consider my arguments and tried to persuade me that Goering would not have countenanced any participation by the Armed Forces High Command in the affairs of the Luftwaffe, that he would have termed it interference and forbidden it. There can be no doubt of the inaccuracy of this contention. To be sure, Goering was not a man to countenance interference, but he would certainly have welcomed constructive support and assistance from the Armed Forces High Command in improving the Luftwaffe's armament situation.

The above passage clearly illustrates the unhealthy tendency of the Armed Forces High Command leaders—most of whom were from the Army General Staff—to refuse to interest themselves in the problems of the Luftwaffe. In fact, one often had the impression that the Army was considered the sole decisive branch of the Armed Forces and that the other two—particularly the Luftwaffe—were merely auxiliary troops and expected to get along on their own. If Luftwaffe and Navy leaders had been given more responsible posts in the Armed Forces High Command, this attitude might have been avoided. Hitler would never have permitted a reshuffling of his planning staff to this end, because his views on war and its problems were very much those which had prevailed during World War I, and at that time, of course, the Army was the most important military force. On the other hand, neither the Luftwaffe nor the Navy was much interested in having greater responsibility in the Armed Forces High Command, since it would have meant a certain loss in their quite considerable independence of action.

It is a well-known fact that the top-ranking members of the Armed Forces High Command had no influence over the fantastic plans of the Fuehrer. History cannot but reproach them for this. From the vantage point of today it seems incredible that these men let themselves be hypnotized into acquiescence by Hitler's demoniacal fantasies, whose lack of military soundness must have been obvious.

The lower echelons of the General Staffs of all three branches of the service gained little if any accurate knowledge of what was really going on. Few of these lower ranking officers were acquainted with the personalities and military prowess of the men at the top. Fuehrer Directive No. 1 made it impossible for them to obtain adequate information regarding the overall policies governing the conduct of the war and domestic politics. The troop general staffs trusted their superiors and comrades at the top because they traditionally assumed them to be men of character and officers capable of sound and objective planning. The gradual change in these men, brought about by Hitler's unbelievable successes in both the military and political spheres and by the tremendous influence which his personality exerted over the persons around him, was never clearly recognized by the men in the lower General Staff posts. The change in Field Marshal Keitel, however, became generally apparent, as is indicated by the widespread use of the nickname "Lakai-tel"* during the last years of the war.

GOERING AND HIS GENERAL STAFF

The relationship of the Luftwaffe General Staff to its Commander in Chief was subject to various and changing influences. Basically, the tone was set by the extremely friendly association existing between Goering and his first General Staff Chief, Wever. Wever's personal integrity and his tremendous efficiency made a lasting impression on his chief, and were certainly instrumental in inspiring the attitude of trust and confidence which Goering displayed towards all the Luftwaffe General Staff officers. The success of this early relationship influenced Goering to grant the Luftwaffe General Staff officers complete independence in carrying out their work—at least during the early developmental years.

Kesselring describes the early relationship as follows:

> In Reichsmarschall Hermann Goering, the Luftwaffe had a former flight officer, a National Socialist, and a generous man as its Commander in Chief. He required a great deal from us generals in the Reichs Air Ministry, but he gave us complete freedom of action and shielded us from all political criticism. In my long years as a soldier, I have never been so free of outside influences and so able to act independently as during this early period of Luftwaffe development (from 1933 on), when I served as Chief of the Luftwaffe Administration Office, Chief of the Luftwaffe General Staff, and as a field commander.

The personal respect which Goering felt for the leading officers in the Reichs Air Ministry facilitated his decision to approve the forma-

---

* Translator's Note: This is a play on words; the word "Lakai" (accented on the last syllable) means "lackey."

tion of a Luftwaffe General Staff. In a sense, this decision represented a sincere vote of confidence on Goering's part, especially since all his friends from former days and particularly his State Secretary, Milch, were bitterly opposed to a General Staff for the Luftwaffe.

The confidence which Goering felt in his first General Staff Chief certainly had some effect on his attitude towards the subsequent Chiefs. The friction which later developed was not due to a basic change in this attitude, but rather to specific events of the war which will be discussed more fully later on. It is understandable, of course, that Hitler's antipathy towards the General Staff may have influenced Goering to a certain extent; however, Goering's antipathy was restricted more or less to the Army General Staff, and a certain feeling of closeness and solidarity—as well as a personal need to belong—bound him to his own General Staff. On the other hand, he was easily swayed by the comments of close friends and younger, inexperienced combat officers (particularly those who had distinguished themselves in combat), and when under these influences was quite capable of turning against the General Staff as the proper instrument of command. These moods never lasted very long, however, for he was shrewd enough to realize that he was wholly dependent upon the General Staff in matters of command.

Goering's alleged rages at the General Staff—particularly after a Luftwaffe defeat—were not taken too seriously by that organization; they helped, however, to disrupt his relationship to it on more than one occasion during the war.

Goering's almost pathological vanity made it impossible for him to permit the achievements of his General Staff Chiefs to be praised in public. It was the duty of the Chief to remain in the background—even as far as the Luftwaffe itself was concerned. Jeschonnek, as the first wartime General Staff Chief, was the one to suffer most as a result of Goering's hunger for personal fame. Goering almost never recommended his General Staff officers for decorations, "after all, they were only aides, and aides have no right to decorations . . ." Under no circumstances were the General Staff members permitted to appear publicly as leading personalities within the Luftwaffe—which did not deter Goering from demanding the maximum from them in performance and self-sacrificing devotion to duty. Inasmuch as this practice was a part of the ancient General Staff tradition, they accepted it in fairly good grace. In the long run, however, the rod is not enough to ensure continual top performance—an occasional pat on the back is also required.

During the course of the war, the Luftwaffe General Staff gradually built up a kind of defense front against its Commander in Chief. Thus,

Goering gradually lost the confidence of the Luftwaffe General Staff as the war progressed. When Korten died of injuries sustained in the unsuccessful plot against Hitler's life on 20 July 1944, Goering was hard put to find a willing successor for him. Again, after Kreipe's comparatively short incumbency as General Staff Chief it was only with difficulty that Goering was able to persuade Koller to take over the job.

When Koller took office as General Staff Chief on 25 November 1944, Goering delivered a speech before the assembled General Staff officers (an unprecedented thing for him to do). Goering's remarks reveal better than any other source the total picture of his personality, his views on Germany's position, and his concept of the General Staff and its mission. His comments are indicative of a certain basic primitiveness, combined with healthy common sense and flavored with humor; the speech is filled with somewhat long-winded argumentation, which may be interpreted as an expression of his feeling of insecurity towards the General Staff. Now that he was alone, abandoned by many of his former friends and associates, fallen from Hitler's favor, and facing the complete collapse of his Luftwaffe, Goering was desperately eager to reassociate himself with that group which had done such a fine job of building the Luftwaffe, i.e. with the Luftwaffe General Staff! The reassociation was not to be of long duration, however, nor did it spring from an inner desire on Goering's part, but was motivated rather by the urgency of the moment. This is clear from a study written by Deichmann, in which he has the following to say regarding the position of the Chief of the Luftwaffe General Staff during wartime:

. . . The relationship existing between Goering and his General Staff Chiefs during the war had little in common with the classic examples of history, such as Blucher-Gneisenau, for example. It resembled much more the legendary relationship between a sultan and his grand vizier, whereby the latter lived in constant dread of being beheaded or thrown into prison at his master's whim. In his book *Der letzte Monat* (The Last Month), General Koller describes Goering's continual threats of court martial, concentration camp, and execution.

We must admit in all fairness that this unsatisfactory relationship between the Commander in Chief, Luftwaffe, and his General Staff Chiefs only developed gradually as the war took its course, particularly from that time on when the Luftwaffe began to suffer defeat. However, even at the beginning of the war, the association of these two personalities was not entirely what it should have been. The reasons for this are probably the following:

Goering considered himself the sole creator of the Luftwaffe. Moreover, he was determined that he, and he alone, should receive credit for its successes; he had no intention of sharing this credit with anyone else. It was for this reason that he limited the power of decision of his General Staff and retained personal control over many minor details. He objected strongly whenever the General Staff Chief dared to make inspection visits to subordinate headquarters or to troop units without him in order to orient himself on conditions.

In the beginning Goering usually attended the conferences with the Fuehrer himself; whenever he was unable to do so (or preferred not to do so, as was almost always the case later on, when the air situation had become so desperately critical), he sent as representative not the General Staff Chief, but some other officer from his staff (frequently the intelligence officer from the Luftwaffe High Command). When he did finally agree to send the General Staff Chief—probably at Hitler's insistence—the latter no longer had any authority to make a final decision anyway.

Whenever Goering made inspection visits together with the General Staff Chief, it was apparent to all observers that the latter functioned only as an order-taker. "Write this down . . ." "See that such and such is done . . ." were the usual remarks addressed to the General Staff Chief by his Commander in Chief on these occasions.

The General Staff Chief, who had quite enough to keep him busy, spent a great deal of time in fulfilling social obligations and in waiting for Goering. If the latter was in conference with Hitler, for example, the General Staff Chief was expected to wait hours on end at Fuehrer Headquarters in case he might be needed to furnish information on some particular matter.

Goering's penchant for retiring to remote places, such as the Reichs Hunting Lodge at Rominten (East Prussia), often made it necessary for the Chief of the General Staff to work with a diminished staff in Goering's railroad car for months at a time. In this connection, General von Waldau's diary gives us a further hint:

"I've been trying to keep my distance from the Chief (i.e. Goering); it's not compatible with work to have to keep company with him and to eat all the time . . ."

It would be unfair if we should try to make the General Staff Chief responsible for certain events over which he had little or no influence. This is particularly true of technological matters, in which the leading role was played by the deputy Commander in Chief, Luftwaffe, the State Secretary and Inspector General Erhard Milch. Ernst Heinkel, in his memoirs (the value or rather lack of value of which it is not my province to judge) states:

"The creation of the new position (i.e. Milch's appointment as Goering's deputy) was rather unfortunate in that it prevented the development of a real top-level command agency within the Luftwaffe.

There were countless occasions when close contact between Goering and the Chief of the General Staff would have been profitable; in every case Milch's robust figure stood between them and could not be circumvented."

Heinkel's remarks are essentially accurate. Ever since 1937, when the General Staff was removed from its position of subordination to the State Secretary (after a serious disagreement between Milch and General Staff Chief Kesselring), Milch had been jealously on guard to see that no one from the General Staff should have any say in the technological matters nominally entrusted to him. Thus, since 1937 the General Staff had hardly been in a position to push through its thoroughly justifiable armament requirements (particularly in regard to the development of new aircraft models). The only way was to go directly to Goering, but this involved numerous difficulties and, in any case, was rarely successful. A further factor which served to weaken the position of the General Staff Chief was Goering's penchant for using his personal friends as unofficial advisors. As a result, the General Staff Chief not only had to convince Goering of his views, but also had to struggle against prejudices and preconceived notions planted in his mind by these advisors. As the fortunes of war varied, Goering resorted to other advisors as well—a colonel whose hobby was graphology, for example, and a professor from Kassel with an allegedly clairvoyant wand whose gyrations influenced Goering's decisions . . .

After the war, Goering came to realize the unhealthy influence of the individuals with whom he had surrounded himself—as is indicated by his comment that "now he knew who his real friends had been . . ."

We need add little to the foregoing comments—made by a man who witnessed much at first hand during his association with the Reichsmarschall—in order to obtain a full picture of the personal relationship between Goering and his General Staff Chiefs. The only thing we might point out is the fact that an older officer, such as Wever or Kesselring, would not have countenanced such treatment from Goering; and this is precisely the reason why Goering preferred to have a younger officer as General Staff Chief, and as a matter of fact, to surround himself with younger men. Jeschonnek cannot escape a good deal of the blame for encouraging this tendency. He deliberately called Goering's attention to younger officers who had distinguished themselves in action—men like Storp, Diesing, Harlinghausen, and Peltz*— in order that the Reichsmarschall might obtain an accurate picture of

* Generalmajor Walter Storp, Generalmajor Ulrich Diesing, Generalleutnant Martin Harlinghausen, Generalmajor Dietrich Peltz.

actual conditions at the front. The result, however, was not quite what Jeschonnek intended. As the war continued, Goering tended more and more to go directly to these young men, without consulting his General Staff Chief, and to solicit their advice. Goering overlooked the fact that these young officers could not possibly possess more than limited specialized experience, but that—in their confident immaturity—they might easily be tempted to voice an authoritative opinion in matters of which they had no real knowledge.

In this way the General Staff Chief himself brought unofficial, and in part, irresponsible advisors into the Reichsmarschall's vicinity. One of them, Diesing, went over to Goering's camp entirely and worked so openly against Jeschonnek that the latter was constrained to term him a traitor.

Goering's so-called "Kindergarten," a group of young officers under the leadership of Chief Adjutant von Brauchitsch* (all of them much decorated for valor in action) who had succeeded in working their way gradually into the personal staff of the Reichsmarschall, had a decidedly detrimental influence on Goering's attitude towards his General Staff Chief and thus on the work of the General Staff itself.

Not only was their influence—exerted during the course of evening discussions around the fireplace—unhealthy, but they also managed to form a tightly-knit clique with other younger officers and comrades serving in various headquarters staffs and at the front. The collective influence of this clique on Goering made the work of the General Staff unbearably difficult and played a not inconsiderable role in the final break between Goering and Jeschonnek.

The influence exerted by the Reichsmarschall's personal circle of friends was also highly undesirable. The majority of these were officers whom Goering had known during World War I, men whose knowledge of modern military operations was sadly limited, but who—thanks to Goering's patronage—had been promoted with comet-like rapidity. A number of them were constantly in Goering's vicinity, and the influence which their comments exerted on him was anything but conducive to a smooth relationship with the General Staff. A report by Koller serves to enlighten us further in this respect:

> The Reichsmarschall must also be blamed for the frequency with which conferences and orientation periods were simply broken off before a decision had been reached. He solicited the advice of anyone and everyone—the Chief of Luftwaffe Procurement and Supply, the State Secre-

* The son of Feldmarschall von Brauchitsch.

tary, any young squadron captains or unit commanders who happened to be around—no matter how fantastic and immature his ideas might be. None of them knew what any of the others had said, and the Chief of the General Staff was almost always the last one to hear (often quite by accident) what it was all about. Then, too, Goering was very receptive to the remarks of the often irresponsible men making up his circle of associates, most of whom were totally incompetent and had absolutely no idea of the problems involved . . .

Koller, who served for many years as Chief of the Luftwaffe Operations Staff and ultimately as Chief of the General Staff, was in a particularly good position to observe events at first hand. He has the following to say regarding the role played by the younger General Staff officers in Goering's personal staff:

It was extremely unfortunate that the Reichsmarschall preferred to fill his personal staff with such young officers, men from the flying forces, antiaircraft artillery units, or signal troops who had had only a few years' experience as soldiers. Most of them had had no really thorough training—at least no all-around training—and at most only a few weeks of General Staff experience. It is no wonder that their views were immature and their professional experience painfully limited. Their training spotty and incomplete, they tended to be conceited and the heady atmosphere into which they came often had the effect of turning them into megalomaniacs and spinners of intrigues. They were taken into the General Staff even before they had had any basic training and given the right to wear the coveted crimson stripe on their trousers; they were promoted with astonishing rapidity—over the heads of their comrades; and they were accorded a position of influence which they were totally unqualified to fill. These youngsters were infuriatingly quick to pass judgment on anything and anyone—commanders in chief, generals to whom they were abysmally inferior in professional knowledge and personal savoir faire, men who could have been their fathers. They were just as quick to pass judgment on technical matters or on questions pertaining to the employment of forces. That Goering's "court clique" came in for a great deal of adverse criticism from troops and command as well as from leaders in the top echelons of the Luftwaffe itself is a well-known fact.

The several passages which have been cited in this section, stemming from men who had ample opportunity during their period of service as Chiefs of the General Staff to become intimately acquainted with Goering's professional qualifications and personal attitudes, require no further comment. They provide a complete picture of Goering's rather extraordinary personality and of the relationship between him and his General Staff Chiefs, who by rights ought to have been his closest coworkers. He was a man of tremendous energy, quick to explode in impulsive rage, and then—in smug self-conceit—to sit back and let things run their course; a personality characterized by an inordinate degree of self-confidence out of all proportion to his actual professional ability and, at the same time, by a feeling of insecurity in keeping with his lack of ability. Outwardly brutal and ruthless, he was filled with an almost childlike reverence, tempered by fear, for his Fuehrer, which made him constantly eager to anticipate the latter's every wish, regardless of whether or not it might be capable of practical realization.

For the General Staff Chiefs, Goering was an extremely comfortable superior so long as things were going well but an unbearable burden in a crisis—precisely the time when the positive qualities of a strong commander in chief are most urgently needed to support his co-workers. Instead of doing everything in his power to strengthen the instrument which had performed so well for him, he viewed it with mistrust, belittled it in public and before the troops, blunted it by continual amateurish interference, and, ultimately, was responsible in good part for its defeat and collapse.

MILCH AND THE GENERAL STAFF

The position of the State Secretary Erhard Milch within the Reichs Air Ministry had little in common with the post of State Secretary within the parliamentary government of a democratic state. This position was created as an aid to Goering, whose many and varied obligations prevented him from devoting as much time to his duties as Minister of Aviation as seemed desirable. Besides, it was necessary to create some sort of post for the director of the Lufthansa (Milch), to whom Hitler had incurred certain obligations during the early struggles of his political career, and the position established had to be one which would utilize his experience in the field of aviation and, at the same time, satisfy his ambition. It is for the latter reason that the State Secretary was designated as the permanent deputy of both the Minister of Aviation and the Commander in Chief, Luftwaffe. In the latter capacity, of course, he had authority over the Chief of the General Staff, with his various departments, as well as over the chiefs of the troop staffs.

In keeping with ancient tradition, the Chief of the General Staff is the primary advisor of his commander in chief—a function for which his personality, training, and experience ideally should suit him; obviously, then, serious friction is bound to develop when the post of State Secretary is held by a man who has none of the above-mentioned qualifications, but who insists upon being recognized as the first and only advisor of the minister, even in purely military matters. Thus it is no wonder that the poor relationship between the State Secretary and the Chiefs of the General Staff is an ever-recurring theme in this study.

In order that the reader may have a more thorough understanding of the situation, the extraordinarily strong position enjoyed by Milch as a result of his close connection with the Party and with Hitler himself should be emphasized. Taking this fact into consideration, it is easy to understand why Goering—who was anything but fond of Milch—was unable to rid himself of the State Secretary. All attempts to reduce Milch's authority in favor of the Chief of the General Staff were doomed to failure by the State Secretary's ruthless determination to hold on to his position and the privileges appertaining thereto. Once the war had begun, however, and particularly after 1944, Milch's position grew gradually less important.

In order not to jeopardize the closeness of the ties which bound him to the Party (and also in order to keep himself fully informed on the latest political developments), Milch employed a high Party functionary as a special duty staff assistant on his personal staff. He gained the man's loyalty by giving him civil service status and by arranging to have him promoted to high ministerial rank. No one was deceived as to Milch's true purpose, of course, but in the last analysis this man proved to be a boon to the Luftwaffe as a whole; because of him, Milch was able to handle any attacks on the Luftwaffe made by the Party right in his own office and the Luftwaffe officers did not need to bother about them.

In order to compensate for the fact that his qualifications for the post of deputy to the Commander in Chief were painfully few, Milch did his best to impress the General Staff Chief and his colleagues with his admittedly unusual talent for organization and his allegedly all-encompassing knowledge of technological matters. Inasmuch as his experience in both fields was based exclusively on his activity as director of the Lufthansa, his audience was less impressed than irritated, thinking —quite correctly—that the principles applicable to the operation of a commercial enterprise such as the Lufthansa could not be entirely applicable to military conditions.

The first serious disagreement began to develop when Kesselring took office as Chief of the General Staff, and had its climax in Kesselring's voluntary resignation from this post; Stumpff then became General Staff Chief. The State Secretary had won, but his victory was Pyrrhic in that he was relieved of his authority over the General Staff Chief. In a letter dated 21 February 1954, Milch describes the effects of this move as he saw them and evaluates the influence on subsequent events of the overall reorganization in the Luftwaffe top-level command apparatus:

> . . . In the summer of 1937, Goering reorganized the top-level command apparatus of the Luftwaffe; some of the results of his reorganization were the following:
>
> 1. The close cooperation previously existing among the General Staff, the office of the Chief of Luftwaffe Procurement and Supply, the Personnel Office, and the rest of the departments of the Reichs Air Ministry was diminished considerably. A further factor in this connection was the high rate of turnover in the incumbency of key positions, e.g. during the years 1933 through 1945 there were no fewer than eight Chiefs of the General Staff.
>
> 2. The Junkers and Dornier four-engine bombers were not approved for mass production, despite the fact that the test models had proved highly promising. As a result Germany had no really adequate aircraft model for use in strategic operations; without any doubt, this is one of the reasons for the failure of the air offensive against Britain and for the Luftwaffe's inability to provide adequate air protection for German submarines at sea.
>
> 3. The production of aircraft instruments, which had increased steadily until 1937, was allowed to level off and was not stepped up again until 1942. The same was true of research and developmental activity on new aircraft types and modern aircraft equipment, such as power units for turbojet engines (a project assigned to Junkers and the Bavarian Motor Works in 1936), new piston-driven engines, etc.
>
> 4. According to the plans developed in 1933, bomber aircraft were to have first priority in order to build up a minimum deterrent force to discourage the Western Powers from interfering in Germany's rearmament activity. After 1937-38 top priority was to go to the fighter aircraft, first the day fighters and then the night fighters. This shift in emphasis never took place. And neither the technical performance nor the airborne armaments of the few fighters being produced (approximately 200 per month by the end of the second year of war) had taken full advantage of the technological possibilities.

5. During the period from 1 September 1939 through 15 November 1941, the aircraft production program was subject to no fewer than sixteen thoroughgoing revisions, not a single one of which was carried through as planned. As a result, the industrial plants concerned were thoroughly confused regarding series production and developmental work. During the year 1942, for example, there was no fixed schedule for delivery of new or refitted aircraft and engines to the front. The technological aspect of Luftwaffe development had come to a full stop, both quantitatively and qualitatively, by the end of 1941. A complete reorganization was urgently needed and, indeed, it began to have a favorable effect after about eight months until all progress was stopped by Allied bombardments on the one hand and interference from above on the other (e.g. the ban on developing and producing the Me-262 as a fighter) . . .

So much for the State Secretary's personal views. While the items which he mentions are certainly contributing factors to the final collapse of the Luftwaffe, he still (21 February 1954) insists on blaming them all on the reorganization of 1937, which removed the Chief of the General Staff—and, incidentally, Udet as well—from his immediate command. He neglects to mention, however, that this situation was changed six months later—at the suggestion of Stumpff, Kesselring's successor—and that from that time on Milch was once more exclusively responsible for technical air armament, without any possibility of interference on the part of the Chief of the General Staff. Thus, one might be tempted to interpret his statement regarding the stagnation of technological development in late 1941 as an attempt to fix the blame retrospectively on Udet. Even so, Udet—despite the fact that he had direct access to Goering—was technically subordinate to the State Secretary, and it would be manifestly unfair of the latter to try to make Udet entirely responsible for the collapse.

It is difficult to understand the reasons for the State Secretary's hatred of the General Staff and its Chief. Goering once said to him, "Milch, you don't know what you're talking about! You're simply jealous of the General Staff because they wouldn't accept you when you tried to get in in 1917!"

In view of Milch's desire for power and prestige, it may well be that this was the basis of his antipathy. Thwarted ambition is always a bad thing and it can become dangerous when the person concerned is given a position of power in which he can avenge his wounded feelings. There is no doubt that the disharmony existing between the State

Secretary and the General Staff was one of the chief factors in the failure and final downfall of the German Luftwaffe.

During Jeschonnek's period of service as Chief of the General Staff, the relationship between Milch and the General Staff grew noticeably more difficult. In a questionnaire dated 2 September 1955, Milch gives his reasons as follows:

> . . . This is the way it happened. One day I received a report from the Training Wing that an airplane had crashed out of control in a low dive over the *Bach**. The next day two more machines, with their crews, were reported missing for the same reason. I requested copies of the orders and in them I read the following sentence: "In practicing low-altitude flight, the pilot should make certain that the propeller tips touch the water." It was reported to me that the comment "Anyone who doesn't do it this way is a coward!" was added orally.
>
> I now faced the decision of whether or not to initiate court martial proceedings against Jeschonnek. I decided against it, however, and gave him a severe reprimand instead. From this moment on, he was my deadly enemy. If I had gone ahead with court martial proceedings, he could have been sentenced to several years' imprisonment. Ambition and vanity are the basic causes of his enmity towards me. Incidentally, only a man with no experience whatsoever in technical matters could have issued the orders he did.

In the same questionnaire, Milch had the following to say regarding the effects of Jeschonnek's attitude towards him:

> . . . The only time I took Goering's place during the war was in the winter of 1940-41, when he went on leave. At that time I spent about two months at his headquarters near Beauvais, in France. The day I arrived, Jeschonnek took off for Karinhall. His orders were transmitted by telephone to von Waldau . . .

Goering did nothing to ease the tension between his two chief colleagues. On the contrary, he did his best to stir up friction between them in order to keep them from joining forces against himself. In this respect he was following in the footsteps of his lord and master, even though he may not have been consciously aware of it. Hitler, too, was a past master in the art of sowing the seeds of dissension in such a way as

---

* *Bach* (stream) is Luftwaffe jargon for ocean; in this particular case, it refers to the Baltic Sea bay off the shore from Greifswald.

to keep the political leaders, the Party, and the Armed Forces continually at each other's throats and thus too divided to represent a real danger to him.

FRICTION WITHIN THE GENERAL STAFF

In the early days under Wever, Kesselring, and Stumpff there was no internal friction of note within the Luftwaffe General Staff. There were occasional differences of opinion, of course, as is the case in any group of intelligent individuals, but these were never of such nature as to give rise to lasting tensions. The first situation of a more serious nature arose in early 1939, when Luftwaffe leaders were requested to submit their plans for a so-called Fuehrer Program. This program called for the rapid expansion of the Luftwaffe on a scale far beyond any practical possibility.

Kammhuber—at that time Chief of the Organization Staff—describes the conference on the Fuehrer Program and its effects in a report dated 11 October 1954:

> . . . On 6 December 1938, Goering relayed to us Hitler's order that we begin work on a new Fuehrer Program for the Luftwaffe. I, that is to say, the Organization Staff of the Reichs Air Ministry, was to be responsible for planning in this connection. I was to have the help of all the office chiefs and of several specially designated branch chiefs in the Ministry.
>
> After a week's discussion with the various office chiefs, I had reached the conclusion that the Fuehrer Program was of such tremendous scope that we simply did not have either the materiel or the personnel necessary to accomplish it within the foreseeable future. For this reason I set up an alternative program of lesser scope, which we termed the Kammhuber Program.
>
> During the first week of January 1939, Milch called a meeting of the office chiefs of the Reichs Air Ministry in order to discuss the Kammhuber Program. Without exception, all of the chiefs (including Stumpff, Chief of the General Staff) disapproved the Fuehrer Program because it required far too much. Most of them however, also disapproved of the Kammhuber Program for the same reason, although it represented only about one-third of the Fuehrer Program in scope.
>
> After the discussion, before Milch and I left to report the results to Goering, Milch asked once more whether all those present were

V) became more and more tense. The reason for this was the unwilling-ness of Branch V to depart from its tradition of objective evaluation of information.

Intelligence Reports. Unfavorable reports submitted by intelligence officers at the front were simply dismissed as inaccurate. On the other hand it was rather embarrassing for us to have to correct the exagger-ated reports of successes sent in by certain corps.

Evaluation of Conditions Abroad. Our reports on the development and expansion of the Russian Air Force during the campaign in the East were interpreted as an expression of a "defeatest attitude on the part of Branch V." We were unable to convince Luftwaffe leaders of the tremendous capacity for armament production in Soviet Russia. Our evaluation of the significance for Russia of the supply routes via Arch-angel, the Far East, and the Persian Gulf was brushed aside as incon-sequential.

The recovery of the British aircraft industry and the establishment of a four-engine bomber fleet in England were considered unimportant. Countless oral reports and written memoranda dealing with the Ameri-can armament program went entirely unnoticed. Our reports on the establishment of a huge American fleet of four-engine bombers, on the first appearance of American aircraft in England and Africa, and on the construction of a large number of airfields in Great Britain (air reconnaissance over Britain had been all but discontinued because of the efficacy of the British fighter aircraft defense; thus we had no aerial photographs to present in support of the last contention)—all of which were of the greatest importance in planning the future conduct of the war—were not only doubted but held up to ridicule.

Our reports regarding the number of British aircraft appearing over Germany at night were not believed. The importance which the Chief of Intelligence had attributed to the attaché service was dismissed as grossly exaggerated, and the traditional attaché conferences, which ad-mittedly took these people away from their posts temporarily, were se-verely criticized. Those memoranda submitted by the attachés and re-porting on the dissatisfaction of Bulgaria, Rumania, Hungary, and Turkey at the small amount of German support they were receiving wandered into the wastebasket, and the attachés were told to omit all references to political matters from their reports in the future.

Finally, when the Chief of Intelligence dared to confirm—by means of a detailed report and several diagrams—a statement made by Churchill to the Lower House to the effect that England had employed a force of 1000 aircraft in a night raid on Cologne, his "defeatest at-titude and tendency to theorize" were proved beyond any doubt. The Fuehrer and his immediate staff arbitrarily termed all reports coming from Branch V "reports of lies." By this time none of us really enjoyed our work any longer. In addition the Chief of the General Staff ordered that the personnel strength of the Intelligence Branch be reduced to a minimum in order to cut down the "pointless evaluations of conditions abroad" and to do away with the reports "which made such unpleasant reading." It was time for a change and it was not long before the opportunity presented itself.

The irresponsible casualness with which the Chief of the General Staff, Hitler, and Goering treated the carefully prepared reports on conditions abroad is a clear indication of the arrogant and criminal optimism with which they led an entire nation to ruin. It is understandable that clear-thinking General Staff officers, particularly the older ones, were unable to share this optimism, especially if they were familiar with the overall picture and acquainted with the methods employed by the top-level military leaders. Although open disagreements were avoided, Jeschonnek was simply incapable of maintaining that feeling of trust and confidence which had bound the General Staff officers to their former chiefs.

PART II
Seeds of Defeat

by its very nature time-consuming and directed to the future, interested him far less than the employment of already available forces, in other words, of the strategic-tactical force in being. This occupied his interest to the exclusion of almost everything else.

And this attitude of his, although incidentally coinciding with his personal makeup and inclinations, was based primarily on his unshakable conviction of the proper way for the Reich to conduct a potential war. In his opinion, Germany was capable of conducting successfully only a short, limited war. In order to do this, she would have to commit all of her forces, including reserves, at the very beginning. The enemy must be overrun by a blitz campaign before he had a chance to make full use of his potential strength.

This was clearly an oversimplification of Hitler's own views. In the event of a war with the western powers, England and France, Hitler had spoken of a war to the end, and had warned that the leaders of state might have to be prepared for a struggle of ten to fifteen years' duration.

Undeniably there was a certain element of truth in Jeschonnek's opinions. The concept of a blitz campaign inevitably calls for the immediate commitment of such overwhelming strength that all enemy resistance is nipped in the bud. And Germany's campaigns in Poland and in the Balkans were actually classic examples of an avalanche-like employment of superior strength. During the campaign in France, the numerical superiority of the German Luftwaffe assured a relatively quick victory, and as a matter of fact, moved the British to keep their Spitfires at home in self-defense and to utilize them only sporadically over Dunkirk in rescue actions in behalf of the British Expeditionary Force.

These same principles of concentration on the force in being and commitment of all available strength, however, were bound to be unsatisfactory as soon as the time factor became important, i.e. as soon as it became apparent that the enemy could not be subdued within a matter of days or weeks, but would have time to recover and to build up his own air armament.

In other words, to use an expression more strictly applicable to World War I, the situation changed as soon as the mobile war turned into a war of position. It is true, of course, that only geographically extensive nations such as Russia or America could indulge in this type of warfare indefinitely. Even so, the British Isles managed to maintain itself in the face of German blitz attacks during the summer and fall of 1940. It turned out to be impossible for the Luftwaffe to gain air supremacy over Britain or even to deliver blows sufficiently crippling to put her out of action for any length of time.

The Luftwaffe General Staff had more or less completely given up any claim to influence over the training program in 1939. The creation of the new office of the Chief of Training, however, was hardly a suitable substitute in case of war, especially in view of its extreme decentralization. The Chief of Training himself had no direct supervision over the training program. The Pilot Training Commanders were subordinate to the Air Fleet Commands, which meant that the latter had direct control over the schools and training equipment. In the last analysis, the training program was under the supervision of what we might term all-powerful stepfathers, who naturally were far more concerned with immediate fighting preparedness than with the pampering of a training program whose effects could not be felt right away.

When the war began, the air fleet commanders in chief, no doubt having discussed the matter thoroughly with one another, began their ruthless raid on the schools to requisition Ju-52's* (for use as transport aircraft) as well as other types of training aircraft (for use as courier planes). In this way the Chief of Training lost not only the Ju-52's for the C-schools [advanced flying schools of the Luftwaffe] and instrument flight schools, but also their crews, made up of highly trained instructional personnel. It was not until much later that aircraft and crews found their way back to him and even then in nothing like their full numbers. Finally, the Chief of Training succeeded in persuading the Commander in Chief of the Luftwaffe that the air fleet commanders should have nothing to do with training as long as the war continued.

And with all this, it must be remembered that from the beginning, the base of the Luftwaffe training program had not been very broad. At the time the office of the Chief of Training was set up, there were only three bomber schools, one naval aviation school, and—fantastic though it seems—only one fighter school. Deichmann, former Chief of Staff of the Chief of Training, writes as follows: "In early 1939, when the office was first created, the Chief of Training prepared a report for the Chief of the General Staff and requested authorization for new pilot training schools. The General Staff refused his request, stating that all

---

* The Ju (Junkers) 52, a three-engine, low-wing, transport monoplane, was used by the Luftwaffe from the beginning of the Spanish Civil War until the end of World War II. It was Germany's standard transport aircraft.

technical resources were being wholly utilized in the activation of new front units."

Immediately after taking office, the Chief of Training tried to improve the situation by parcelling out training assignments to the active units, which did have access to training aircraft at their assigned air fields. Even so, there was then and remained a serious discrepancy between the need for training, as evaluated by the Chief of Training, and the facilities available for training. There could be no thought of building up a trained reserve. The effects began to manifest themselves in January 1941, when German losses suffered in the air battle against Britain began to increase steadily. The reports issued by the Quartermaster General of the Luftwaffe for this period repeatedly emphasize the lack of crews capable of operating the Ju-88's. Beginning with 22 May 1941, the phrase "growing scarcity of bomber crews" occurs with ever greater frequency.

It was no secret that a good fighter pilot needed one year of training, and a bomber crew as much as two years. These facts should have served as a warning in the event of war.

One question remains unanswered. After the Munich conference Hitler, impressed by the scope of Britain's armament program, ordered an immediate reinforcement of Luftwaffe strength—almost a fivefold increase. His order was quite logical, for two reasons. In the first place, England's all-out armament program was certainly an indication of the fact that Europe was not fully satisfied by the outcome of the Munich conference. On the contrary, one of the strongest participants in the Munich pact thought it necessary to build up her military preparedness. And such an act could be directed only against Germany; thus, it was a clear indication of the political atmosphere. If Hitler was to maintain Germany's military superiority, i.e., the basis for the bloodless victories he had enjoyed so far, the only way he could meet the British bid was by producing an even higher card. However, the superiority of Germany's modern air force was already the highest card he held. If this superiority should be placed in doubt, as it was—quantitatively and qualitatively—by British air armament activity, then Germany's situation might soon experience a change for the worse.

This is presumably the motivation behind Hitler's request to Goering of October 1938; it is incomprehensible that the latter did not pass it on to his closest associates until 6 December.

The branch chiefs entrusted with the execution of Hitler's order found it totally infeasible in view of the available aircraft factories, schools, raw materials, and funds. As a compromise, the Chief of the Organization Staff, Kammhuber,* worked out a modified program of development. Even Kammhuber's program would have been difficult enough to achieve, but it did guarantee a tremendous increase in Luftwaffe strength.

But Kammhuber's program was doomed to disapproval. Jeschonnek, at that time Chief of the Luftwaffe Operations Staff, insisted that Hitler's original plan be followed to the letter. Jeschonnek managed to convince both the State Secretary and Goering of the rightness of his views and shortly thereafter, on 1 February 1939, was promoted to Chief of the General Staff. Goering's approval, to be sure, was qualified; he stated that "everything possible" must be done to realize Hitler's plan. In the last analysis, however, "everything possible" turned out to be nothing at all. It was simply a comforting phrase, which one could afterwards ignore.

In reality, the action taken resulted in no more than an acceleration in the buildup of units recently activated. In other words, the force already in being was brought more rapidly up to full strength; the vitally necessary potential force (dependent upon more aircraft works and an intensified training program) was not affected.

The excuse that the beginning of the war (September 1939) made all further preparatory activity impossible is invalid. It is true that neither new aircraft nor trained crews were available in the sense of Hitler's demands. Even so, a program of expansion was feasible in many areas. If those in charge had been able to foresee the developments of late 1940 one thing is certain; the General Staff would have accustomed itself to thinking in terms of overall events and large-scale requirements in the fields of aircraft production and personnel training. In reality, however, Germany's leaders had gotten into the habit of tolerating apathy, improvisation, and stopgap planning in both the air armament and pilot training programs, and this at a time when England was making an all-out effort in air armament, Russia was building up a tremendous air force, and America was beginning to develop its gigantic potential strength to a scope hitherto unimagined.

Nowhere do we find evidence of the Luftwaffe General Staff's having made a reasonable attempt to meet Hitler's demand for a fivefold increase in Luftwaffe strength. It was not until Milch's intervention in 1942 and thereafter that the German air armament industry was finally roused from its unfortunate apathy. But the results of this intervention did not make themselves felt until 1943 and 1944 and by then it was

* Later to become the first post World War II chief of the German Air Force.

already much too late. The training program, in spite of Milch's efforts, lagged far behind the requirements made upon it.

In its defense, though, we must admit that it had a number of very serious setbacks to overcome. These began with the raid on the training schools by the air fleet commanders. The second blow came when the Chief of Training was ordered to release his Ju-52's and his instructional crews for the setting up of special duty bomber groups for employment in the air landing operations in Norway and Holland and later—during the Balkan campaign—for the conquest of Crete.

No attempt was made to replace the losses thus incurred; it was not until months later that the requisitioned aircraft, i.e. those which had escaped destruction, were returned to the Chief of Training. As regards the crews—consisting of carefully selected and carefully trained instructional personnel—it was an entirely different story. The best men among them obviously felt themselves far more attracted by service at the front than by training duty far behind the front lines, and pulled all the wires at their disposal to keep from returning to the schools. This source of loss, together with the death suffered by a great many instructors during their employment in air transport duty, represented a depletion in instructional personnel from which the office of the Chief of Training simply could not recover.

An attempt was made by Deichmann—then Chief of Staff for the Chief of Training—to substitute the twin-engine Ju-86, which was not needed by any other Luftwaffe branch and for which the aircraft industry still had component parts for 1,000 aircraft, for the Ju-52's requisitioned during the air fleet raids on the training installations. Although Milch gave his approval to this plan, it was disapproved by Goering. Deichmann redoubled his efforts in this direction after the Norwegian campaign and defended his views during a conference with Goering. According to Deichmann:

> . . . Strangely enough, the Ju-52 transport aircraft had come to be the standard training aircraft for course in the C group (multi-engine aircraft) as well as for courses in instrument navigation. This was understandable in the early years of Luftwaffe development for the simple reason that there were no other aircraft models available. The retention of the Ju-52 in this capacity, however, was less comprehensible since it had three engines and a steering wheel, while all the other models used in the Luftwaffe had either one or two engines and stick control.
>
> In the early months of the war the practice developed of borrowing the Ju-52's and the instructional personnel of the C Schools and In-

strument Navigation Schools to take part in air transport operations. The aircraft which survived were returned several weeks later, some of them badly damaged, and instructors killed in action were practically irreplaceable. As a result, the training of replacement crews for bomber and long-range reconnaissance units stagnated just at the time when such replacements were most urgently needed at the front.

In 1940, while I was Chief of Staff to the Chief of Training (after the campaign in Poland), I took advantage of a conference with Goering to suggest to him that the Ju-86 be adopted to replace the Ju-52 as a training aircraft. The Ju-86 was a twin-engine bomber with a crude oil engine and had been introduced in a number of bomber units shortly before the war. Since the crude oil engine had not proved entirely satisfactory, and since newer, faster models had become available, the Ju-86 was no longer being used at the front. It would have taken only a few man-hours to adapt the Ju 86 as a trainer by installing double controls and a second instrument panel. By replacing the crude oil engine with a gasoline engine, the Ju-86—with its highly satisfactory flight characteristics—could be made into an ideal training machine. There was one disadvantage involved in the conversion from crude oil to gasoline: the fuel tanks, of course, had been constructed for crude oil and would hold only enough gasoline to keep the aircraft aloft for one and a half hours; however, I did not feel that this was a serious obstacle to its use as a trainer. Moreover, auxiliary fuel tanks could be installed in the wings without any difficulty. Another thing in its favor was the fact that large supplies of the necessary raw materials were available, since its removal from the armament program had come as a surprise. A single small aircraft plant could easily have produced the quantity needed for the C Schools.

Field Marshal Milch, who was also present at the conference, objected strongly to my recommendation, ostensibly on the grounds that the Ju-88 program required every bit of available industrial capacity. He explained that the new aircraft procurement program called for the production of eighty Ju-52's per month, which would easily be enough to meet front requirements for transport aircraft as well as the needs of the schools. He brushed aside my objection that the needs of the front in transport aircraft were practically unlimited. Goering decided against my suggestion. The only concession I was able to obtain was the promise that control of the distribution of all Ju-52 aircraft would be given to the Chief of Training. In this way, he could at least see that the schools had sufficient training aircraft.

It is a well-known fact that the practice of requisitioning Ju-52's from the training schools continued unabated and, in fact, became more and more common as the war progressed. As a result, of course, the schools were simply unable to fulfill their mission of providing trained replacement personnel for the bomber and long-range reconnaissance forces.

The Battle of Britain provided the earliest indication of the catastrophic consequences of Goering's decision.

In this instance, too, it is obvious that Milch deliberately sabotaged an excellent suggestion with flimsy arguments. Milch was not so foolish that he could have failed to see the advantages to be gained by adopting this suggestion. One can only assume that he turned it down so vehemently in order to impress Goering, who of course had no idea of the issue involved, with his own superiority to the General Staff officer. The fact that he could do such a thing without taking the possible effects into account throws rather a revealing light on his character and on his attitude towards the General Staff.

Deichmann's plan would have freed the Ju-52's for the air transport forces, and the training program could have proceeded without any uncertainty as to the availability of its most important training aircraft.

With disapproval of the Deichmann plan, an old evil (peacetime neglect of air transport) became apparent, and its consequences grew all the more painful as the demands for air transport services increased. It all began with the activation of a number of special duty bomber groups (in effect, air transport groups) in December 1941, when a major crisis on the Soviet front made it imperative that reinforcements be flown to the seriously threatened Army Group Center.

The second setback in the training program was not so justifiable as the first had been. When the decision was taken to initiate air supply services to certain isolated Army elements in Russia (a small group at Kholm and a larger unit—and for a period of more than several months —at Demyansk), it was the Chief of Training who was ordered to help out with newly activated units, some of them already equipped with He-111 bombers.

The air transport missions, which continued without hope of respite on the Russian front and were also beginning to be necessary in other theaters of war (Africa, the Channel ports), reached a peak with the air supply operations at Stalingrad, during which no fewer than 500 aircraft were lost.

A further setback in the training program, already seriously weakened by continued requisitioning of its aircraft and instructional crews, was the gasoline situation. Ever since the middle of 1941, the training program had been treated like a stepchild by the powers responsible for allocating gasoline, and in 1942 the allocation to the Chief of Training was restricted so tightly that only certain categories of personnel (and these only in limited number) could be trained. Every effort was made to conserve the dwindling gasoline stores, all the way down the line. In 1942 von Seidel, the Quartermaster General, urged Jeschonnek to permit a more generous allocation of gasoline for training purposes. The General Staff Chief's reply was disheartening: "First we've got to beat Russia, then we can start training." This incredible lack of understanding for the necessity of a training program as an integral part of the business of waging war can be explained only by the almost pathological blindness of an otherwise intelligent man, clinging to the forlorn hope that Russia could be conquered in a short war; and this in spite of Germany's experiences in the Soviet theater of operations.

The Chief of Training, whose prospects of functioning effectively were thus curtailed at every step, produced only a small number of trained fighter and bomber crews in the fall of 1942. This was the year in which the training program all but ceased to exist as an effective entity.

In 1943, in order to keep up with the increase in aircraft production, the training program had no choice but to intensify its efforts and, by such measures as doubling up on training lessons, the lack of training aircraft and gasoline were compensated for to a certain degree. During 1944, however, when fighter aircraft production reached an unprecedented high, the training program—measured in terms of the effectiveness of the fighter crews trained—was hopelessly behind.

These, then, were the difficulties faced by the training program at a time when developments at the front—especially as regarded the need for fighter aircraft and crews and in home air defense becoming more critical day by day—were giving the Luftwaffe no time to recuperate its strength in the unequal battle against superior numbers and superior quality. What good did it do to point out that there were finally ten fighter training schools, all producing crew after crew in the shortened, hectic, and often interrupted training periods made necessary by existent conditions? The pilots' and crews' lack of familiarity with their aircraft and with the vagaries of weather caused a high incidence of loss and damage through crashes and crash landings. In addition, the enemy inflicted heavy losses by attacking with numerical superiority and superior machines. This is no wonder in view of the fact that the average German fighter pilot enjoyed a training period of 160 flying hours completed in aircraft which sometimes bore very little resemblance to the fighters which he would later be required to fly. The British fighter pilot, on the other hand, was given 360 flying hours of training and his American counterpart over 400, both in the most up-to-date fighter aircraft.

Milch may have exaggerated somewhat when he stated: "The Luftwaffe training program, and with it the Luftwaffe itself, was throttled to death by the gasoline shortage." So much is undeniably true, however; the turning point in the air war was certainly due in great part to Germany's neglect of the training program and to the constant raids made upon its resources.

11
The Chimera of Dive-Bombing

PRIOR TO THE OUTBREAK of war, Germany had no really adequate bombsight at her disposal. The Goerz-Visier 219 was effective "only in closely-limited areas and after a good deal of practice," and the optical sights of Lotfe 7 and 7D were available only in a few experimental aircraft. The latter had not yet been incorporated into the training program.

Not even the best bomber crews from the Training Wing, using the Goerz-Visier 219, were able to achieve satisfactory results in area bombardment. The bomb-carrying capacity of the German bombers was relatively low (one 550-lb. bomb for the Do-17; four 550-lb. bombs for the He-111).* Thus, even though a bomber unit might drop an impressive number of bombs in an area bombardment action, the individual performance of each aircraft was comparatively slight. In dive-bomber attacks, on the other hand, the results achieved by the Training Wing during its practice runs were impressive indeed.

Consequently, the technique of attack by individual dive-bombers seemed to be an extremely appropriate method worthy of further development. The Luftwaffe had at its disposal well-trained, enthusiastic crews, accustomed to the carefully tested Ju-87,** and it is quite understandable that Luftwaffe leaders had great confidence in the immediate effectiveness of this weapon in case of war.

Pinpoint bombing, with the dive-bomber releasing its load directly over the target, seemed to promise a high degree of bombing precision and appeared to be exactly the right method for Germany's situation. For Germany, in the words of a member of the Luftwaffe command hierarchy, "was so limited with regard to raw materials and gasoline that her production capacity and, in turn, her war potential, simply did not

---

* The Dornier-17 and the Heinkel-111 were both twin-engine bombers.
** The Ju (Junkers)-87 was the famous "Stuka" dive-bomber, a two-place aircraft with a low, inverted, gull wing.

permit the construction of sufficient numbers of heavy bomber fleets. She had no choice but to limit herself to medium and light bombers with the highest possible degree of hitting accuracy." Eberhard Spetzler, from whom the foregoing was quoted, goes on to say that a preference for precision bombing "was quite natural to Germany, since it was in keeping with the continental concept of the conduct of war," and as this concept applied to air warfare, it called for maximum precision in hitting a militarily significant target—normally a relatively small area—with a minimum of danger to the surrounding countryside. Spetzler continues, "Hitler, who repeatedly spoke up for the abolition of the bombardment war, was just as eager as Goering to spare the civilian population of both sides the horrors of air warfare insofar as possible. . . ."

In view of all this, it is perfectly understandable that Jeschonnek and the colleagues whom he had recruited from the Training Wing (particularly Captain Helmuth Pohle) were just as enthusiastic about this bombardment technique as the crews of the dive-bomber groups themselves. Further, it is understandable that a daring pilot like Udet was much more deeply impressed by the tactical offensive possible with dive-bombers than by the mere releasing of bombs by a fleet of heavy bombers flying in a horizontal line at high altitude. In fact Udet—a devotee of broad humor—even invented special whistles (the so-called Trumpets of Jericho) to attach to the bombs carried by the Ju-87's, their purpose being to put the fear of God and the Last Judgment into the victims of the attack.

The enthusiastic champions of the dive-bomber technique were blind to its disadvantages. Chief among these was the dive-bomber's vulnerability at the moment in which the pilot pulled out of his dive. And this became more and more dangerous as the defenders became accustomed to dive-bomber attack and persisted in their antiaircraft artillery fire. Moreover, during the moment when the pilot was pulling out of his dive his machine was completely defenseless against attacking fighter aircraft.

"The dive," writes General Krauss, "presents an extremely difficult problem in aeronautics. Only the best pilots are capable of carrying it through so that they really hit their targets, and that only after long practice. . . ." Krauss continues: "In the concentrated demand for dive-bombers, one fact was completely overlooked: the hitting accuracy achieved during a dive depends necessarily upon the bomb-release altitude and upon the pilot's knowledge of wind conditions at that altitude. The reflector sight was effective only at relatively low release altitudes. The BZA-2* was still in the developmental stage. . . . In addition, the Luftwaffe did not get around to setting up a bombardment school (in Anklam) until the war began in 1939."

The Luftwaffe General Staff had rejected the concept of area bombardment and had decided to concentrate on pinpoint bombardment. In the tactical requirements summary issued by the General Staff in the spring of 1938, the following appears: "The emphasis in offensive bombardment has clearly shifted from area to pinpoint bombardment. For this reason, the development of a bombsight suitable for use in dive-bomber aircraft is more important than the development of any other aiming device."

The step from pinpoint bombing by a unit to pinpoint bombing by a single aircraft was a short one, and as a matter of fact, quite a logical one. For example, if the target was that particular part of a factory which was indispensable to the operation of the whole, then a single, highly-qualified crew was all that was needed. In addition to being effective, the method also gave promise of being the most economical.

During the Battle of Britain, when the early bomber fleet raids had resulted in heavy losses without achieving any decisive results, Jeschonnek—the foremost champion of the pinpoint bombardment technique—picked out particularly efficient crews to carry out individual raids. As a result, British air defense elements (fighters and antiaircraft artillery) were able to concentrate all their efforts on these individual aircraft, which were, of course, picked up by British radar in plenty of time. The losses thus incurred—irrevocable losses, since the very least that could happen was that the crews were taken prisoner—involved the elite among Luftwaffe flying personnel and even at that time they were difficult, if not impossible, to replace.

Without really intending to and perhaps without even realizing it, the General Staff Chief and his staff—in their shift from the concept of area bombing to that of pinpoint bombardment and individual attack—got farther and farther away from the idea of strategic air warfare to which they still adhered in theory. But strategic air warfare, with its goal of paralyzing or destroying the enemy's sources of military strength, had very little in common with these individual attacks (pinpricks!), which were usually ineffective and never decisive and could almost always be repulsed if the enemy marshalled his antiaircraft defenses cleverly. Success in strategic air warfare, on the other hand, depends upon the employment of concentrated forces of ever-increasing

* Bombsight, type 2.

strength in an effort to destroy all the enemy's military potential, and such employment must be repeated again and again until a decision is reached.

It has already been seen how Jeschonnek and the General Staff had pledged themselves to the concept of the dive-bomber and its employment against pinpoint targets and had rejected the concept of area bombardment. As has been pointed out, this development was chiefly responsible for the inadequacy of the German bombsights.

As a matter of fact, under the limitations already described, the dive-bomber idea was a reasonable one. Yet its development provides a perfect example of the way in which a perfectly good idea can be so exaggerated that it leads to the downfall of an entire service branch.

The idea was originally Udet's. In 1933, with Milch's approval, he brought back to Germany two American dive-bombers (Curtiss Hawks). It was due to Udet's foresight that the dive-bomber principle was modified for use with a single-engine machine. The German Ju-87, ready for production by 1936, was a dependable instrument and its stability and robust construction were points in its favor. It was relatively slow, however, and for this reason had to be withdrawn from commitment against the British as early as 1940. On the Eastern front, on the other hand, it remained in action until the autumn of 1943 and rendered valuable assistance to the hard-pressed German ground forces in close-support operations.

All this was still far in the future in 1938, however, when the Luftwaffe General Staff, enthusiastic over the target accuracy demonstrated by the Ju-87 Group at Greifswald-Barth, ordered Junkers engineers to modify the twin-engine bomber they were working on (a longer-range, fast bomber) to include diving performance. As a result of this new requirement, which necessitated a more stable fuselage construction as well as the installation of diving brakes and a number of other extras, the flying weight of the Ju-88, originally planned for six tons, increased to twelve or thirteen tons. The good old Ju-87 weighed only about one-third as much, 4.2 tons. It was obvious that a dive with the Ju-88 was going to be a far more difficult undertaking than it was with the Ju-87. Even an average crew could manage a creditable dive with the latter.

An additional warning occurred when Captain Rudolf Freiherr von Moreau, an experienced pilot who had seen service with the Condor Legion in Spain, crashed to his death in a Ju-88 at Rechlin. At this juncture, Jeschonnek ordered Pohle to set up a testing group and to fly the machine himself. This gave an experienced pilot who was himself an avid champion of the dive-bomber idea a chance to try out the Ju-88. After a two weeks' trial, Pohle reported to the General Staff his confidence that even an average crew could learn to negotiate an 80° dive with the Ju-88 with sufficient training and practice; unfortunately, Pohle's confidence was never justified. In action over Malta and against naval targets, the Ju-88 did attain the performance promised for it. On the whole, though, the tendency in the field was towards "far too shallow dives . . . some of those measured were no more than thirty degrees." At this angle, of course, rocket bombs were completely ineffective against armored targets, and the painstaking work devoted to their development was in vain.

If the General Staff had not ordered these modifications in the spring of 1938, the Ju-88 would no doubt have been ready for use far earlier and the Luftwaffe would have had a fast, long-range bomber at its disposal.

General Marquardt (Engineer Corps), who is firmly convinced that it was the dive-bomber concept which brought ultimate ruin to the Luftwaffe, speaks of the two Curtiss Hawks which Udet brought back from the United States as ". . . Trojan horses within the walls of traditional aircraft design." Goering, "as an old fighter pilot, was understandably enthusiastic about the idea of a dive-bomber."

Marquardt continues, "the bomber pilots from World War I, no longer active pilots but holding important positions in the Luftwaffe command hierarchy, didn't dare to object to the dive-bomber concept for fear of being thought 'old-fashioned.'" According to Marquardt, the General Staff simply did not understand the principle pointed out by the technical experts, namely that "in aircraft development, those qualities ought to be emphasized which serve to make the aircraft different from all other military vehicles, in other words those attributes which enable it to overcome the obstacles of distance and time and so to achieve its maximum effect."

"In the dive-bomber," Marquardt points out, "it is precisely these attributes which are sacrificed, because it must utilize brakes to reduce its attacking speed and because, in order to be able to release its bombs from a relatively low altitude in the interests of maximum accuracy, it is forced to descend into the effective range of enemy antiaircraft artillery fire."

Yet Luftwaffe leaders clung to the dive-bomber concept with a stubbornness explainable only on the basis of sheer blindness. Horizontal bombardment was completely out of the picture as far as they were concerned.

Once an idea has taken exclusive possession of men's minds, fate itself is powerless to drive it out again; the mind becomes inaccessible to the lessons of experience, no matter how impressive they may be. The dive-bomber might almost be termed the idol of the Luftwaffe General Staff. Before experience with the Ju-88 had begun to reveal its unsuitability as a dive-bomber, the General Staff had already given instructions to incorporate diving ability into the long-range bomber He-177 (which had a flying weight of thirty-two tons), then in process of development at the Heinkel works. Because of this new requirement, Heinkel engineers decided to make use of a design already developed in connection with a twin-engine model, in which two engines were combined tandem-fashion to drive one propeller, instead of utilizing the more stable design of four independently functioning engines.

In practice, however, the use of the two engines with a single propeller proved to be a source of danger since the engines repeatedly caught fire. As a result, crashes involving the loss of both aircraft and crew were common. Finally—but far too late in view of the overall military situation—the decision was made to return to the original four-engine design for the He-177. In this connection Goering, when it was explained to him on 13 September 1942 that tandem engines were a prerequisite if adequate diving performance was to be achieved, told Heinkel in no uncertain terms: "What an asinine idea, to demand diving ability of a four-engine aircraft! If they had consulted me, I could have told them right away that that was nonsense. A four-engine bomber doesn't have to be able to dive. I'll be satisfied when we have a twin-engine model that far along. So far we've managed perfect dives only with a single-engine machine, the old Iolanthe [Ju-87] . . . It's perfectly idiotic to expect a four-engine bomber to dive. If I had known, I would have gone right to the top. . . ."

To Heinkel's rejoinder, "A dive with a machine weighing thirty tons is a colossal undertaking; it's never yet been done in the history of the world . . .", Goering replied: "And it isn't going to be done in the history of the world—at least not under my supervision . . . I'm grateful when a four-engine bomber can even fly at a thirty degree angle—it would be sheer madness to try to dive in one!"

On 22 February 1943, Goering once more spoke out against the tandem engines. But in order not to lose all the work which had gone into their development thus far, it was decided to keep on experimenting with them. By the time the General Staff finally changed its mind and made the reluctant decision to go back to the original design of four independently functioning engines, it was too late to do very much good. An experimental model was ready for testing by 1944, but it never reached the stage of mass production. In the report of a fighter staff conference which took place on 3 July 1944, the following appears:

> . . . In a conference lasting nearly five hours with the Reichsmarschall on Saturday, we were told that the old He-177 will be pulled out of production as soon as those few machines now being finished are out of the way, and that the entire labor force concerned will be freed for our use in other programs. Moreover, it was decided not to start production on the new He-177, not even in limited numbers. This means that the entire working plant—labor force, equipment, and everything else—is at our disposal.

A little more than ten months later, Germany's ruin was complete. It is certain that the tragedy of the He-177 was one of the factors which had contributed to her downfall.

The He-177 was not the only aircraft model involved, however. According to Heinkel, Udet once told him that the He-111 would be Germany's last horizontal-flight bomber. When it was decided to construct a more modern engine for the Me-110 long-range fighter* in order to fit it for commitment as a fast bomber (the idea was that it would ultimately replace the Ju-87), the General Staff was on hand once again with its demands that diving performance be included in the requirements. It was partly this requirement which rendered the new model, the Me-210,** perfectly useless. Because industry had made extremely time-consuming and expensive preparations for the production of the Me-210, the waste in labor hours and working area and the losses involved in scrapped materials were particularly conspicuous.

Marquardt estimates that approximately 10,000 aircraft engines of the DB-601 type went to waste during the period 1941-43 (the very years during which the basis for subsequent military events was being established), partly of course, as a result of circumstances beyond anyone's control, but also because of the fact that the General Staff remained adamant in its requirement of diving performance for the He-177 and the Me-210. As Marquardt points out, if this requirement (which was beyond fulfillment in any case) had not existed, Germany could have sent 10,000 more fighter aircraft to the front.

* A low-wing, twin-engine fighter manufactured by Messerschmitt.
** A twin-engine, long-range fighter-bomber also made by Messerschmitt.

Marquardt expresses himself as follows: "The military situation would have been entirely different if we had had 10,000 more fighter aircraft—this would have been twice as many as we really had—at the front at that time. As it was, all our material was tied up in useless equipment; this is the real reason for the defeat of the German Luftwaffe."

Marquardt's words should perhaps be modified in one or two minor respects, but it cannot be denied that the decision of the two most influential Luftwaffe agencies, the Technical Office and the General Staff, to concentrate exclusively on the dive-bomber was one of the factors, originating before World War II even began, which were to lead to a turning point in the air war.

12
The Neglect of Air Transport

DURING THE EARLY developmental days of the new Luftwaffe, Hitler and Luftwaffe leaders were confronted by the problem of air transport, and their handling of it was a foreshadowing of events to come.

On 26 July 1936, while Hitler was in Bayreuth for the Wagner Festival, he was visited by representatives of General Franco who was then engaged in the struggle against the popular front government in Madrid. Franco requested that Hitler place at his disposal a number of Luftwaffe transport aircraft to bring the Spanish Foreign Legion, as well as Moroccan troops, from Tetuan to Seville. Hitler immediately approved the loan of twenty Ju-52's and their crews. The first one (under the command of Lufthansa Captain Jenke) took off from Berlin-Tempelhof the very next day, 27 July 1936, and the other nineteen followed shortly.

The tremendous significance of this undertaking was soon apparent. Each machine was capable of transporting twenty-two to thirty men with their equipment and, if necessary, could make the Tetuan-Seville trip four times a day. There is no question but that the air transport service furnished by Germany, coming as it did during the first, most decisive days of the Franco uprising, was one of the main factors enabling the Spanish Dictator to consolidate his position so quickly, i.e. to secure a firm base of operations for his offensive against the government.

In the face of this object lesson, carried out by German transport aircraft with an escort of German fighters before the eyes of an interested and observant Europe, it seems incredible that the German General Staff—and particularly the Luftwaffe General Staff—should not have been immediately won over to the importance of air transport. Franco's action in transporting military forces over long distances by air gave ample evidence of the feasibility, in the event of a future war, of sudden attacks in unexpected areas. Even during World War I the importance of troop transport had been clearly demonstrated when General Maunoury's army was transported by the Paris taxis to the right flank of the German offensive wing (the German First Army under Generaloberst von Kluck).

Even so, Franco's air transport of the Moroccan troops failed to move the Luftwaffe to create an independent air transport force, with its own corps of specially trained officers. Nor did it give rise to transport aircraft. On the contrary, in 1937, when production was curtailed because of a reduction in steel and aluminum allocations, the Ju-52's were the hardest hit of all aircraft types.

This was particularly unfortunate because, as has already been mentioned, the Ju-52 played an extremely important role in the Luftwaffe training program and was never replaced by an aircraft model created exclusively for training purposes. As a result, the training program was pretty well tied to the Ju-52, and the Ju-52, unfortunately, was very attractive for all sorts of other uses. Until 1943, all the requests for Ju-52's were filled at the cost of the Chief of Training.

New production of Ju-52's never reached the point at which the requirements of both, i.e. of the training program and the air transport forces, could be filled adequately. Ever since the setbacks suffered by Germany on the Russian front (and especially after Stalingrad, which frustrated completely all subsequent attempts to stabilize the front), there had been more and more requests for air transport forces—for troop transport, air supply missions, and airlift actions—and all of these took their toll of the overall strength of the Luftwaffe. The air transport forces, already overburdened with their missions in Tunisia, were unable to get back up to full strength. They were swept on into the catastrophe to its very end (the air supply action at Breslau), and by the close of the war they were totally depleted.

Although they were finally (1 October 1944) consolidated under the command of an Air Transport Chief directly subordinate to the Commander in Chief, Luftwaffe, the air transport forces still had no channel through which they could argue for refusal of undertakings which were obviously hopeless from the beginning, i.e. in which the end result was not sufficiently important to justify the sacrifices involved. They had no choice but to obey, to sanction the commitment of their very last forces, until the end came.

In view of this unfortunate—indeed, fatal—course of development, it seems utterly grotesque that from 1 October 1941 until April 1942, the Chief of the Instrument Flight Schools, Office of the Chief of Training, was understandably reluctant to relinquish his influence over the Air Transport Chief (otherwise he probably would never have gotten his training aircraft back); the latter had his own air transport staff and was stationed with it at Smolensk. At the same time, as Chief of the Instrument Flight Schools, he headed a training staff (to which, of course, he could devote no time whatsoever) located in the office of the Chief of Training. This is a particularly good example of the violation of the traditional proverb which warns against attempting to serve two masters at the same time.

When Germany finally instituted a training program for air transport personnel, it was not due to the object lesson presented by Franco or even to Germany's own belated recognition of the necessity for some means of rapid troop transport; it was due exclusively to the Russian experiments with paratrooper forces which were so disquieting that Germany even set up paratrooper units of her own.

It was at about this time that the German bomber wings were converted from the Ju-52, never ideal as a bomber, to the He-111, which had recently gone into series production. The only unit to retain its Ju-52's was the IVth Group of the Bomber Wing Hindenburg. The IVth Group was placed at the disposal of the paratroop battalion then being activated and was intended to serve as a nucleus for the formation of additional units of the same type. In October 1937, the IVth Group was rechristened the 1st Special Duty Bomber Group and was later assigned to the 7th (Paratroop) Division. On 1 August 1938, the Group was divided and each half-group then brought up to full strength, and during the summer of 1939 (just before the beginning of the war), the 1st Special Duty Bomber Group was expanded into a "fully-recognized, active air transport unit," the counterpart of the paratroop regiment. At about this time, preparations were begun for the activation of a second paratroop regiment; a corresponding second special duty bomber group, however, was not activated.

The status of the air transport forces was rather an inferior one; they did not even have an air fleet of their own to take its place among the other four air fleets already in existence, but were merely a wing subordinate to the 7th Air Division.

It is obvious that the air transport forces, by virtue of their ridiculously subaltern position on the organizational scale, were deprived of a good many advantages which they might otherwise have enjoyed. The establishment of an independent air transport fleet would have necessitated the appointment of an air fleet commander in chief with a staff made up of General Staff officers. The problems of day by day administration would have necessitated greater clarity in organizational think-ing. Automatically, the problems faced by the air transport forces would have been taken into consideration and solutions worked out during the periodic war games. Experienced and high-ranking specialists, whose opinions could not be brushed aside without further ado, would have been on hand to consider the questions arising in connection with the first large-scale air supply operations in the Russian theater of war. The existence of such a staff would have provided a certain measure of pro-tection against the uneconomical employment of air transport aircraft in senseless air supply actions such as the ones at Kholm and De-myansk, not to mention the completely hopeless ones, of which Stalin-grad is the best example.

The actual situation was quite different. Unfortunately, even the highest-ranking air transport officers were nothing more than recipients of orders from above; because of their comparatively lower rank, they were not even consulted as to the feasibility of the large-scale transport operations ordered by the Luftwaffe top-level command. Let us consider the example of Stalingrad. If there had been an air transport fleet, is it likely that Hitler would have consulted only the Commander in Chief of the Luftwaffe and the latter's General Staff Chief? Or, if Hitler had not turned to the transport fleet commander on his own initiative, is it not reasonable to suppose that Generaloberst Zeitzler, for example, who was dead set against air supply operations on behalf of the encircled Sixth Army, would have persuaded Hitler at least to listen to his opinion?

In a study by Generalmajor Fritz Morzik, former Air Transport Chief, the author states that before launching an airlift, ". . . every possible effort must have been made to obviate the necessity for one." Morzik, who wrote this study in close collaboration with the officers who played important roles in air transport activity, continues: "Dur-ing World War I air transport had no opportunity to make a place for itself. . . ." It was not until the period between the two wars that this opportunity presented itself in the form of the tremendous increase in commercial flying. It is incomprehensible that military leaders paid so little attention to the military possibilities of this new mode of trans-port.

In any case, it was not until World War II that the versatility of an aircraft type designed for transport purposes and its consequent poten-tial value to a modern military force could be demonstrated. The em-ployment of transport aircraft was not the result of a planned period of systematic development; there was no body of past experience on which to build, and no guidelines had been developed regarding the potentialities and limitations of transport aircraft. What little systematic planning that had been done viewed the commitment of transport aircraft as a means of transport for parachute and air landing forces. It must be emphasized at this point, as it has been elsewhere, that Germany's failure to recognize the potentialities inherent in the transport aircraft was a basic and serious mistake. And one cannot resist the temptation to add that this mistake not only led to the decimation of the air transport forces, but was also responsible in good part for the loss of the war.

13
Bomber Decisions

EVER SINCE 1933, the German air armament program had concerned itself with the construction of a four-engine bomber. Wimmer, then Chief of the Technical Office, was successful in his efforts to persuade Wever—at that time Chief of the Miscellaneous Branch of the Reichs Air Ministry—of the need to develop a heavy bomber. Wimmer pointed out that it would take at least three years' work before even a small number of bombers could be ready for testing in the units. Failure to take the necessary steps right away would result in valuable time irrevocably lost once the problem became acute.

Wever was convinced. He began to count on the heavy (four-engine) bomber as a decisive weapon in the event of serious hostilities. Within the Reichs Air Ministry the machine was christened *"Uralbomber"* (Ural bomber), a clear indication of the range expected of it.

By 1936 the two firms entrusted with its development had two designs ready, the Ju-89 and the Do-19. According to Deichmann, who at that time was Chief of Branch 1 (Operations) of the Luftwaffe General Staff, both models were perfectly adequate as a basis for further development, although both were equipped with relatively weak engines. Milch concurs in Deichmann's evaluation. At this point, however, instead of going ahead with the developmental work (and designing more powerful engines), Goering ordered a halt on all work concerned with the four-engine bomber. And this despite the fact that both models appeared in the Technical Office (Development Branch) priority list (dated 26 April 1937 and reflecting the status of 15 March 1937) as "SV" (models ready for testing). According to the testimony given by Milch at Nuremberg, Kesselring (then General Staff Chief) had requested and obtained a halt from Goering on 29 April. Deichmann, on the other hand, emphasizes Milch's role in this decision. Udet, who became Wimmer's successor as Chief of the Technical Office on 10 June 1936, must also be ranked with the enemies of the four-engine bomber, as must his branch chief, von Massenbach, and a number of other Technical Office engineers.

Milch probably did the most damage through his decisive influence on the development and production of aircraft models. Here he often used his influence to counter the recommendations made by the General Staff, as the two examples given below will indicate. The following is an excerpt from a report by Deichmann concerning the General Staff request for a four-engine bomber:

. . . Realizing that any future war would involve operations against targets lying in Russia, near and perhaps beyond the Ural Mountains, Luftwaffe leaders submitted a request for the development of a long-range bomber. In keeping with its contemplated employment, General Wever and his colleagues termed this model the "Ural bomber" both orally and in internal correspondence.

The technological requirements established for the Ural bomber were such as to enable it to reach the target indicated in its name.

Even at that early date, the Luftwaffe General Staff was firmly convinced that the standard bomber of the future would have to be a long-range machine.

The next few years of developmental work on bomber aircraft revealed clearly that the necessary technical performance could not be attained by a twin-engine bomber. Very soon thereafter, once Colonel Wimmer, at that time Chief of the Technical Office, had persuaded General Wever of the urgent need for a four-engine aircraft, the Luftwaffe General Staff amended its original request to encompass the larger airplane. The initial research and developmental work was assigned to three separate aircraft manufacturing firms.

In 1937, after I had become Chief of Branch I, Operations, I learned that the Technical Office was planning to give up any further work on the four-engine bomber. Hereupon I requested permission to present my views on the subject to the Commander in Chief, Luftwaffe, Hermann Goering. General der Flieger Milch also participated in the ensuing conference. I asked Goering to authorize further work on the bomber at all costs, pointing out that information received from abroad as well as the views of a number of recognized engineers indicated clearly that the performance of the four-engine bomber was expected to be so far superior to that attainable by a twin-engine machine that the four-engine aircraft would certainly develop into *the* air weapon of the future. I emphasized that the four-engine bomber was capable of a far greater flight range than could ever be developed for its twin-engine counterpart, and that the presumably remote targets involved in any future war could be reached only by a four-engine bomber. I continued, explaining that a four-engine bomber was capable of attaining a sufficiently high service altitude to keep it safely out of the range of antiaircraft artillery fire; its considerably greater carrying capacity would permit it to carry not only a greater number of bombs, but also heavier armor plating and more and better airborne armaments. Its higher speed would help to reduce its vulnerability to attack by enemy fighter aircraft.

General Milch interrupted, demanding to know where I had gotten all this information on the "fantastic" performance of the four-engine bomber. He told me that his own aeronautical engineers had come up with far less favorable prognoses. I replied that I was aware of the views held by this particular group of engineers within the Reichs Air Ministry, but that a considerable number of the engineers connected with the Technical Office were of quite a different opinion. The only way to determine which group was right was to let the developmental work continue. At this Milch declared that all available industrial capacity was needed for the production of Ju-88's. I replied that during the course of my tour of the aircraft plants to inspect camouflage measures, several directors had assured me that they had both the space and the manpower to work on a four-engine bomber in addition to their other projects. Milch's rejoinder was that the men with whom I had spoken obviously were not aware of the full scope of the Ju-88 program.

In summary General Milch pointed out the following facts: 1) the much vaunted advantages of the four-engine bomber were far overrated, both in Germany and abroad; 2) what would be the point of its being able to fly at 32,800 feet? . . . according to statistics, in Germany the sky was overcast for so and so many days per year, so that it would be impossible to aim bombs from this altitude (I no longer recall the fantastically high number of days per year mentioned by Milch, but a subsequent check with the weather service revealed that he had exaggerated by thirty to forty percent); 3) our industrial capacity would permit a fleet of only 1,000 four-engine bombers, whereas several times that many twin-engine bombers could be produced; 4) the development of a four-engine bomber, even for limited production as test models, would endanger the Ju-88 program.

In reply I voiced the opinion that 1,000 four-engine bombers, whose longer range, greater speed, and higher degree of invulnerability to enemy attack would enable them to reach their targets safely, were of far more value than 10,000 twin-engine bombers which would probably be shot down by the enemy before reaching their destination. I begged Goering not to decide against the four-engine bomber without further evidence, but to let the developmental work on it continue.

Despite my pleas, Goering determined that work on the four-engine bomber should be dropped inasmuch as it might interfere with successful accomplishment of the Ju-88 program . . .

Deichmann's report certainly refutes the charge that the Luftwaffe General Staff never made any definite request for the development of a long-range bomber. The conference described above shows quite clearly that the General Staff had indeed taken the proper action but that its request was deliberately scrapped by Milch. Only a layman—and Goering was one—could base such a far-reaching decision on the flimsy arguments advanced by Milch. Milch's contention that the Ju-88 program would be endangered by the production of a few four-engine bombers for testing purposes is so utterly ridiculous that one is curious to know what the real reasons may have been. At any rate, it seems strange that Milch now labels Germany's failure to develop a four-engine bomber as a grave error on the part of Luftwaffe leaders and attempts to blame it on the reorganization which took place in Luftwaffe top-level command agencies in the summer of 1937.

Suffice it to say that the four-engine bomber was definitely dropped in the spring of 1937. As a result, Germany never developed this particular weapon, perhaps the most important instrument in strategic air warfare.

To be sure, soon after this unfortunate decision had been made (even earlier, in the fall of 1936, according to Huebner, who at that time was a staff assistant for development in the Technical Office), the General Staff began to call for a long-range bomber, its range to be approximately double that of the two four-engine models already designed. Most unfortunately the idea of making this long-range bomber a twin-engine machine soon gained a foothold, whereupon Heinkel (who, in addition to Junkers, had been asked to work on development) suggested that his test model, the He-119, might be used as a starting point. Careful study of the He-119 resulted in the decision to solve the problem of four engines by utilizing two sets of engines in tandem arrangement. It was chiefly due to the use of this system that the He-117 was never developed into a satisfactory model.

In part, of course, the catastrophe was also due to a lack of consistency in overall aims. From the very beginning, political aspects were permitted to interfere in the development of the long-range bomber. For it was largely political considerations which dictated the constant alternation between high and low developmental priority; one day work would be slowed down because the machine was not urgently needed, and the next day orders would be issued to go ahead on it as rapidly as possible. Conditions were hardly conducive to a well-rounded, carefully thought-out course of development.

Prior to the beginning of the war, the prevailing mood was one of optimism. There would be no war with England because . . . well, simply because Germany did not want war with England. And if the British should adopt a hostile attitude towards Germany, there was always Hitler, whose genius would certainly manage to find a peaceful solution. Under these circumstances, Luftwaffe leaders did not consider the development of a long-range bomber to be particularly necessary or urgent, especially since they were confident that the range of the Ju-88 would enable it to cover not only the British Isles in their entirety but the coastal waters beyond as well. And at that time, of course, no one had any idea that a war with Russia was even remotely possible. The name Ural bomber was forgotten and with it all the significance which Wever, in his astute evaluation of future events, attached to the long-range bomber for Germany.

The He-177 was the victim of this optimistic attitude. Its development was not pushed hard enough before the war began. With the sobering shock of England's declaration of war, efforts were redoubled, only to subside again as the blitz attacks on the London area proved to be so successful. As war with Soviet Russia loomed imminent and finally became a reality, new and even more urgent efforts were made to push ahead on the He-177. Apart from all this uncertainty, however, there still remained the problem—never fully appreciated—of the unfeasibility of the tandem-engine design. Because of this, Germany failed to make the shift to four independently functioning engines in time. This failure in the armament sector—and the losses attributable to it— was one of the deciding factors in the outcome of the war.

Pausing for a moment to consider the possibility so casually renounced in 1937, of a genuine four-engine bomber at the disposal of the German Air Force, it can be seen that its significance in naval warfare (North Sea, Polar Sea, Atlantic) could have been enormous, especially during the early stages of the war; later on, the Allied convoys to Murmansk would have been vulnerable for a far longer stretch of their route to a hail of bombs from these powerful, high-altitude, heavily-armored bombers. In the Battle of Britain, too, long-range bombers could have created an entirely different situation, due to the qualities pointed out above and to their ability to appear anywhere over the British Isles. British antiaircraft defenses, admirably developed for use against the German medium bombers, would have been so thoroughly dissipated by long-range bombers that defeat would have been inevitable. In the Russian campaign, with the tremendous distances inherent in its geographic scope, long-range bombers would have been able to search out and destroy the centers of Soviet military armament. Heavily armored as they were, they would have been relatively invulnerable to Russian fighter aircraft; their flight altitude would have been sufficient to render antiaircraft artillery useless. There is one other aspect to be considered: if Germany had had four-engine bomber units at her disposal, her Army forces in Russia—no matter how enamored of the concept of ground-air operations—would never have thought of requesting close-support action from the larger aircraft.

What effect would the employment of four-engine bombers have had in the Mediterranean, against the Suez Canal and other weak points in the British line of defense? The thesis can be amply illustrated by one example. Prior to the Allied landing in North Africa, German leaders were fully aware of the fact that the Gibraltar airfields were crowded with enemy aircraft; however, because of the limited range of its bombers, the Luftwaffe was unable to launch an attack, although this would have been tremendously successful and would have made an Allied occupation of western North Africa extremely hazardous. Such an attack would have presented no problem for four-engine bombers. In addition, the enemy's transport fleet could have been under continual attack.

But enough of these potentialities which never reached fulfillment. The fact remains that the sins of omission and errors in judgment in this particular field were one of the factors leading to the final collapse. One more point lost to the German Reich in the field of armament planning!

In July 1939, in time for the campaign in Poland, the office of the Special Duty Air Commander was established as an operations staff for close-support actions. General von Richthofen, a veteran of the Spanish campaigns with the Condor Legion, was selected to head this office. The units assigned to von Richthofen were those which had shown particular promise in close-support actions, chiefly dive-bomber, twin-engine, and ground-support aircraft units.

In Southern Poland, von Richthofen was given command of all operations designed to furnish direct and indirect support for the ground forces, and it was chiefly due to his efforts that the campaign in Poland came to a successful end so quickly. It was his energetic intervention, for example, which served to obviate the development of a serious crisis within the sphere of action of the Tenth Army. The VIII Air Corps, which came into being as a result of the grouping together of these ground-support units with the addition of a fighter wing (the 27th) and a bomber wing (the 77th), repeatedly proved itself worthy of the highest praise for its action during the campaigns in France and Greece and finally for its role in the occupation of Crete. The VIII Air Corps, in fact, may be termed one of the most important instruments of the German blitzkrieg technique. It was, after all, the primary characteristic of blitzkrieg warfare that enemy resistance should be broken at the point of advance of the armored elements by close-support air units, while the bombers prevented the enemy from bringing reinforcements and supplies up to the battlefield.

By concentrating their efforts at the focal point of the enemy advance—a technique at which von Richthofen was a past master—the close-support forces could save their own advancing troops a good deal of bloodshed and could guarantee a rapid push forward. The bomber units, the so-called strategic element of the Luftwaffe, were thus freed for commitment "against the larger, more tightly massed targets in the enemy's rear area, such as, for example, the enemy communications system."

Any attempt on the part of Luftwaffe leaders to evaluate the experience gained thus far in terms of planning for future operations was bound to be confronted with the decisive factor represented by the VIII Air Corps. The results of the campaigns in Poland and France were unmistakably clear in their implications. Beginning with the summer of 1940, however, Luftwaffe leaders were fully occupied with plans for the Russian campaign envisioned by Hitler. Hitler, as well as the Army High Command (which apparently raised no objections to his plan), was convinced that a blitzkrieg of no more than three to five months' duration would be sufficient to subdue Soviet Russia. The Commander in Chief, Luftwaffe, did indeed raise a number of objections to the plans devised by the Fuehrer; however, he failed to defend his point of view successfully and refused to accept the logical consequence, i.e. to resign from his post in protest after his objections had been brushed aside.

In accordance with Hitler's plan the German Army, divided into three Army Groups, was to attack along a front more than 1,250 miles in length, in a theater of war which was naturally divided by the extensive Rokitno Swamps into three main areas, each of them containing an important military target (Leningrad, Moscow, and Kiev, the latter closely followed in importance by the cities of Kharkov and Rostov). The campaign in Poland had been directed against one main target only, Warsaw; the campaign in France, against the Channel coast and Paris.

At that time the strength of the one special duty air corps was sufficient to meet the needs of a concentration of ground effort against one main target. In view of the tremendously extensive operational area assigned to each of the three Army Groups in Russia, and taking into consideration the fact that successful penetration of the Eastern front was bound to create even more extensive operational areas as the German Army left western and central Europe behind and pushed on into the endless wastes of the Eurasian continent, there could be only one logical conclusion—to establish additional close-support air corps (or tactical Luftwaffe commands), at least so many that each Army Group would have one at its exclusive disposal. New activations of this type would have gone hand in hand with the consolidation of the bomber units into strategic air corps.

Fuehrer Directive No. 21 ("Barbarossa"), dated 18 December 1940 and dealing with the campaign in Russia, envisioned two points of main effort as far as Luftwaffe operations were concerned. It forbade any attack on the Soviet armament industry "during the main operations," so that "all forces could be marshalled for action against the enemy air forces and for direct support of the ground forces." This indicates full awareness of the fact that the Luftwaffe, once it had fulfilled its primary objective of subduing the Russian Air Force, would have to provide direct (and no doubt indirect, as well) support for the German ground forces and this for the duration of the hoped-for "lightning" campaign. The Luftwaffe, as it well knew, had no choice but to accept this mission as a necessary evil; we cannot give credence to the theory that the Luftwaffe was thrust into close-support operations on the spur of the moment and without any preparation whatsoever. On the contrary, Hitler made it perfectly clear from the very beginning that direct support of the Army would be an important Luftwaffe mission throughout the entire Russian campaign—for this is the significance of the phrase "main operations." The only unforeseen complication was the fact that the Russian campaign did not turn out to be a short one, but lasted until the downfall of Hitler's empire.

We may assume, then, that the Luftwaffe was fully aware of the type of performance expected of it, and this no later than 18 December 1940 (in all likelihood even earlier, since Luftwaffe leaders must have had a hand in the preparation of the Fuehrer Directive). In view of the experience gathered during the campaigns in Poland, France, and Greece, Luftwaffe leaders should certainly have realized, from the moment that Hitler informed them of his plan to attack Russia, that close-support operations would be required.

In short, the Luftwaffe had sufficient time for the planning, organizational, training, and procurement programs needed to fit it for its new mission. The Commander in Chief, Luftwaffe, was certainly informed of the plans for a Russian campaign no later than the Commander in Chief, Army. (This was on 21 July 1940 in Berlin, when von Brauchitsch mentioned to Halder that the conference took place "under the usual circumstances." This gives us no clue as to whether or not Goering was present, but it is quite unlikely that he was.) Considering the fact that the relationship between Hitler and Goering was very close during that period, we may assume that Goering was aware of the plans for Russia at a much earlier date. Further, it can be taken for granted that Goering passed on this information, in strictest confidence, to Jeschonnek.

Thus Luftwaffe leaders had a good ten months in which to prepare their forces for the inevitable conflict with Soviet Russia, a conflict whose outcome—whether favorable or unfavorable—was bound to have tremendous significance for the fate of Germany. Their first step clearly should have been the firm organization of the new tactical Luftwaffe commands on a basis which would permit their immediate and smooth activation when the time came. This would have required early selection and training of the officers who were to be in charge of the new mission, concentration on the pilot training program for single-engine aircraft, and last but by no means least, a timely increase in the production of single-engine machines, even if it meant using up the last material resources available; for it was obvious that at least three new tactical commands, with a number of new close-support wings (i.e. dive-bombers and ground support aircraft), would have to be activated and equipped. Existing difficulties, including the Luftwaffe's relatively low priority for the allocation of raw materials, would simply have to have been overcome somehow. This first step, however, was never taken. Instead, faced with the demands bound to arise out of a campaign against Soviet Russia, Luftwaffe leaders placed their reliance on half measures.

The VIII Air Corps was the only real close-support unit available. The other air corps assigned to the Eastern front (the IV, V, II, and I) had been given the mission of providing direct support for the Army, but had not been issued the equipment necessary to fulfill this mission.

As we can tell from the organizational chart of the Fourth Air Fleet, neither the IV nor the V Air Corps had any dive-bombers at its disposal. The IV Air Corps, with four bomber and three single-engine fighter groups, was comparatively weak to begin with. The V Air Corps had eight bomber and three single-engine fighter groups. The Second

Air Fleet, in addition to the VIII Air Corps (with three bomber, five and one-third dive-bomber, two twin-engine fighter, three single-engine fighter, and one air transport group), also had at its disposal the II Air Corps, with its five bomber, three dive-bomber, two close-support (Me-110), and one air transport group. The First Air Fleet, assigned to the northern sector of the Eastern front, had no dive-bombers whatsoever, but only eight bomber and three and one-third single-engine fighter groups.

Thus it was only the Second Air Fleet, with its two Air Corps, which was adequately equipped for close-support operations. The Fourth and First Air Fleets, on the other hand, were forced to employ their bomber (the First Air Fleet had only the vulnerable Ju-88; the Fourth was a bit better off—the IV Air Corps was completely equipped with the more robust He-111 and the V Air Corps had two wings of Ju-88's and one of He-111's) and single-engine fighter aircraft in ground-support operations, all of them machines which could not land just anywhere with impunity.

In addition, in low-altitude flight (which was often necessary in this type of operation) the heavy bombers presented a far better target than their lighter, single-engine counterparts for the implacable Russians, who were wont to let fire with everything they had. In view of the size of the crews and the cost and time which had gone into their training and the amount of materiel and armament carried, the loss of a heavy bomber was more painfully felt than that of a light close-support aircraft. Then, too, the heavy bombers were far more vulnerable to damage while landing on the often unsuitable airfields in the East than were the Ju-87's and He-123's.

Even the He-111's were not ideal for close-support operations, but in spite of this they were utilized in air transport missions to Demyansk and Stalingrad. The losses incurred were correspondingly high. During the air supply operations to Stalingrad alone, 165 He-111's—more than one entire bomber wing—were destroyed.

The result, quite simply, was a continuing wear and tear on bomber aircraft on the Eastern front due entirely to their being employed in a type of operation for which they were not suited. The losses incurred could have been avoided to a very large extent if Luftwaffe leaders had been wise enough to insist upon an increase in the production of single-engine bombers in 1940. Such an increase could have been balanced by a temporary decrease in the manufacture of heavy bombers, and—considering the lower rate of loss with lighter bombers (a factor which could and should have been foreseen)—the final result would have been more favorable.

The facts defy understanding. The Luftwaffe General Staff had already seen, in Spain, the decided advantages to be gained from the tactical employment of air forces and had even taken steps to establish a special force for close-support operations. This is evidenced by the activation of the V Special Duty Air Command in 1939 and its later expansion into the VIII Air Corps. These actions occurred during the course of the campaigns in Poland and in France; and in both instances, the Luftwaffe was committed in only one limited theater of operations. In 1941, however, when the Soviet theater of operations—with its enormous geographic extent—began to spread out, at a time when fighting was going on in the Mediterranean theater and when the West and Germany herself were being subjected to British terror raids —in short, when the war had spread to a number of separate fronts— German military leaders contented themselves with reinforcing only one Air Corps (the II) with additional close-support forces. Moreover, the difficulties created in command channels as a result of this particular action are clearly evidenced by the fact that it was found necessary to appoint a special close-support commander within the II Air Corps to take care of the single-engine bomber forces (because of the total lack of uniformity in the equipment issued).

The Luftwaffe was resigned to the necessity of providing direct support for the Army ground forces, as indeed it had to be in view of the fact that the plight of the German armies had become steadily worse since their defeat at Stalingrad and also as a result of unrealistic orders from the Fuehrer to hold indefensible areas. After all, it was a matter of saving German soldiers and holding back the Soviet avalanche. Unfortunately for the forces assigned to close-support operations as well as for the outcome of the entire war, the measures taken in regard to organization and equipment were no more than half-measures. The General Staff, the brain of the Luftwaffe, had failed to think through to its logical conclusion the thought which inspired the creation of the VIII Air Corps.

14
The Wrong Priorities

AS FAR AS WARTIME ERRORS and wrong decisions on the part of Luftwaffe leaders are concerned, we are dealing with events which, although they occurred well before the actual turning point, had a significant influence on the history of the Luftwaffe. For these events, far more than those which occurred prior to the beginning of the war, were to play a vital role in subsequent military developments. The Luftwaffe, despite the tremendous successes it was to enjoy in the eyes of the world, already bore the seeds of defeat in the form of defects traceable to faulty prewar planning. And these defects, as we have seen, were by no means minor, incidental ones.

The Luftwaffe, still new and untried, had been designed for blitzkrieg operations, and in three brilliant campaigns of this type was to prove its value as the backbone of the Wehrmacht. It must not be forgotten, however, that the Luftwaffe was far less capable than the Army of recovering from serious setbacks or heavy losses. The replacement of both materiel (aircraft and equipment) and personnel was far more difficult, for the production of aircraft and the training of crews were both time-consuming affairs. Everything depended upon timely preparation. Above all, it was vital that the development of new weapons be systematically planned and brought to fruition in order that they might be ready for employment at the front before those already in use were outmoded and inferior to those used by the enemy.

In the case of the Luftwaffe, the mistakes and instances of neglect which occurred during wartime and which were based, in part, on the Luftwaffe's prewar weaknesses, were to have far-reaching consequences.

As early as 1935, specific instructions indicating the steps to be taken in case of war had been issued to the German air armament industry. Even during peacetime, this so-called mobilization plan was recognized as having "highest authority for overall planning." While the peacetime production program was based on a single work shift of eight hours per day, the mobilization plan called for two shifts of eight to ten hours per day. Peacetime and wartime production programs had been carefully planned so that a smooth and rapid shift could be made to the latter without the necessity of constructing and equipping additional work space. The industry had been instructed ahead of time to install the equipment necessary to meet the scope of production called for by the mobilization plan, to see that construction projects outside the main works were protected insofar as possible from the danger of bombardment, and to keep on hand sufficient raw materials to last for six months. Each factory had a mobilization planning office staffed by personnel trained by the Defense Inspectorates and found to be competent and reliable. This office was responsible for the preparation of a mobilization calendar which was subject to periodic inspection by Defense Inspectorate officials; these in turn, were empowered to adjust it in keeping with any changes made in the overall program. In this way difficulties and bottlenecks—to a certain extent at least—could be foreseen and eliminated. During 1935 and 1936 the Technical Office carried out test mobilization in a number of factories and the experience thus gained was of great value.

Thus thoroughgoing planning, characterized by the careful attempt to eliminate in advance any possible difficulties, was carried out to prepare the German aircraft industry for an immediate increase in production as soon as the war should begin.

It was highly unfortunate, of course, that by the beginning of 1937 the available construction capacity allotted to the aircraft industry had already been used up, and because of the shortage in iron (still readily available, however, for a number of other projects), the buildup of the air armament industry was forced to a stop. This was followed by a "far-reaching curtailment of funds for the Armed Forces," which naturally necessitated a curtailment in aircraft production. "If the buildup could have proceeded systematically and without interruption," says Generalingenieur Walter Hertel, "there is no doubt but that aircraft production capacity would have been much greater by the time the war began."

During the war itself, "the independence of the various Armed Forces Branches and the lack of uniform guidance of the armament program" continued to be an unfavorable factor "as far as maximum exploitation of the available work-force and construction capacity was concerned." It was not until 1 May 1944 that the entire construction program was placed under the supervision of Ministry Director Dorsch of the Reichs Ministry of Armament and War Economy. This action came too late. The mobilization of the economy, the plans for which had been so carefully laid, never materialized. It is not within the purview of this study to investigate the reasons for this failure;* its consequences are obvious from the positively pitiful production figures recorded during the early years of the war. Total aircraft production for the first four months was less than during the corresponding period of 1944, at a time when the Reich was nearing final collapse, and having lost large portions of her territory, was almost entirely defenseless in the face of enemy air attack. The increase in production during 1940 was slight, but even at that it was greater than the increase recorded for 1941, despite the fact that this was the year in which Germany dared to pit her strength against that of Soviet Russia. Furthermore, we find these same figures for years during which the Polish and French campaigns had already brought the raw materials and the production capacity of the West into the German camp, years in which the following factors existed and should have been exploited:

1. The German aircraft and aircraft engine factories were able to carry on their work in relative freedom from any disturbance.

2. No serious inroads in Germany's work-force were required and her transportation network was undisturbed.

3. The raw materials allocated to the Luftwaffe were still intact, i.e. had not yet been destroyed by enemy air attack or captured by the enemy.

4. The destruction by the enemy of German aircraft on the ground was a rare occurrence.

5. Aircraft damage by inadequately-trained crews was far less common than was later to be the case.

* The failure of economic mobilization seems to be a fact which is taken for granted; no attempt is made to explain the reasons behind it. Presumably it had something to do, at least in part, with Hitler's self-deception in regard to the will for peace of his enemies in the West. General der Artillerie Walter Warlimont has the following to say in a letter under date of 27 December 1957: "In the face of the successful Polish campaign, Hitler refused to order mobilization in the full sense of the word; later on, partial mobilization was ordered, but the economy was specifically exempted. This business of the 'gradual establishment of increased military preparedness,' as it was called, in preparation for 'special commitment of the Armed Forces' brought nothing but confusion, as I can testify from personal experience—the tragedy of which I shall never be able to forget. To put it briefly, none of the carefully thought-out measures designed to protect the armament industry by keeping its skilled workers on the job was put into effect. Not until it was no longer possible to ignore the fact that the West meant business was any attempt made to undo the damage. By then, of course, it was no longer a matter of putting a certain paragraph of the mobilization plan into effect, but of ordering back every single skilled worker from the front, provided of course, that he was still among the living."

6. Military operations were either at a standstill or were taking place far beyond the borders of the Reich.

In short, although these were war years they were also years in which the aircraft industry could have exploited the advantages of near-peacetime conditions.

And in spite of all this, production was pitifully small. The fault lies clearly with the Technical Office whose lack of initiative cannot be ignored and with the Luftwaffe General Staff (including Jeschonnek), which failed completely to provide the guidance expected of it.

Lest one is tempted to think that it was Germany's irrevocable fate to fall behind in air armament, as is indicated by the production figures for the period 1939-41, one must consider Milch's period of service as Chief of Luftwaffe Procurement and Supply. His first act after taking office was the establishment of definite production goals and in 1942, after the short period of decrease made inevitable by the unproductive confusion which he inherited, he managed to achieve a considerable increase in production over the previous year. In 1943, without neglecting bomber production, he pushed fighter production figures to a new high. Production planning for 1944 envisioned 4,000 fighter aircraft per month in comparison with Udet's average of 250 per month in 1941.

And all of this Milch achieved during a period when:

1. Germany's home air defense was falling apart.

2. German aircraft factories, one after the other, were being attacked and were suffering heavy losses in materiel and in work force.

3. The destruction of raw materials through enemy air attack was becoming more and more common.

4. Working conditions in the factories were becoming more and more difficult.

5. The western, eastern, southern, and southeastern fronts, as a result of the territory lost during 1942, were coming closer and closer to Germany.

The production figures for the year 1944 were nothing less than heroic, but their tragedy was that they came too late.

During the early stages of the war, Germany, by failing to bring into play the mobilization measures designed for the eventuality of war, condemned herself to an eventual irrevocable numerical inferiority in the field of armaments.

In early 1940 this incomprehensible instance of neglect was followed by another blow—equally incomprehensible—which effectively prevented any further action on the part of the Luftwaffe and which robbed it of any chance it might have had of winning the armament race in time. It was the Technical Office in which this second blow originated. On 7 February 1940, Udet requested approval for certain restrictions, as set forth in his letter to the Commander in Chief, Luftwaffe:

> The present shortage of aluminum as well as of other nonferrous metals such as copper, tin, molybdenum, and chromium leaves me no choice but to recommend the following:
>
> I consider it imperative that everything possible be done to increase the production of those aircraft models which are in active use at the front. It is my opinion that a decrease in the production of aircraft models not in use at the front (i.e. training aircraft and reconnaissance machines), which could be replaced by converted single-engine and twin-engine fighters, can be justified for the near future.
>
> This change in our production program would result in a shift within the overall production to those models chiefly in use at the front.

Two days later, on 9 February, a meeting was held under Goering's chairmanship (presumably in his function as chairman of the Ministers' Council for the Defense of the Reich). Among those present were Keitel, Milch, and Funk. The following appears in the minutes of the meeting:

> The Reichsmarschall announced as policy new instructions to the effect that the materiel resources presently on hand will be utilized to the maximum in order to produce as much armament equipment as possible within the shortest possible time. This takes precedence over previous instructions to conserve our available stocks of raw materials. *Those projects slated for completion in 1940 or 1941 at the latest will receive priority.* Projects of longer range than this will be approved only within the framework of the Krauch Plan, designed to insure our ultimate independence of the necessity of important materials from abroad. All other long-range programs will be reevaluated carefully. Reassessment of our present areas of main effort in the armament program, such as has already been carried out by the Luftwaffe in its recommendation to discontinue the production of certain aircraft models, will be of paramount importance.

Unless we construe the reference to "long-range programs" as such (and this interpretation is hardly justified), there is no specific mention of any "stoppage of development" in the above record. Somewhere else, however, the minutes must have contained explicit instructions to the aircraft industry, forbidding it to carry on further developmental work on its own initiative. "The development of new aircraft models was systematically throttled by order of the Reichs Air Ministry, which considered such development to be of secondary importance, 'because it could not be expected to bear tangible fruit before the war was over.'"

Surprisingly enough, there are no documents on record which shed any light on the question of whether Goering acted on his own initiative or whether the new policy merely represented official confirmation of certain instructions already issued to the aircraft industry. There is much mention of a stoppage of development, and presumably its consequences were of vital significance, but no one seems able to provide any detailed information concerning it. Generalleutnant Erich Schneider, for example, even places it at the wrong time when he states, "In the fall of 1940 Hitler issued what was certainly one of the most senseless orders of all time. Developmental work on all Wehrmacht equipment which could not be promised for use at the front within one year was to be stopped."

The Fuehrer Directive of 11 September 1941, which was implemented by Keitel in a detailed summary of instructions to the Wehrmacht High Command under date of 10 October 1941, deals chiefly with procurement. Keitel's instructions call for careful appraisal of the areas in which procurement effort was to be concentrated and make it clear that procurement policy was to be based in part on the ability of industry to deliver. A stoppage of development is mentioned only once, in the sentence "In order that these measures may be carried out effectively, I direct that all Wehrmacht requests for the procurement and development of equipment be forwarded to the appropriate procurement agencies through the office of the Chief, Wehrmacht High Command." Keitel's instructions continue, "The Chief, Wehrmacht High Command, will be responsible for evaluating each request, together with the Reichs Minister for Armament and Ammunition, in order to determine its feasibility and to decide, as my representatives, the type and scope of the contract to be awarded." Thus, the Chief, Wehrmacht High Command, is authorized "to prescribe curtailment of nonessential projects advanced by individual Wehrmacht branches. In the event that a certain project can be carried out only through the curtailment of other, more urgent programs, I [i.e. Keitel] shall make the appropriate decision personally."

In a publication dated 8 January 1942, the Commander in Chief, Luftwaffe, adapted the Fuehrer Directive and Keitel's instructions into a special order applicable to the Luftwaffe. Goering gives developmental work a good deal more scope than was implied in the first two orders. He points out the necessity for "more careful guidance of the Luftwaffe development program. The presentation of contemplated development programs to the Wehrmacht Armament Office, 'as was required by Keitel's order,' is no longer necessary. The State Secretary and Inspector General, Luftwaffe, however, is required to evaluate all development projects in terms of their feasibility as regards the current status of raw materials and production capacity."

The State Secretary was also empowered "to take any organizational measures necessary to the accomplishment of this order and to issue any instructions he deems appropriate." No such instructions have come to light so far. From the material at hand—the Fuehrer Directive, Keitel's order, and Goering's decree—we cannot deduce any systematic stoppage of development. Goering's decree states clearly that "if air armament or the conduct of air warfare will be influenced materially *by any restrictive measures,*" such measures are to be reported in advance to the Chief, Luftwaffe General Staff.

Objectively considered, these documents do not in any way justify speaking of a general stoppage of development. There were, of course, individual instances in which development was halted on the general basis of the four directives cited.

Milch has the following to say in connection with the stoppage of development:

> It is still quite clear in my memory that Hitler was interested only in calling a halt on those developmental projects (in which he included research programs) which could not possibly be completed in time to be of any use during the war. This is the way in which I interpreted his instructions in my capacity as Chief of Procurement and Supply, as the record of development of the Messerschmitt jet fighter and, above all, of the V-1 rocket (which was not ready for use until the summer of 1942) clearly indicate. The number of developmental projects carried on by the various Wehrmacht branches after the so-called "stop" was very considerable; these projects were continued with Hitler's permission and approval. Goering's attitude in the matter agreed closely with Hitler's, and his active role was restricted in general to the further transmittal of Hitler's expressed opinions.
>
> During his conversations with me, Hitler often mentioned his fear that highly-qualified technical personnel and valuable raw materials were being expended on projects which were admittedly interesting but had very little to do with winning the war. As an example, the

Navy secretly prevailed upon the Messerschmitt Works to develop and build tropical barracks of duraluminum (which, incidentally, was Luftwaffe property), so that it would have termite-proof billets available when the time came to occupy the recovered German colonies. The construction of the aircraft carrier "Graf Zeppelin" and the development of certain highly-specialized artillery pieces were also cases in point.

It is my feeling that some of the reproaches which have been directed at our handling of this phase of armament since 1934 are unjustified.

This serves to illustrate the care which should be exercised in utilizing the term "stoppage of development." So far, this term has been used much too loosely so that it has degenerated into a glib cliché.

Until 1939, it was the responsibility of the Director of the Four-Year Plan to distribute the Reich's resources among interested applicants, i.e. the various branches of the Wehrmacht as well as nonmilitary applicants. The Luftwaffe had always been able to achieve a fairly high priority rating, partly because the Commander in Chief, Luftwaffe, and the Director of the Four-Year Plan were one and the same person and partly because the Army's requirements were so modest.

This situation changed rapidly as soon as the Wehrmacht High Command was entrusted with the allocation of resources and the exigencies of war gave rise to more significant demands on the part of the Army High Command. The Navy, traditionally all else but modest in its requests, was also driven to increased requirements as the submarine war became more and more acute. For a while, to be sure, the Luftwaffe was able to hold on to its favorable priority, at least as far as preferred production for the Ju-88 was concerned; however, once victory in the West was a foregone conclusion, the Luftwaffe was demoted to fifth place on the priority scale, despite the fact that the Battle of Britain was yet to come. Hitler, of course, was already completely absorbed in his plans for Russia, and it was obvious that the German Army would have to be expanded considerably if his plans were to be realized. Forty new divisions would have to be formed and equipped, and under these circumstances there was no doubt but that the Army's requirements would have to come ahead of those of the Luftwaffe and the Navy. As Hitler explained to the Commander in Chief, Army, once the lightning campaign had been brought to victorious conclusion, fifty or sixty divisions would be sufficient to occupy those parts of Russia which Hitler hoped to bring under his sway. It would then be possible to disband a part of the land force and to utilize the manpower thus freed in armament work in behalf of the Luftwaffe and the Navy.

Even before the end of 1941, it was obvious that Hitler's plans were going awry. Instead of surrendering at Moscow, the Russians pushed on in a series of attacks against the hard-pressed German Army Group Center. As a result, the projected release of large contingents of manpower for utilization by the Luftwaffe and the Navy never came to pass. On the contrary, it was more imperative than ever that the production of armored equipment for the Army be increased to the utmost. The problem of replacing the high materiel losses sustained by the Army during the Russian winter understandably took first priority.

To be sure, with the revised priority table issued by the Chairman of the Reichs Defense Council, Goering (in concurrence with the Reichs Ministry for Armament and Ammunition), on 7 February 1941, two new special classifications were added; "S" and—even higher—"SS," and the Luftwaffe was given "SS" rating for the production of all vitally important aircraft models. In addition, the "SS" rating was assigned to work in progress on experimental models of the Ju-252, Ju-288, Me-161, Me-321, FW-191, DFS-331, and Go-242 types and to the production of Luftwaffe ammunition, antiaircraft artillery, aiming sights, and searchlights. A number of other important projects were included in the "S" category.

Thus, Luftwaffe armament activity managed to retain a certain degree of independence, both under Todt and under Speer. Allocation of raw materials, however, was becoming more and more exclusively the prerogative of the Reichs Ministry for Armament and Ammunition, and it is natural that the Ministry tended to favor the Army and the Navy, neither of which had shown itself so aggressively independent as the Luftwaffe. And once Hitler assumed command of the Army (after the resignation of its Commander in Chief, von Brauchitsch) and came into more direct personal contact with the desperate situation on the Eastern front, it was naturally the Army—whose plight was continually before his eyes—which claimed the greatest share of his attention. A close second was the Navy with its submarines, by means of which he hoped to achieve the victory over England which the Luftwaffe had failed to bring in 1940.

As a matter of fact, it was not until 1944, when the Luftwaffe finally capitulated to Speer by setting up a fighter aircraft staff and abolishing the office of the Chief of Procurement and Supply, that it was able to obtain top priority for its fighter program and for the transfer of its armament works underground. Inevitably, one is tempted to wonder whether the Luftwaffe might not have been better off if it had given up its independence in armament activity at a far earlier date.

By the time the Luftwaffe agreed to subordinate itself to Speer, Germany's air cover had already fallen to pieces. The enemy enjoyed uncontested air supremacy, and the products of the enormous increase in armament activity which took place in 1944 were destined to land on the rubbish heap.

15
The Lost Chance—Jets

THE MOMENT the American long-range fighters were in a position to escort the American, and then the British, bomber streams to any target in German-held territory, it was clear that the German fighter forces faced certain defeat if they continued to utilize traditional aircraft models and equipment. The only instrument capable of effectively meeting the enemy onslaught (which threatened to annihilate Germany sooner or later) was a jet fighter aircraft with a substantially higher rate of speed than that of the enemy fighters.

It will always remain one of the inexplicable puzzles of World War II that Germany had just such a weapon within her grasp, and that the inconceivable blindness of her top-level leaders resulted in a six-months' delay in its release for production—coming on top of the developmental delays already occasioned by high-level indecisiveness and exaggerated caution.

Even before the beginning of the war, the Heinkel plant had begun to work in this—at that time—futuristic direction. Its He-178, as a matter of fact, had already been tested on 24 and 27 August 1939. During the course of the war, Heinkel developed a twin-engine jet fighter, which was tried out for the first time in 1941. Messerschmitt, however, with his designs for the Me-262, forged ahead of the Heinkel works, which then retired from the jet fighter race. One of Messerschmitt's experimental models had already passed two tests on the efficiency of its jet motors (although, in the interests of safety, a conventional piston engine had been installed in the gunner's cockpit). During the spring or summer of 1941, when Messerschmitt reported to Udet and Milch on the progress of the Me-262, the latter refused to order a speedup in developmental work, despite Messerschmitt's warning that England or America might be working in the same direction. "If they decide to concentrate on development of jet-propelled aircraft," Messerschmitt is supposed to have said, "it could easily mean catastrophe for Germany."

The refusal on the part of Luftwaffe leaders to push the development of his Me-262 did not disturb Messerschmitt too much; he continued with his experimentation. Taking care to move "as secretly as possible," he had already made arrangements with the Junkers and BMW engine works to go ahead with development of the jet engines. By mid-1942, according to its creator, the Me-262 had already been flown as a jet aircraft without piston engine.

Soon afterwards, a Major Opitz applied for and received permission from Messerschmitt to try out the Me-262. His reaction was one of unqualified enthusiasm. Through him, Galland was led to fly the machine himself, which he did in April and again on 22 May 1943. Three days later, he reported the following to the Reichsmarschall:

1. This model is a tremendous stroke of luck for us; it puts us way out in front, provided the enemy continues to utilize piston engines.

2. As far as I could tell, the fuselage seems to be entirely satisfactory.

3. The engines are everything which has been claimed for them, except for their performance during takeoff and landing.

4. The aircraft opens up entirely new possibilities as far as tactics are concerned.

Galland recommended that production of the Me-209 be discontinued, inasmuch as the FW-190-D, which was as good if not better than the Me-209 in all respects, was rapidly being developed. He suggested that single-engine fighter production should be limited to the FW-190 in future, some of them equipped with the BMW-801 engine and others with the DB-603. He goes on to urge that "*the production capacity thus freed*" should be "*switched to the Me-262 program.*"

In a meeting conducted by the Chief of Procurement and Supply on 2 June 1943, it was decided to release the Me-262 for series production "because of its superior speed as well as its many other qualities." On 17 August 1943, when Milch announced a fighter production goal of 4,000 per month (calculated to raise 1944's fighter readiness to an unprecedented peak), Galland demanded that 1,000 of them be jet fighters. Milch demurred, however, explaining that he could not be expected to stop all other developmental projects just because of the Me-262. He continued, "the Fuehrer feels that the risk is too great. . . . I, personally, would go ahead and produce it, as we had planned, without all this business of discontinuing the Me-209. However, as a soldier I have no choice but to obey orders. If the Fuehrer orders caution, then we must be cautious."

Milch's statement, based on stenographic notes, flatly contradicts information provided by Galland to the effect that the Fuehrer had ordered full-capacity production of the Me-262 in the early spring of 1943, and that all the necessary preparations had been made. According to Galland, the Messerschmitt works were obviously too poorly organized to carry out this order, since they were continually getting into difficulty by failure to meet delivery dates.

One fact seems sure: the Technical Office hesitated far too long, partly in memory of previous disappointments and partly in its inability to break away from tradition. Galland was the one who kept calling for action; finally, Hitler intervened, but unfortunately—tragically for the exciting potentialities of the new model—to demand an impossible (at first, anyway) modification.

On 2 November, Hitler sent Goering to the Messerschmitt plant at Augsburg in order to broach the question of equipping the Me-262 to carry bombs. Messerschmitt replied that the original plans had always envisioned the installation of two bomb release clips, for either two 550-lb. bombs or one 1,100-lb. one. This equipment, however, including the necessary wiring, had not yet been installed because the machine was being prepared for mass production. Pleasantly surprised, Goering assured him that this was all the Fuehrer wanted to know. The Fuehrer wanted the aircraft to carry a bomb load of two 154-lb. bombs; if it could manage two 550-lb. bombs, so much the better. Goering then asked how soon the first models would be ready.

Faced with a direct question such as this, Messerschmitt had no choice but to admit the truth—the bomb release clips had not yet been designed. As soon as the design could be finished, there would be no difficulty in installing them in the test models.

Goering's next words to Messerschmitt hit the nail on the head: "You stated that the original plans envisioned the installation of bomb release clips; surely that must mean that you've given the problem some study!" Messerschmitt replied that all the data were included in the appendix to the construction plans.

Again the Reichsmarschall touched upon a sore point when he inquired exactly how great the delay would be "in case of dire emergency."

Messerschmitt's reply was casual—one is tempted to term it criminally casual—"Oh, not very long—two weeks, perhaps. It isn't really much of a problem; just a matter of camouflaging the clips."

Goering continued with a question as to how many machines were available for testing, to which Messerschmitt replied that none from the latest production series was ready as yet. The model had been designed in 1938 and flown for the first time in 1941. It was obvious that the production guidelines had needed revision. At the present time, there was one experimental model available; there would have been more but for the fact that one had been totally destroyed in a crash landing and two others seriously damaged. Messerschmitt went on to say that one model had been constructed on a stable nosewheel, but that its takeoff and landing performance seemed to be no better than that of a normal machine.

On 2 November, a special commission was established to guide the development of the Me-262. The Chief of Procurement and Supply was beginning to be seriously concerned at the manpower which was being requisitioned for work on the fuselage, engines, and equipment of the new model. On 12 November 1943 Milch asked for Vorwald's opinion of the following question: "The one thing we are not yet entirely sure of is the problem of whether the Me-262, with its jet engines, is so foolproof that we can go ahead with production next year. Are we ready—not only in point of development but also in point of production?"

Vorwald's answer was an unqualified "Yes!" Major Knemeyer, on the other hand, warned of the catastrophic situation in the Messerschmitt plant, where everything had run into a bottleneck. On 30 November, the Chief of Procurement and Supply complained bitterly of the delays in delivery, and of the juggling of numbers, dates, and deadlines by the Messerschmitt firm.

Soon Hitler's own influence in the affair of the Me-262 became apparent. In a telegram to the Reichsmarschall, dated 5 December 1943 and signed by Hitler's Luftwaffe aide, the following appears:

> The Fuehrer has called our attention once more to the tremendous importance of the production of jet propelled aircraft for employment as fighter-bombers. It is imperative that the Luftwaffe have a number of jet fighter-bombers ready for front commitment by the spring of 1944. Any difficulties occasioned by labor and raw material shortages will be resolved by the exploitation of Luftwaffe resources, until such time as existing shortages can be made up. The Fuehrer feels that a delay in our jet fighter program would be tantamount to irresponsible negligence. The Fuehrer has directed that bimonthly written reports, the first due on 15 November 1943, be made to him concerning the program of the Me-262 and the Arado-234.

The above gives us a clear indication of just what Hitler had in mind. The Me-262 was to be a fighter-bomber. In a conversation with Milch on 5 January 1944, he emphasized once more that he needed jet bombers and modern submarines in order to meet the expected Allied invasion.

Under the circumstances, it is easy to visualize Hitler's rage and disappointment when he learned in April 1944 (on the occasion of a conference with Milch, Fighter Staff Chief Saur, and Goering) that the Me-262 was not being built to carry bombs. Thoroughly upset, he shouted: "Not a single one of my orders has been obeyed!" Milch's comment that the Me-262 was designed to be a fighter, and not a bomber, did nothing to placate the Fuehrer's rage, but did serve to weaken Milch's prestige.

Goering, who—once upon a time—had maintained a certain degree of independence towards Hitler, had been brought through the many failures suffered by his Luftwaffe to the point where he was no longer morally capable of an energetic protest, bolstered by the threat of his resignation. Hitler, angry, feeling betrayed and stubbornly insisting on the need for a "blitz bomber," saw, in the Reichsmarschall, someone who no longer needed to be taken seriously, who might be buffeted about at will. Goering's authority was gone; his original independence of thought had been replaced by an exaggerated, abject obedience which he hoped would permit him to maintain his position.

Goering's attitude was clearly illustrated during the May conference on the Obersalzberg. On 29 May, immediately after the talks were concluded, Goering spoke to a group consisting of Messerschmitt, Bodenschatz, Petersen, Galland, Korten, etc., "In order to avoid a misleading designation, I suggest that we call the new aircraft a 'superspeed bomber,' rather than a fighter-bomber. Accordingly, the further development of this model will be entrusted to the General of the Bomber Forces." The Fuehrer would decide "which of those experimental models equipped with armaments should be developed further as fighter aircraft."

This is confirmed by Bodenschatz, when he says, "The Fuehrer ordered expressly that its development as a fighter should be continued." Galland, arriving on the scene, was informed by the Reichsmarschall that ". . . it is not that the Fuehrer wants the new model to be only a bomber—quite the contrary, he is aware of its potentialities as a fighter. However, he does want all of those presently in production to come out as superspeed bombers until further notice. It is his desire that we concentrate on the bomber question and that the problems of bomb-carrying capacity, bomb release clip design, bombsight development, and bombardment tactics be given paramount consideration."

Goering went on to explain that the superspeed bomber might be used in the coming invasion, ". . . on the English coast, for example, to bombard the beach while the invasion force was going aboard and the boats and already landed equipment during unloading operations. As I see it, our aircraft would fly along the beach, dropping their bombs into the confusion below. This is the way in which the Fuehrer envisions employment of the new model, and this is the way it will be!"

The Reichsmarschall was afraid of incurring Hitler's wrath again; once, during the course of the subsequent conversation, Messerschmitt inadvertently used the word "fighter" in conjunction with the Me-262, and was interrupted immediately by Goering with the words, "Will you please stop using that word 'fighter'!" The Reichsmarschall almost begged those present to do nothing behind his back which might upset his plans. "The commands of the Fuehrer must remain inviolable!"

The minutes of a discussion between Hitler and Saur on 7 June 1944 confirm the Fuehrer's demands in connection with the new aircraft model. All attempts to change his mind were of no avail. Speer tried it and failed; on 30 August, Kreipe, sixth Chief of the Luftwaffe General Staff, tried his luck and did manage to obtain one minor concession—that every twentieth Me-262 would be equipped as a fighter. Hitler did not give final permission to begin series production of the Me-262 as a fighter until 4 November 1944, and even then he stipulated that each aircraft "must be able to carry at least one 550-lb. bomb in case of emergency."

The dates mentioned in the foregoing are enough to tell us that there was no chance of Germany's having her superspeed bomber ready in time for the Allied landing in Northern France. On 22 June, at a meeting of the Fighter Staff, Saur lectured his colleagues:

> . . . we deserve to be soundly reproached; during September and October of last year we made certain promises which we based not on fact but on pure wishful thinking. We simply assumed that we would have a goodly number of machines available for rigorous testing by January or February; we assumed that we would produce at least thirty to forty aircraft during March, sixty per month by May, and soon thereafter seventy-five to eighty per month. It is now June, and we do not have one single machine. We have only ourselves to blame —we were incapable of concentrating our efforts, and incapable of approaching the problem with the energy and determination warranted by its vital importance. . . . The development and production of the Me-262 has been attended by a number of mysterious machinations—this sort of thing must come to an end immediately! I refuse to let myself be lied to and deceived any longer!

Hereupon, the Fighter Staff established a new production schedule: 60 aircraft in July, 100 in August, 150 in September, 225 in October, 325 in November, and 500 in December.

But even these figures were never to be achieved. By the end of 1944, the German aircraft industry had produced a grand total of 564 Me-262's. It was simply too late. Even Hitler's firm intercession (as, for example, on 22 November) came too late to have any influence.

For the purposes of this study, there is no point in going into the last desperate measures (such as the appointment of special representatives of the Fuehrer and of the Reichsmarschall for the jet fighter program) which were initiated as the implacable waves of destruction began to break over the Reich. During the first three months of 1945, Germany achieved a total production of 740 jet fighters.

Germany had lost the race against time. Both Hitler and the leaders of the Luftwaffe had taken far too long (from 1941 until 1943) to realize that a race against time was even involved. The time lost in the delays prior to 1941 could no longer be recovered. And, in retrospect, it seems clear that these delays in the field of aircraft engine development were of the greatest and most decisive importance. In the last analysis, it was Milch's exaggerated (though, when one considers the bitter experience behind him, perhaps warranted) skepticism, a certain inexplicable aversion on the part of the Technical Office, and Hitler's stubborn insistence on a superspeed bomber which combined to prevent the timely production of the Me-262 fighter and—as a result—the establishment of air cover for the Reich. (Air cover for all of Europe was no longer thinkable.)

Timely production, in sufficient quantity, of the Me-262 as a fighter aircraft not only would have prevented untold suffering on the part of the civilian population and enormous property destruction, but it might well have averted catastrophe in the scope which it assumed in 1945. Saur, and his Fighter Staff, as well as Galland, whom Saur called "father of the Me-262," did their best. Circumstances, however—and here we must include Galland's unwillingness to accept the limitations of reality and Saur's inability to overcome the desperation of the overall situation—were simply such that they could no longer succeed.

PART III
The Lost Battles

Ju 86: A twin-engine bomber with a crude oil, not gasoline, engine; not entirely satisfactory and not used much after 1940. (Army Air Force Photo, National Archives)

Ju 86: A proposal to convert the oil engines to gasoline and to convert the plane from a bomber to a trainer was rejected by Milch. (Army Air Force Photo, National Archives)

Ju 88: Designed as a high-speed bomber with a long penetration range (620 miles); released for mass production in 1938 at the time of the Czechoslovakian crisis. (Official U.S. Air Force Photo)

Ju 88: Once again the Luftwaffe General Staff demanded that the Ju 88 be equipped for dive-bombing capability. That raised its flying weight from six to thirteen tons and it became, as Milch said, "a flying barn door." (Army Air Force Photo, National Archives)

He 177: A long range bomber; it became a monstrosity because engineers decided to use the design of a twin-engine plane for a four-engine bomber. Twin-engines in tandem fashion one behind the other drove the propeller. (Official U.S. Air Force Photo)

He 177: In practice the use of two engines with one propeller proved to be a source of danger since the engines repeatedly caught fire. The plane never reached the point of mass production. (Army Air Force Photo, National Archives)

Ju 89: As early as 1937, the Technical Office of the Luftwaffe listed the Ju 89 as a model of a four-engine bomber ready for testing. But Goering ordered all work halted in favor of shorter range twin-engine bombers. (Army Air Force Photo, National Archives)

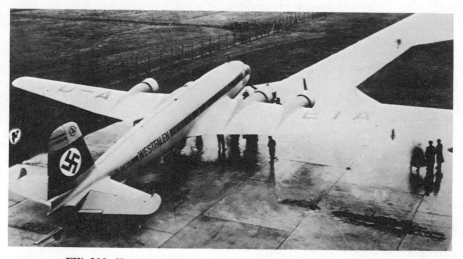

FW 200: Known as the "Condor," it was a four-engine converted commercial plane. Used by Hitler as his personal transport plane. (Army Air Force Photo, National Archives)

FW 200: Primarily a long-range plane; used for reconnaissance and as an anti-shipping bomber. Its range was 2,100 miles. (Official U.S. Air Force Photo)

Ju 290: A four-engine transport; considered for conversion into a high-altitude bomber, but never produced in large quantities because of the German emphasis on dive-bombing. (Official U.S. Air Force Photo)

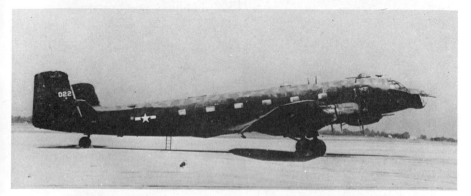

Ju 290: With a range of 3,700 miles, it had missions similar to the FW 200—harassing the sea lanes. (Army Air Force Photo, National Archives)

Hitler in an uncharacteristic (friendly) pose. His obsession with dive-bombing led to serious delays in the production of many of the Luftwaffe's proposed fighters, including a jet fighter. (National Archives Collection of Foreign Records Seized, 1941)

Hermann Goering, the commander of the Luftwaffe from its beginning to the end. A strong leader in the pre-war years, he personified the rise of the Luftwaffe; but his egotism and indifference in the war years was a major factor in the decline of the Luftwaffe. (National Archives Collection of Foreign Records Seized, 1941)

Erhard Milch (left), Goering's deputy as head of the Luftwaffe, on an inspection tour with unidentified civilians and other officers. His feuds with the Luftwaffe General Staff led to bickering and dissension in the top leadership of the Luftwaffe. (National Archives Collection of Foreign Records Seized, 1941)

Milch (center) in the field with Kesselring (right) and unidentified officers. Internal politics in the Luftwaffe resulted in a shake-up in which he was "organized out" of his post in 1944. (National Archives Collection of Foreign Records Seized, 1941)

Ernst Udet, chief of Luftwaffe Procurement and Supply; a job for which he was tempermentally unfit. The first of the top leadership to see the handwriting on the wall, he committeed suicide in November 1941. (National Archives Collection of Foreign Records Seized, 1941)

Hans Jeschonnek, chief of the General Staff during most of the war (right) with von Richtofen (left). One of the youngest of the Luftwaffe generals, Jeschonnek was unable to cope with Hitler and Goering and committed suicide in 1943. (National Archives Collection of Foreign Records Seized, 1941)

Hitler at a conference with Jeschonnek (third from left), von Richtofen (second from left) and Student (left). (National Archives Collection of Foreign Records Seized, 1941)

Hitler in a friendly conversation with Mussolini (right) and Kesselring (center), who had been a Chief of Staff of the Luftwaffe in pre-war days and who became a top commander of German forces at the war's end. (National Archives Collection of Foreign Records Seized, 1941)

16
Baptism of Fire

JESCHONNEK had been Chief of the Luftwaffe General Staff for exactly seven months when on 1 September 1939 the war broke out against Poland, followed two days later by a declaration of war by Great Britain and France. According to a carefully-considered deployment, which committed the massed concentration of forces solely to the Eastern Theater of Operations, the Luftwaffe set out against Poland at 0445 hours, 1 September 1939, with a total of 1,929 aircraft, including 897 bombers. The attacks on Polish airfields by the First Air Fleet (General der Flieger Kesselring) in the northern areas and by the Fourth Air Fleet (General der Flieger Alexander Loehr) in the southern areas succeeded in throwing the Polish fliers completely into a state of hors de combat, or in effecting such disorganization that their effective commitment in the future was so severely hampered as to be of little importance. The forces of both Luftwaffe air fleets were immediately able to give indirect and direct support to the Army's operations and, by cooperating during assaults and by overcoming a temporarily threatening situation, were able to contribute to the lightning-fast course of the campaign, which even exceeded the expectations of the Army General Staff. In eighteen days the strong Polish Army was destroyed.* The employment of the Luftwaffe also forced the quick capitulation of the futile, but stubborn, resisting Polish forces in Warsaw.

A strategic employment of the Luftwaffe did not follow this campaign. Because of the short duration of the Polish operation, it was unnecessary, and indeed, seemed even undesirable to think in terms of strategic air power, since Germany wished to have the conquered nation with its industry intact and its business back in running condition in short order.

---

* The term "strong" is perhaps appropriate if one speaks from the point of view of determination and bravery, but is otherwise inappropriate. Poland was almost pathetically lacking in automatic weapons, the best and most modern small arms and artillery, armored equipment, and supporting air units. Polish cavalrymen, trained and ready for a war which had already passed into the mists of history in World War I, had to combat German armored units.

The Luftwaffe acquitted itself gloriously in Poland,* and its leadership proved itself equal to the mission at hand. The "Stuka" tactics were responsible in great part for the swift pace of victory. The campaign ran its course entirely according to Jeschonnek's concept of war.

The Norwegian Campaign and, to an even greater extent, the French Campaign (10 May-25 June 1940) justified the deep-rooted confidence of the German people in the young air service. In France everything again ran like clockwork. Douhet's theories were once more applied with devastating attacks against enemy airfields and in a framework of air superiority won by German fighters. Thereupon the German Air Force carried out almost uninterrupted support of the German armored spearheads in their swift breakthroughs. Following the panzer forces marched the infantry columns, no longer fearful of enemy airmen and protected by the spectacular Luftwaffe dive-bombers, while bomber wings provided air cover for the flanks of the spearheads.

These operations benefited from the fact that, as soon as the British took cognizance of the irresistible advance of Guderian's tanks, they no longer continued to send large numbers of fighters to France and the Low Countries, but anticipating German air attacks on England, began to hold aircraft back for home defense purposes. Thus, the first real encounter between German Me-109's and British Spitfires took place over the Dunkirk area when the battle for France was nearing its end. The blame for this initial failure of the Luftwaffe to gain air supremacy is attributable to Goering.

On 24 May 1940 Hitler stopped the German armored advance before Dunkirk. In these circumstances, Goering's offer to use the German Air Force to smash the British forces concentrated near Dunkirk was certainly decisive. According to Schmid, Goering and Jeschonnek were "unshakable" in their conviction that the Luftwaffe would succeed in this undertaking. However, the inclement weather, which impeded not only the German takeoffs but also visibility within the combat areas, the absence at that time of German airfields close to the front, the negligible effectiveness of bombing the sandy beaches, and the intervention of the highly maneuverable Spitfires, which inflicted heavy losses on the German Stukas and twin-engine fighters and bombers, were factors which enabled the British Command (27 May-4 June 1940) to evacuate by thousands of small craft a total of 338,226 men to the safety of British soil.

* If the defeat of a third-rate air force in a backward state can be considered "glorious," the Luftwaffe was covered with glory. Not only was the Polish Air Force under strength, but its few aircraft were almost entirely obsolete.

But, since the Dunkirk days were immediately followed by the second phase of the French Campaign (which had been successfully ushered in with a great Luftwaffe strike on 8 June by 600 bombers and 500 fighter aircraft against airfields and aircraft factories in the Paris Sector), and since the German attacks led to the rapid and complete collapse of the French Army, and the campaign ended gloriously in the armistice at the historic site of Compiègne (21-22 June 1940), the significance of the hazardous venture of Dunkirk was completely misunderstood. Even so critical a mind as Hoffmann von Waldau saw only the extent of the devastation on the beaches caused by the German bombers. He wrote in his Journal on 25 May 1940: "One hundred percent success not achieved, particularly because of the two-day period of bad weather." He believed, however, that "a subsequent annihilating effect was, nevertheless, achieved. Losses through sinking of ships and through bombing of the troops concentrated on the beach and quay must be estimated as enormous." Farther on he wrote, "Degree and scope of the devastating effect of our Luftwaffe impossible to describe. The Dunkirk area presents the picture of a frightful catastrophe. . . . Some 50,000 motor vehicles lie around wedged together higgledy-piggledy." It was not immediately recognized that the enemy had succeeded in rescuing his manpower, the main body of his irreplaceable regular army, in spite of Luftwaffe action.

There is no doubt that for Hitler himself the days of Compiègne (21 and 22 June 1940, together with the conclusion of the Armistice there on 22 June) represented the zenith of his life. So, too, for Jeschonnek the overwhelmingly glorious outcome of the French Campaign meant the fulfillment of his fondest hopes: the prestige of the Fatherland restored through the unprecedented splendor of the victories and his own work crowned by the Luftwaffe's very great share in them, his having proven himself despite his youth and the very short time of his tenure as Chief of the Luftwaffe General Staff, and his confidence in and his faithful devotion to the Fuehrer, whose views were vindicated despite the Army General Staff's opposition, particularly to the offensive in the West. And, on 19 July 1940, on the occasion of the great wave of promotions to marshal, Hitler, who now stood like a constellation in the zenith of the German heavens, spoke very special words of appreciation for Jeschonnek's services and announced the promotion of the Chief of the Luftwaffe General Staff (then only a little over forty years of age) to General der Flieger.

Even in the sunny days of this new blitzkrieg shadows began to cast themselves over events to come, events which were quite apart from the

Dunkirk intermezzo. Early in the war the air fleets wrought havoc with their inroads into the personnel and materiel strength of the Luftwaffe pilot training schools by depriving them of their instructor crews, technical cadres, and aircraft in order to activate additional new combat units which were not provided for in the mobilization plan. The Chief of the Training Command (who had become involved in the affair) appealed in vain to the air fleet commands as well as to the Chief of the Luftwaffe General Staff. The latter could not be persuaded to safeguard the Training Branch once and for all against these incursions. And yet, training held a heavy responsibility for an important part in the war's denouement in case the conflict should become of long duration or more extensive in scope (a possibility which sober reflection should have taken into account). On the contrary, this case and numerous later ones were classic examples of how the principle of armament in breadth attained ascendancy at the expense of armament in depth, and also by making inroads into the medium which fostered future armament, namely, the training program.

According to Deichmann, the above reason explains in part the decline of training after the outbreak of war. Yet, if the Luftwaffe desired to remain prepared for any contingency, that was the precise time when training, in all of its aspects, should have been stepped up. It was only after many attempts that the Chief of the Training Command was able to recover some of his aircraft and his instructor personnel from the flying units. But, efforts to get back the Ju-52's (which had been requisitioned as transports) were for the most part unsuccessful.

A similar cannibalizing resulted from the demands of Student's 7th Parachute Division which carried out the phenomenal airborne operations in the Netherlands and Belgium during the early part of the Battle of France. The creation of a separate air transport fleet had been neglected during peacetime so that at the outset of war only one wing of Ju-52's (1st Special Purpose Bomber Wing) was in being. This was naturally insufficient for the great tasks that lay ahead. Again, demands were made upon the Training Command, which had to make available several hundred (about 378) Ju-52's, together with the appropriate instructor crews. This occurrence, at the beginning of training exercises many weeks before the operations in the Low Countries, was followed from the opening of the Norwegian Campaign in April by additional bloodletting of the Training Command. Thus the sensitive training instrument, which had already received shabby treatment, again suffered grave injury. It can be emphatically stated that this became one of the concomitant reasons for the terrible outcome of the entire war.

To replace the Ju-52's, the Chief of the Training Command made an effort to utilize the discarded Ju-86's, which he was convinced would be particularly suitable as training aircraft if certain modifications were made. This proposal was rejected out of hand by Milch, even though spare parts and cutout material was on hand to construct 1,000 Ju-86's. Goering concurred in Milch's decision. There was no apparent initiative on the part of the Chief of the General Staff to put air transport services on its own legs as a separate command, thereby relieving the hard-pressed Training Command. It must therefore be assumed that the problem did not seem urgent enough to Jeschonnek, who must have thought that the war would not be of long duration. This then was the basis of the fatal self-deception of the German Command.

The extent of the victory achieved against France had surprised even Hitler, who had been very optimistic from the first. He therefore assumed that the war was as good as won. Hitler's well-known Anglophilism also played a part in his efforts and hopes for a quick peace with Britain. For weeks he waited for the answer to his peace offer of 19 July 1940. This man, who seemed to be such a shrewd judge of the facts of life, politics, and war, had in this instance become the slave of his own wishful thinking! Far into the Russian campaign of 1941 the deliberations of both Hitler and his colleagues were governed by the greatest and most tenaciously held optimism and by that most dangerous enemy of all successful leadership in war, underestimation of the adversary.

After the French Campaign, instead of girding up their loins, many German leaders relaxed their efforts. The loss of a whole year's time (in terms of operations as well as armament) from the conclusion of hostilities in France until the beginning of the war against Russia (22 June 1941), a year in which production could have been carried out without interference, became one of the main reasons for the subsequent German defeat. The tremendous victory in France caused many a top commander to lose his head and to allow soldierly conduct to go by the board.*

Jeschonnek undoubtedly shared Hitler's optimism, but he was not a man to relax his efforts. On the contrary, given his austere and soldierly point of view, he must have inwardly sincerely rejected the progressive slackening of effort by his Commander in Chief. However, Jeschonnek was unable to exercise any decisive influence over Goering.

* The reference is to the luxurious living and acquisition of various items and objets d'art, especially in occupied France, by some German officers.

It is not known how the Chief of the General Staff reacted to Goering's order of 7 February 1940 and to Hitler's of 11 September 1941 stopping all development that could not be completed in order to get the aircraft to the front within a year. Jeschonnek apparently made no protest against this truly fateful order, an edict which did not reflect a careful consideration of the hard reality of the war which still had long to run. By this stoppage, work was delayed on the new weapons planned by the Luftwaffe, particularly the jet fighter.

Disappointed by his failure to force Britain to sue for peace, Hitler ordered preparations to be made for an invasion of the British Isles, Operation Sea Lion (*Seeloewe*). This plan entailed a very difficult assignment for the Luftwaffe from the very outset. Quite apart from the protection that the waters of the English Channel offered for the United Kingdom, and apart also from the advantage enjoyed by the British from having radar defenses, German forces were simply inadequate for the task at hand. They could have accomplished it only if Germany's optimistic estimates of the RAF's inferior strength had been correct, but that did not prove to be the case.

Only two German air fleets were capable of making the attack. The Fifth Air Fleet (under Stumpff in Norway) was almost completely disqualified because of the limited range of German bombers and escort fighters. But the fighter forces in the South (in northern and northwestern France under Sperrle) and in the Second Air Fleet in the North (Netherlands, Belgium, and northeastern France under Kesselring) lacked coordination. As Deichmann commented, "The inappropriate splitting up of German fighter units into three separated groups permitted only the Luftwaffe group located in the Calais area to reach the decisive combat area over London."

Since the very vulnerable German bombers each required three or four fighter escorts, the number of operationally serviceable bombers was necessarily reduced while dive-bombers (Ju-87 Stukas) could no longer be committed because of the heavy losses they had suffered. The attacks on British fighter airfields south of London were not decisive, and the airfields north of London could not be attacked because of the limited range of German escort fighters. Then, too, the Luftwaffe was not in a position to cover the whole of Great Britain, since the Ju-88's, which were finally brought into action, did not have the range which had been expected of them and no other long-range bomber had enough range to span the distances. Jeschonnek, who to some extent was at fault for dropping the four-engine project, was therefore responsible for the dilemma.

The commitment of individual bombers with select aircrews for the destruction of specific highly important targets—this was a favorite idea of the Chief of the General Staff—amounted to mere pinpricks for the British, although for Germany it meant losing many an irreplaceable crew.

All in all, the long-drawn-out Battle of Britain, which was not ended for all intents and purposes until the Russian Campaign, was a defeat for the aggressor, since Germany failed to achieve its objective of wearing down the British will to resist and its armed forces. Although German bomber and fighter losses were heavy, the aircraft losses were less grievous than the loss of aircrews, since carefully selected and well-trained airmen could not be easily made good. German bombers were generally shot down over Britain, and the crews that parachuted to safety became prisoners of war, whereas many of the RAF fliers, shot down over their native soil or in the adjacent waters, could soon be back in aerial combat again. Too, the total losses of flying personnel were made additionally lighter for the British than for the Germans because the former used almost exclusively single-engine, one-man fighters, while the Germans used many twin-engine fighters and bombers with from two to four men in each crew.

During the Battle of Britain, how was the state of confidence of the Chief of the Luftwaffe General Staff, who, after the initial rather pompous pronouncements of Goering, soon had to bear the brunt of abuse again? Unfortunately, there is little information about what transpired within the Luftwaffe's headquarters at this time. Wherever the slender, aloof Jeschonnek appeared, he radiated confidence. This is confirmed by Ministerial Director von Hammerstein:

> At the end of the French Campaign we sat in the dining car of Goering's train and the talk turned to the impending attacks on England. Then Goering turned to Jeschonnek and asked him if he thought these attacks would be successful. Jeschonnek answered quite positively, "I certainly think so." Another time I heard him tell Goering, "I count on only six weeks more!" Goering doubted that, and stressed the fact that since the German would fight on even if Berlin were destroyed, the Britisher would not be any softer than the German, and would fight on even if London were destroyed.

No strengthening of German armament had begun with the outbreak of war, and all too few aircraft were being produced. After the outbreak of hostilities in 1939 production went on completely undisturbed by the enemy just as it had in peacetime, yet in the first four months of the war production amounted to only 1,869 aircraft. By contrast 8,462 aircraft were produced in the first three months of 1945, even though at that time Germany was literally dying, its factories demolished and innumerable machines and huge stocks of materiel destroyed, while work was constantly jeopardized by allied air raids, and transportation was continually interrupted at one point or another, making it difficult to transport materials and to move workers to job sites.

Only a powerful increase in production and training immediately after the British-French war declaration would have assured the Luftwaffe of maintaining the advantage it had had upon entering the war. Since both production and training required much time, they should have received immediate attention but this was not the case for either. On the contrary, training immediately declined to a great extent and once the crisis was overcome, suffered further cannibalization. These facts indicate clearly how early the German Air Force was in trouble.

It is important to know whether a man as observant as Jeschonnek failed to see this and to know if the General Staff failed to demand in good time an appreciable augmentation of forces and numerous new units. Hitler's Luftwaffe Adjutant, von Below, and von Hammerstein, the Luftwaffe's Judge Advocate General, say that Jeschonnek did make such a demand. Unfortunately, despite the convincing sound of Hammerstein's testimony, the documents do not confirm any such conclusion. (It is a fact, however, that Hitler, because of the Army's requirements for the Russian Campaign, reduced the Luftwaffe's armament priority to fifth place.) Moreover, there is neither proof nor an available witness to testify that Jeschonnek demanded a strengthening of the Luftwaffe after the heavy losses of the Battle of Britain, although this encounter should have opened his eyes. The Chief of the General Staff must have persisted in his optimism, remaining essentially a slave to Hitler, who was a man "possessed by a demon."

Although he was clear-sighted enough in his soldier's profession, Jeschonnek lacked imagination and the ability to foresee the possibilities and proportions which a great war could have. Thus, his arms and forces remained at prewar levels while, by the end of 1942, the Allies faced him in three widely-separated theaters with ever increasing strength. It is irrelevant to claim that Jeschonnek, since he was constrained by a dictator, would have been unable to make his voice heard. The truth of the matter is, he honored the dictator, shared his optimistic views, and believed Germany was destined to win. Had he been of another opinion, some trace of this would have survived for posterity. A General Staff Chief does not normally make verbal demands without some accompanying documentary justification. Furthermore, there is no reason to think that he could not have made some demands, had he so desired.

A series of victories can be too much of a good thing when it prejudices good judgment. And he who makes decisions for the future with a veil before his eyes courts failure. Moreover, the greater the object of the decision, the more serious will be its consequences. The last German blitzkrieg, the Balkan Campaign (6-27 April 1941) occurred in such a way as to increase once more the fatal optimism.

Again the Luftwaffe, with its Fourth Air Fleet (Generaloberst Alexander Loehr), provided close support for Army operations. The result was a magnificent victory over two courageous opponents who had been aided by difficult terrain. The Fourth Air Fleet's contribution to this achievement was considerable. In the Battle for Crete, which followed shortly thereafter (20 May-1 June 1941), the XI Air Corps (Student) and the VIII Air Corps (von Richthofen) performed in an exemplary manner. In the Balkan Campaign the special ability of the VIII Air Corps to perform close-support work was again in evidence as it intervened in the Army's battles on the ground. Both of these highly proven units (after only a short rest) were to be committed in Russia.

With this, Hitler's greatest and most fateful operation, the destiny of the Luftwaffe was sealed. The German victories of the first year in Russia served only to extend the Luftwaffe's vast scope of operations and to entangle it in a conflict which was beyond its resources. Were the top Luftwaffe leaders aware of the tremendous significance of this new war?

Since 1939 the Luftwaffe's buildup had lagged. Some German wings lacked a third group in 1939, and these were eventually organized along with entirely new wings, but the British buildup was going forward at a much faster pace. The island Kingdom first reaped a blessing during the Battle of Britain, when it was permitted to increase its air armament program and to organize a number of new squadrons. However, the real gap between the British and German air forces was to become noticeable only at a later date.

There is no doubt that the Luftwaffe leadership, like Hitler and the German Army, underestimated the Russian opponent. The estimate of the number of Soviet operational aircraft was too low, the estimate of Russian industrial capacity was not high enough, and the technical ability of the Russian people was badly underrated.

A psychological factor which perhaps contributed to this underestimation was that most of the officers in the German Wehrmacht who had been in World War I had served on the Western Front against the British, the French, and the Americans. At that time the Russians, by contrast, had seemed to be poorly armed, and by tradition the Germans had known little of the toughness of Russian defenses since the Napoleonic Period. Hitler (like Goering and Jeschonnek) had served on the Western Front and thought of the Russian theater of World War I only as an area in which Austro-Hungarian troops committed a series of blunders and in which the Germans won a number of great victories. Thus, with great and general optimism the war against the Soviet Union was begun. Hitler promised Goering that after the few weeks—he judged that this war would last no longer than that—he would immediately place 150,000 workers at the disposal of the Luftwaffe armament industry.

Nothing is known concerning Jeschonnek's position with respect to the planned Russian Campaign. We have only the testimony of Admiral Wilhelm Moessl, at that time Naval Liaison Officer assigned to the Luftwaffe High Command, who stated: "The Chief of the General Staff was for the mission." The oft-mentioned Schmid reported:

> Reservations concerning the campaign against the Soviet Union were first brought to the Chief of the General Staff's attention by General von Waldau, the former Chief of the Operations Branch of the Luftwaffe. Not known is whether the Chief of the General Staff shared von Waldau's reservations and passed them on to Goering. I consider both possibilities improbable, however.

Nevertheless, on another occasion Schmid quoted Jeschonnek as having said in his presence: "At last a proper war!"

The Chief of the General Staff and his immediate superior were as different as fire and water in their views of the world, in their attitudes toward duty and work, and in what they demanded of life. In all of these attitudes Goering (grown soft) could not be compared with Jeschonnek. Goering did surpass him in one respect, however. His intuition against Germany's involvement in a two-front war led him to warn Hitler about the dangers of a campaign against Russia. As an alternative, he suggested that Britain's position in the Mediterranean be crushed. Jeschonnek, ensnared by his belief that Hitler was infallible, was incapable of such an intuitive stroke. Instead, he acted as if guided by some immutable physical law, and without a sideward glance, followed Hitler's magnetism to the end.

If it is true, as Koerner recalls, that Goering pointed out to Hitler that the Luftwaffe needed a period of rest and rehabilitation, and an opportunity for internal development before taking on any new enterprises, then Goering was much more farsighted in his views than Jeschonnek. Directive No. 21 (Operation Barbarossa) instructed the Luftwaffe to:

> . . . make such strong forces available for the Eastern Campaign as to assure both an early termination of ground operations and the restriction of damage from air raids in eastern Germany to an absolute minimum. This concentration of forces in the East is to be limited by the need to provide sufficient protection against enemy air raids in all combat and armament areas controlled by us [Germany], and to ensure that the offensive operations against England, particularly against her supply lines, do not come to a standstill.

Since, by the opening of the campaign in Russia (22 June 1941), Germany had been obliged to support its weakening ally Italy in Africa —this required transferring the X Air Corps to Sicily and opening the Mediterranean Front—the Reich was faced with a three-front war. The British were unconquered and defiant, and were clearly waiting for an opportunity to strike a telling blow from the West. When this was combined with the massive Soviet opponent in the East, the ever-troublesome Balkans, and the vast Mediterranean area, the Luftwaffe was immediately forced to improvise.

Directive 21 immediately shackled the Luftwaffe and prevented its strategic commitment by ordering it to concentrate upon operations in support of the Army's advance. Only after this was completed could the air forces strike at the Soviet's industrial heart. The Luftwaffe had only five months in which to consider the organization of its forces for the Russian war, and it had only one organization, the VIII Air Corps, which was especially suited for the main mission, close support. In view of the expanse of the Russian Front, it should have been obvious that one close-support air corps would not be enough to accomplish the mission. Many of the coming battles were bound to be directed against field fortifications and other positions. These were hardly the proper targets for the expensive Do-17's, He-111's, and Ju-88's, but they were ideal for the more robust, economical and single-engine Ju-87 Stukas and certain other ground-attack planes, aircraft which required only one to three men in each aircrew.

As soon as the planning began for Barbarossa a second close-support air corps should have been formed, and even if such an organization did not get under way until after the invasion of the Soviet Union, it would have been soon enough to have provided another close-support corps by early 1942. However, Hitler was convinced that the campaign would end long before that time. Optimism was the spirit of the day!

At 0300 hours, 22 June 1941, the Luftwaffe began its attacks against Russia, following its old recipe of destroying the enemy's air forces on the ground, and then shifting to direct and indirect support of the Army. What was forgotten was that while a rapid surprise attack against an enemy's air forces was able to achieve lasting results in Poland and France, similar results could not be expected in the vast expanses of Russia. Serious range limitations kept the Luftwaffe from reaching all of the Soviet airfields, and, although the Red Air Force lost thousands of aircraft, it was not entirely eliminated. Most of the aircraft destroyed were on the ground, which meant that most of the flying personnel were saved for later use. With astonishing determination and speed the Russians moved many of their aircraft plants out of range, so that they were beyond the reach of any German aircraft, even if the Luftwaffe had been strategic-minded. As a result, the Soviet Union was able to rebuild completely its air forces on modern lines and to become a real threat later in the war, a most impressive achievement.

Because of the initiative of some of the air fleet commanders in Russia, some strategic missions were flown, eighty-seven of them against Moscow. But these were neither systematic nor consequential, and their effects were virtually nil. No special forces were set aside for such operations. The High Command of the Luftwaffe could have helped to master this situation if, instead of leaving two bomber wings in the West where they were unable to achieve any decisive results, it had utilized these forces from the first as the core of a strategic air fleet in Russia. This would have been a favorable arrangement at the beginning of the Russian Campaign, and proof of this could be seen in 1943, when under much more adverse conditions, the IV Air Corps was set aside as a strategic bomber corps. By then of course it was too late to help the situation.

The opening of the war in the East gave the Luftwaffe an impressive string of victories. The number of Russian aircraft destroyed was so great that Goering could scarcely believe the figures. There were, in fact, more Russian planes reported as destroyed than the Luftwaffe General Staff's estimate for the total Russian air strength. This alone should have given rise to some concern about the future, but the campaign rushed onward in an avalanche of victories so that it appeared once more that Hitler's rash optimism would prove to be justified.

These bold expectations were not fulfilled, even though the operations were carried out with determination. The gigantic victories of Bialystok and Smolensk were followed in August by those of Uman and Gomel, on 16 September by the surrender of encircled Kiev and the capture of 665,000 Russians, and in October by the double battles of Vyazma and Bryansk, which brought in 663,000 prisoners. These triumphs did much to obliterate the idea that the original purpose of the campaign had not been achieved. The plan of a rapid conquest failed with the onset of unseasonably cold weather, which brought the German offensive to a standstill. The surprise commitment of fifteen to twenty Siberian divisions, and the Wehrmacht's inability to link up with the Finns frustrated the effort to take Moscow. A series of crises then set in, which forced the German Army to give ground in the North, Center, and South.

Until the setback before Moscow the Luftwaffe had served as a support arm of the Army, a consequence of Directive No. 21, but as the war dragged on, German air forces became more tightly bound to the ground situation than before. Instead of supporting the Army's offensives, the Luftwaffe soon found itself trying to save it from a repetition of Napoleon's disaster of 1812. Poor flying conditions, snow and ice, and sub-zero temperatures hampered most of the Luftwaffe's activities, and when Hitler took over personal command of the Army on 19 December, the proper utilization of air power became even more difficult. Being army-minded and then assuming direct command of the Army, it was natural that Hitler would seize every opportunity to use the Luftwaffe for this end.

Once the German Army ceased to move ahead there was a grave need for the Commander in Chief of the Luftwaffe, and especially for the Chief of the Luftwaffe General Staff, to review the organization and strength of the air forces in relation to the new situation and to take whatever steps were necessary to permit the Luftwaffe to carry out its mission.

From the beginning of winter in 1941 hard fighting continued unabated in ice and snow all along the Eastern Front. A possible complete rout of the Army was prevented by an uncompromising order of the Fuehrer not to retreat a foot. With the front stabilized, the Luftwaffe Operations Staff was able to consider necessary measures for future undertakings. Re-equipping of units was necessary, and it seemed that there was time to accomplish this. More aircraft were needed, or even better, a number of new air units with replacement crews. Also needed was a clear organizational division between strategic and tactical units.

If Jeschonnek had made the decision to divide the air units into two forces, tactical and strategic, in July of 1940, when he first learned of the plan for a war in the East, or at the very latest in the winter of 1941, the first large, tactical units would have arrived at the front in time to relieve the costly twin-engine bombers in the bitter winter fighting. This would have made possible a hardening of the resistance against the resurgent Soviet opponent, and the losses of the Luftwaffe would have been lightened considerably. In the meantime, the strategic units could have been readied for missions against the Russian armament industry in the spring. A change in the chain of command would have been useful at this time but it was not essential.

Related to this reorganization was the armament problem. Since the end of the fighting in France and the beginning of the expansion program of the Army in expectation of the opening of the war against Russia, the Luftwaffe's armaments were not on a parity with those of the Army. The Luftwaffe ranked fifth in the priority rating. This situation could not be altered in the winter of 1941-42 when the Army needed all of the strengthening it could get. Furthermore, if Hitler had not taken personal command of the Army things might have been better for the Luftwaffe. Whatever could be done for the armament of the Luftwaffe had to be accomplished within the priority which was available to it. After Udet's suicide, Milch had uncovered massive amounts of aluminum which had been hoarded by several aircraft manufacturers, which was sufficient to have allowed Jeschonnek to order an increase in single-engine aircraft for 1942 and to make it possible to organize several close-support corps similar to Richthofen's VIII Air Corps.

At the same time, a considerable increase in the production of fighters was necessary for it was clear that Germany had several fronts to contend with. In such a critical situation it was highly important to build solid defenses for the skies over the homeland in order to preserve the moral and industrial resources of the nation for the further prosecution of the war. To assure this, it was necessary to organize a home air defense which was capable of sustaining day and night operations.

Luftwaffe forces were able to repulse the British air attacks of 1941 without any great damage being inflicted on the Reich. The German night fighters organized by Kammhuber were put to the test, while those fighter units remaining in the West had a relatively easy time of it on the Channel coast. The British appeared ponderous and needed time to get in motion, but they were also obstinate, methodical, and tough enough to bear fairly heavy losses while they gathered their strength.

Was the establishment of a strong German fighter arm impossible? Certainly not! One possibility that appeared on the horizon was Udet's proposal to build more fighters because of the expected Allied heavy bomber attacks. Milch, his successor, in the course of a conference with Goering and Jeschonnek, offered Jeschonnek an increase in fighter production to 1,000 planes a month.

In the life of every man who has reached a high office there occurs a moment when he must prove if he was merely appointed to his post, or if he was predestined to hold such a position. For the Chief of the Luftwaffe General Staff the moment had arrived, surrounded by such urgency that, if he failed to act positively, his reputation as a leader was likely to be severely damaged. Jeschonnek was offered an increase in fighter production, an increase which would have allowed him to remake the home air defense forces into a powerful system. At the same time there was the need to increase the production of ground-attack and dive-bomber aircraft, and to reorganize the Luftwaffe. It is possible that he could not have convinced Goering or Hitler of the necessity for these projects, but, if he had recognized the need and done everything in his power to meet it, he would have assured himself a place in history as a responsible and farsighted air strategist.

Jeschonnek did not accept Milch's offer to increase fighter production, nor is there any evidence that he made any effort to change the indirect support of the Army by creating a close-support corps and concentrating the bombers (which would have been made available by such a reorganization) into a strategic air force. The latter, by attacking Soviet aircraft and tank factories, would have provided much more effective assistance for the hard-fighting Army than they were able to give by indirect support missions over the battlefield.

Once Jeschonnek rejected the requirements mentioned above, his fate was sealed. No doubt his deep belief in Hitler's genius was at fault, for Hitler was then confident that a renewed attack against the Russians in 1942 would crush the enemy once and for all. As a matter of fact, the Luftwaffe, from this time on, was forced to bear a number of burdens which, together, led to its downfall. First of these was its degeneration into a sort of Army artillery arm. This situation, first dictated by expediency, soon became a permanent one as the relentless Russian pressures (with the short respite afforded during the last great German offensive in the East in 1942) never let up. Within the Luftwaffe High Command stopgap actions became the main order of business, while bomber missions were dictated by Army groups with air fleet commanders becoming mere assistants to their senior Army colleagues. Meanwhile, on the home front the Luftwaffe became increasingly handicapped in its action against the ever more serious RAF attacks, while in the Mediterranean area (to which the Second Air Fleet had been dispatched from Russia in November 1941) the vastness of the territory involved and the inadequate strength of the German forces precluded any real progress. Here, too, the shortage of fighters and strategic bombers made itself felt.

In this situation the Chief of the Luftwaffe General Staff slid unnoticed into the role of administrator of the air forces, while the German Army became the real commander of the air forces with Goering and Jeschonnek compelled to make units available for the Army's planned operations. They administered simply because there was no strategic air war and therefore no need for independent leadership!

It was a curious picture indeed. Hitler had burdened himself with the yoke of command over the Army and had permanently withdrawn behind the locked gates of his headquarters near Rastenburg (East Prussia), while the most faithful of his youthful soldiers Jeschonnek, became enslaved to him through his unshakable trust in Hitler's genius and judgment. In fact, Jeschonnek became precisely what von Seidel called him after the war: a "yes-man".

17
The Battle of Britain

THE GERMAN AIR FORCE, which had gained a reputation for invincibility during three campaigns, had, as a matter of fact, failed to perform really adequately during the last phase of the third of these campaigns; namely during the battle for air supremacy at Dunkirk. There, it had missed its goal, the destruction of the British Army, partly as a result of the fight put up by the Spitfires and partly as a result of unfavorable weather conditions and the overambitious scope of the mission. Dunkirk, however, was a single episode, its memory soon blotted out by Luftwaffe successes during the campaign in France. Moreover, the unfavorable aspects of the Dunkirk operation, which could and should have provided food for serious thought, were overshadowed by the memory of the wealth of enemy materiel covering the length of the beach, left behind by an army which was forced to embark too hastily to take along the greater part of its weapons, tanks, motor vehicles, and other equipment.

While the commitment of the Luftwaffe at Dunkirk was the result of a direct, spur-of-the-moment offer which Goering made to Hitler, it can hardly be said that the Reichsmarschall was equally enthusiastic about Directive 17, of 1 August 1940, which was passed on to him by the Commander in Chief, Wehrmacht, and which referred to the Luftwaffe's role in the "conduct of air and sea warfare against England." Kammhuber maintains that Goering's lack of enthusiasm for Directive 17 is clearly visible in the wording of his Instructions for the Air War against England of 30 June 1940.

By intensifying air warfare against England, Hitler hoped to bring the British leaders to the point where they would be willing to discuss peace. What he wanted was an honorable peace, one which would pave the way to a lasting understanding between the two countries. In this way he would have had his hands free for the Russian campaign, plans for which were already under way.

Just how strong was the German Luftwaffe at this point? On 3 August 1940, according to the records of the Quartermaster General, the authorized single-engine fighter aircraft strength stood at 1,171; actual strength was 1,065, and of these 878 (comprising ten single-engine fighter wings with a total of twenty-eight groups) were combat-ready. Two of these ten wings (a total of six groups), to be sure, were tied to home air defense operations, so that the number of single-engine fighter aircraft available at the beginning of the Battle of Britain was reduced to 760.

At the same time, the Luftwaffe had three wings (eight groups) of twin-engine fighter aircraft. The authorized strength was 332 machines, the actual strength 310, of which 240 were in a state of combat readiness. It must be emphasized that this was aircraft strength only; there were not enough trained crews available to man the aircraft on hand. Thus, effective twin-engine fighter strength (i.e. fully manned aircraft) was probably about 230.

According to the Quartermaster General reports, authorized bomber strength stood at 1,638 on 3 August; actual strength was 1,458, 818 of which were combat-ready. Of the latter, however (a total of fifteen bomber wings or forty-two groups), two wings—or six groups—were based in Norway and therefore could have intervened effectively under only very special circumstances. In other words, of the total of 823 bombers, the Second and Third Air Fleets had an average of 700-800 at their disposal during the first two months of the Battle of Britain. The dive-bombers were represented in an authorized strength of 429 aircraft and an actual strength of 446; in reality, 343 were available for action on 3 August. In addition, on 20 September, an experimental fighter-bomber group (the II Close-Support Group, 2d Training Wing) equipped with forty Me-109's, was sent into action for the first time.

British air strength at the beginning of the struggle was made up of sixty single-engine fighter squadrons, or a total of 960 aircraft. To be sure, these squadrons also had reserve forces upon which they could draw if necessary. Due to the fact that there were eight squadrons not prepared for immediate action, the actual strength on 7 August 1940 was 714 single-engine fighter aircraft. This number was subject to alteration during the various phases of the struggle (on 25 September, for example, it was down to 665). According to British data, losses during the period 11 August-28 September 1940 amounted to 669 single-engine fighter aircraft, while a total of 936 was produced during the same period. British bomber strength (actual strength as of 8 August 1940: 471 aircraft) played no role in the Battle of Britain.

By the end of September 1940, this strength ratio had altered so that 665 British single-engine fighters were facing a German force composed of 276 single-engine fighters, 130 fighter-bombers, 100 twin-engine fighters, 700-800 bombers, 343 dive-bombers, and 26 close-support aircraft.

During the period 10 July-31 October 1940, German losses amounted to 1,733 bombers and single-engine fighters, while the British lost 915 single-engine fighters. In terms of personnel, the German loses were far more critical than the British ones, since the fighting took place over British territory. When a German aircraft was shot down, her crew—assuming that it was able to escape from the damaged airplane—was immediately taken prisoner and was thus irrevocably lost to Germany. These losses were augmented by the ones incurred through crashes into the English Channel where rescue operations were often impossible.

Quartermaster General records indicate German losses for the period 3 August-28 September 1940 as 719 bomber aircraft (total destruction and 10 percent or more damage) and 400 crews. (For the dive-bombers, the figures are 97 machines and 61 crews.) When British aircraft were downed, on the other hand, there was a much greater chance that their crews could be salvaged for future reassignment to other aircraft; they were not permanently lost to future operations. The situation for German single-engine and twin-engine fighter crews, of course, was the same as that described above in connection with the bomber crews.

In view of the figures given above, it is clear that the production of aircraft and the training of crews to man them was a key problem for Germany. During 1940 a total of 11,376 aircraft was produced in Germany (this includes new production, conversion of older models, and repair), as reflected in Quartermaster General reports; this total included 2,268 Me-109 fighters, 1,114 Me-110 fighters, 2,741 bombers (all types), and 480 dive-bombers.

In evaluating the course of the Battle of Britain, a comparison of the number of fighter aircraft produced by each side during 1940 is significant. The 3,382 single-engine and twin-engine fighter aircraft reflected in the Luftwaffe's Quartermaster General records correspond to 4,283 fighters produced by the British during the same year. This very revealing figure provides ample proof of England's greater strength in the field of air armament. When we bear in mind that the German fighters, tied to the bombers they escorted, were unable to maneuver with complete freedom and were thus more vulnerable to enemy action than they otherwise would have been, the production figures given above might just as well be considered decisive.

During the month of August, a period of intensive fighting, the German aircraft industry produced 160 Me-109's and 114 Me-110's, a total of 274 new fighter aircraft (together with the aircraft released from repair, the total for the month was 301—222 Me-109's and 79 Me-110's), while the British produced 476. This is particularly interesting when one considers that the British began the year with a production figure of 157 aircraft (for January) and Germany with a figure of 136 (Me-109's and Me-110's together); thus Britain succeeded in trebling her production during the year, while Germany barely doubled hers. Moreover, the import of American aircraft served to weight the numerical balance in Britain's favor.

If we exclude the twin-engine fighters, and base our comparison on the number of single-engine fighters alone, then the ratio is even less favorable for Germany. The 2,268 Me-109's reflected in Quartermaster General records for 1940 are balanced by 4,283 British single-engine fighters, a ratio of nearly 1:2.

As far as personnel losses were concerned, the fact must not be lost sight of that it was the highly-qualified, peacetime-trained crews who were affected first. And the new crop of bomber pilots coming from the flight schools was no longer so well-trained in instrument flight, partly because the Ju-52's assigned to the Chief of Training were continually being loaned out for special missions.

Appraisal of the British-German strength ratio and of the opportunities for development available to both sides would seem to substantiate the conclusion of the military author, Dr. Theo Weber in the Swiss journal, *Flugwehr und Technik:* "It is clear that the Luftwaffe simply did not have the means of solving this problem in the autumn of 1940." Germany did not possess the long-range, heavy bombers which might have struck a decisive blow against the sources of the enemy's military strength.

The goal of forcing England to the point of peace negotiations was not attained during a single phase of the intensified air warfare carried out by the Luftwaffe during the period 8 (or 13) August 1940 to early June 1941. It was not, however, the high losses inflicted by Britain's undeniably efficient air defenses which forced the Luftwaffe to withdraw from the battle; it was rather the fact that the date which Hitler had selected (almost at the same time as he ordered intensification of the air war with England) for the launching of the campaign against Soviet Russia was drawing near, and he was still convinced that Russia would have to be subdued if Germany were to be safe.

One other factor came to England's aid, the advent of the proverbial British autumn weather on 16 September 1940. The two months which

Hitler had waited, in the hope that Britain would capitulate, now took their toll.

The German attackers were handicapped in other ways as well. The Luftwaffe had no ground control system for the ground-to-air guidance of fighter aircraft, whereas the British had a well-functioning one at their disposal. This was compensated for to some extent, however, by the efficiency of the German radio monitoring service.

The British also had a tremendous advantage in their radar equipment, which had been under development since 1936 in the National Physics Research Institute, chiefly at the instigation of the Scotsman Robert Watson Watt who had recognized its significance in time and whose work had been most generously supported. The radar instruments set up along the English coast ranged over the coastal waters and sometimes even as far as the Luftwaffe assembly areas, so that the approach of enemy aircraft could be detected well in advance. Early warning made it possible for the British fighters to intercept the enemy in plenty of time, which of course, could not have been the case without the help of radar.

In addition, British home air defense operations were superbly organized and administered. Unfortunately, the Luftwaffe High Command made no serious attempt to destroy the British coastal radar stations by bombardment, or even to keep them under continuous harassing attack. After 15 August there were no more German attacks on these stations. Five stations had been bombed and damaged but none had been destroyed completely. Actually, the number of aircraft employed (one bomb-carrying twin-engine fighter group from the Second Air Fleet with twelve Me-110's and eight Me-109's) was not really sufficient for such a mission. As Kammhuber says, "The enemy was continually peeking at our cards—and it was our own fault!" This was also the reason why no prospectively successful attacks could be undertaken against the British ground organization.

At Christmas 1940, the British placed their first panoramic-view radar equipment at the disposal of the night-fighter control organization. As a result, the night fighters, hitherto completely helpless, soon began to chalk up records of German aircraft downed. The figure for March was twenty-two, for April twenty, and for May allegedly one hundred. In any case, German air supremacy at night, previously a foregone conclusion, was now seriously threatened. In addition, from March on British long-range fighter operations out over the Channel were highly successful.

* * *

It is not the purpose of the present study to go into the individual phases of the Battle of Britain in order to examine the appropriateness of the decisions taken by command. Far more interesting is the question of whether and, if so, to what extent, the Battle of Britain can be termed a turning point.

In answering this question, the fact must be borne in mind that the Battle of Britain was broken off prematurely by order of top-level command because the German Air Force was needed for the forthcoming war with Soviet Russia. Operations against England were not discontinued because they were recognized as hopeless or because they could no longer be justified in terms of the losses incurred.

Still, it was the first time that the Luftwaffe had brought its main strength to bear in a large-scale operation of many weeks' duration without gaining its objective. For the fact remained that its goal had not been achieved. The myth of Luftwaffe invincibility had been exploded. England had been left in command of the battlefield, and had managed to maintain herself in the face of the sharp decline in morale occasioned by France's dropping out of the war.

And this was significant—particularly in point of morale. By no means, however, could it be viewed as a turning point after which nothing would ever again go right for the Luftwaffe. Even the depletion suffered in the ranks of Germany's best-trained crews was not sufficient to induce such a turning point. Newly recruited, younger crews had been gathering combat experience in the meantime, and during the two years to follow (1941 and 1942), there is still no instance of out-and-out failure on the part of the Luftwaffe in any theater of operations.

Even so, the Battle of Britain does represent a turning point insofar as Germany failed to recognize and appreciate the reasons which had prevented the Luftwaffe from attaining its objective. These reasons are the following:

1. The lack of purposeful guidance in German air armament during the Udet period. At that time, when there was no appreciable difference in the quality of the German and British fighter aircraft, quantity played an important role. And Udet and his staff, primarily interested in the development of new models, failed entirely to recognize this fact. Germany should have kept herself systematically informed of the efficacy of the British air armament program and should have drawn the inevitable conclusions, chief of which was the need for a continuing increase in the production of aircraft. Germany's military leaders, soon to be confronted with the bitter seriousness of war with

Russia, did not even find it necessary to take a closer look at Udet's office of Chief of Procurement and Supply with a view to getting armament production up to wartime levels, nor did they take steps (and this includes the expansion of training) to fill in the gaps left by the Battle of Britain. Thus, there is justification in treating the Battle of Britain as a turning point. As far as aircraft crews were concerned, the Luftwaffe had been eating into its capital, yet its leaders were unable to see the need for revitalizing the training program.

2. Prior to the Battle of Britain, Germany rashly underestimated the enemy's military strength. The Reichs Intelligence Service had drawn far too rosy a picture; the strength figures it worked out were woefully off. Underestimating enemy strength is clearly one of the most frequent causes of military failure. Germany's leaders could have profited by the admittedly unpleasant surprise they received, if they had determined then and there to err in the direction of overestimation of the strength of a potential enemy in the future, in order to be certain that their own preparations would be adequate. But was this the case? As far as Russia was concerned—and to a lesser extent also in the case of America—it most certainly was not.

With incomprehensible stubbornness, Germany's leaders continued to underestimate the military strength of their adversaries until the final catastrophe broke in upon them.

3. Failure to develop a long-range, heavy bomber (and this could have been only a four-engine bomber) capable of employment in strategic air warfare. Again, Germany failed to profit by her lesson. Right up to the time of his death, Udet was still experimenting with the tandem-engine system for the He-177, and even Milch, who inherited what was admittedly a miserable situation, could not bring himself to order a switch to four independently functioning engines until it was too late. Another instance in which the lessons of bitter experience went unheeded. The same thing also happened in the case of the long-range fighter, the unfortunate affair of the Me-210 taking place at about the same time.

4. The superiority of the British radar equipment. In spite of the valiant effort made by General Martini, of the Luftwaffe signal forces, the British had too much of a head start for Germany to catch up with them in time. As a matter of fact, the Luftwaffe, engaged from 1943 to the end of the war in a life-and-death struggle to protect the Reich, was never to have access to radar instruments which were invulnerable to jamming—and thus a match for the Anglo-American equipment—

simply because the German radar industry was incapable of developing radar tubes for the lower centimeter wave ranges.

In a very real sense, the Battle of Britain was the handwriting on the wall. And neither Goering, Jeschonnek, nor Udet had been able to decipher it. If they had understood its significance, there would still have been time to correct the defects and to launch a new and more forceful attack against the West. For conflict with the West was inevitable until such time as the British wasps' nest could be burned out. It was to take a lot more writing on the wall, however, before the Luftwaffe's top-level leaders learned to read even a part of it. By the time that point had been reached, of course, it was already too late.

18
Defeat from Victory—
Malta

DURING THE SECOND HALF of May 1941, the German Armed Forces—Student's paratroopers and the 6th Mountain Division—had seized the island of Crete. The extremely heavy losses suffered during the first few days of this daring action frightened both Hitler and Goering into dropping their original plan of occupying Cyprus immediately afterwards. If this plan had been realized, the balance of power in the eastern Mediterranean would have been weighted in favor of the Axis.

The possession of Crete alone proved to be fairly insignificant in the long run. Malta, on the other hand, a much tinier island than Crete, was one of Britain's most vital bases at that time, despite its remote and isolated position. Possession of Malta decided the fate of shipping from Italy and North Africa and thus the efficacy of the supply line to Rommel's armies. For the British it was also an invaluable intermediate base between Gibraltar and Alexandria, with stockpiles of coal and oil, well-equipped wharves and docks, and—above all—with its location right in the middle of the Mediterranean. Moreover, the island had high morale value as a symbol of British sea power. The scene of some of the proudest moments of British naval history, Malta was a measure of England's mastery of the Mediterranean.

The island is located fifty-six miles south of the eastern coast of Sicily and is approximately 225 miles distant from the African coast at Tunis. Its area is only 153 square miles, and the loftiest peak is no more than 846 feet. The width of the island varies between six and seven and one-half miles. Its population, military and civilian, was about 300,000 during the war. The British had an armed force of approximately 30,000 men on Malta, including the militia made up of Maltese volunteers and the armed labor troops. Its nucleus was the 231st Malta Brigade Group, which in 1941 consisted of three British battalions (2d Battalion, Devonshire Regiment; 1st Battalion, Hampshire Regiment; and 1st Battalion, Dorsetshire Regiment). Its mission was to guard the Maltese coastline of twenty-eight miles, nineteen of which—according to British data—were highly suitable for the landing of an armed force.

Italy neglected to capture the island right after her entry into the war, presumably because she had no wish to test her strength in an inevitable encounter with Britain's Mediterranean fleet. The consequences of her neglect, however, became more and more painfully evident as the conflict in North Africa approached its climax. They became apparent to Germany when she came to the aid of the Italians in 1941, after the latter had already been defeated by British forces and were in danger of losing all of Tripolitania. The later difficulties of the Africa Corps could be attributed almost exclusively to the unreliability of the supply line across the Mediterranean. At various times, fairly large British fleet units were stationed at Malta, and using the island as a base of operations, submarines and bombers were able to attack German shipping convoys—usually not very well protected by their alleged escort of Italian warships—and inflict serious damage. In September 1941, the damage amounted to 38½ percent of the total tonnage shipped; in October the figure was 63 percent, and in November it hit a peak of 77 percent.

Urgently as every single aircraft was needed to assure the rapid success of the Russian campaign in 1941, Hitler, in October of that year, had no alternative but to send the Second Air Fleet to Sicily (where he had already transferred the X Air Corps from Norway in December 1940). He did this to protect shipping activity and to eliminate or at least neutralize Malta, that most dangerous "aircraft carrier." Apparently the Second Air Fleet's presence in Sicily and the force of its first attacks must have had a very salutary effect, for during January 1942 only 20 percent of the total tonnage was lost through enemy action and Rommel had a chance to catch his breath.

It is understandable that Germany's naval leaders submitted their recommendations for the conquest of Malta to Hitler at a very early date, even before the occupation of Crete. Student reports on a conference with Hitler on 21 April 1941 to discuss plans for the Crete operation. Keitel and Jodl unexpectedly raised the question of whether it might not be wiser for the overall course of operations in the Mediterranean to take Malta first and let Crete wait until afterwards. With the reply, "Malta will be taken care of later!" Hitler decided on Crete.

The first member of the Luftwaffe to broach the subject of Malta to Hitler was Kesselring, who insisted that occupation of the island was absolutely indispensable to efficient conduct of the war in Africa. Kesselring reports that he was unable to get Hitler's approval for this project until the spring of 1942, at which time Hitler put an end to Kesselring's impassioned oratory by patting him on the arm and saying, "Just take it easy, Feldmarschall Kesselring; I'll do it all right!"

In February 1942, Germany began making careful preparations for large-scale air operations against Malta. The attacks began on 2 April 1942 and continued throughout the whole month; the last full-scale raid was carried out on 10 May. During April and May, the Luftwaffe flew 11,000 sorties against Malta; approximately one-fourth of the bomb load dropped was directed at the antiaircraft artillery positions on the island. By the end of May, there were no more submarines or warships at the island. All the enemy aircraft bases there had been destroyed, and the antiaircraft batteries, forty of which were concentrated around La Valetta, fired only sporadically. Both troops and civilian population were already feeling the pinch of rapidly diminishing supply stocks and resistance could be considered very weak. Even so, the Luftwaffe had not succeeded in destroying the island's defending forces, since the huge subterranean limestone caves afforded them sufficient protection.

After this initial success, which unfortunately could not be followed up immediately by a landing of German and Italian troops, came the usual tragedy—the advent of war on several fronts. Kesselring writes as follows:

> With the success of the Luftwaffe raids on Malta, the Armed Forces High Command considered the situation to be so well under control that it transferred the majority of the Luftwaffe forces to the East. Naturally, enough units remained in the Mediterranean to keep Malta under surveillance, to harass enemy convoys, and to protect our own convoys—without having to draw upon the units assigned to the Air Commander Africa. In the long run, however, these units were too weak to prevent the recovery of Malta and to keep supplies from reaching the island fortress indefinitely.

In the meantime, the two allies concluded their negotiations for the joint offensive after the Armed Forces High Command had announced Germany's willingness to participate on 21 April. Mussolini arrived at Hitler's headquarters on Obersalzberg on 29 April, and he was soon followed by Marshal Cavallero and Count Ciano. Their meeting had been called to decide on the date of the attack. Cavallero wanted it to take place before Rommel began his offensive. Kesselring, who originally had been of the same opinion, now insisted that Rommel would have to defeat the British first. When the conference ended on 30 April 1942, it had been decided that Rommel's attack, slated for the end of May, should come first. As soon as his initial advance was successfully completed, Rommel was to remain at the Halfaya Pass on the Egyptian border, and the Malta operation would be carried out. The attack on the island, christened Operation "Hercules", was to take place no later than the full-moon period in July.

So much for the agreements reached by the heads of state and their military advisors. Behind the scenes, the picture was quite different. Ciano, who always regarded events with a good deal of skepticism, noted the following in his diary under date of 28 April: ". . . whether the undertaking will ever take place and, if so, when, is quite another matter. . . ." On 31 May, after an interview with General Carboni, who was to be in command of the attacking divisions, he writes "He is dead set against it (the operation). He is convinced that we'll suffer very high losses and that we won't accomplish anything at all. He blames Cavallero for everything and seems to think that he is an intriguer and not to be trusted."

Far more important, however, were Hitler's feelings in the matter. The losses sustained by the Luftwaffe during the occupation of Crete had made him very skeptical about paratrooper operations, and besides he was not at all certain that Malta was ripe for attack. Then, too, if the island were captured, the necessity of maintaining it would arise— still another area to eat up Germany's resources.

Rommel, in the meantime, who had launched his offensive on 26 May 1942, had succeeded, after heavy fighting against the British forces around Bir Hakim, in gaining a clear victory and had taken Tobruk by storm (on 20 June). In accordance with the agreement reached, Rommel should have brought his operations to a halt and certain air units assigned to the Air Commander Africa should have been released for commitment in Operation Hercules.

The conference of marshals on 26 June at Sidi el Barani, Rommel's headquarters, attended by Kesselring and Rommel (for the German side) and Bastico and Cavallero (for the Italian), showed very clearly the discrepancy between Kesselring's and Rommel's views. Kesselring's warning that it was dangerous to advance against the enemy air bases on the Nile (manned by fully prepared fresh forces) with nearly exhausted Luftwaffe units which urgently needed time to rest and recover was impatiently brushed aside by Rommel. When Bastico asked for his appraisal of the situation, Rommel gave his word that he could be in Cairo within ten days. Under these circumstances, Bastico and Cavallero, heretofore against immediate continuation of operations in Africa, gave in. The other dissenter, Kesselring, was ordered to stop objecting in a radiogram from Hitler.

Hitler, to whom Rommel had direct access, wrote to Mussolini in order to obtain his approval for the immediate continuation of Rommel's operations and the postponement of Operation Hercules. At this stage of operations Mussolini still had unlimited confidence in Hitler's military genius. Cavallero and his objections were simply brushed aside. He had no alternative but to alter his orders and to postpone the Malta undertaking until September.

According to a report prepared by Koller, Goering accepted the credit for having persuaded the Fuehrer to drop the plans for the occupation of Malta. Unfortunately, the motivating factor was his fear of losing paratrooper forces. This attitude on Goering's part is confirmed by Kesselring's personal experiences during this period and can be accepted as an established fact.

Malta, then, although it was near to surrender in April 1942, was never taken; it remained an extremely sharp thorn in the side of Germany's conduct of war in the Mediterranean and helped immensely to make final victory possible for the Anglo-American task forces.

What preparations were actually made for Operation Hercules? According to information provided by Student, who had been placed in charge of the airlanding operation, the plan was to begin with a paratrooper landing along the southwestern coast of the island. This phase of the action was to be carried out by Student's own XI Air Corps, together with the Italian Parachute Division "Folgore," which General Ramcke had trained "in record time and very effectively." The airlanding force was to be brought to the island by freight gliders, of which 1,000 were available for the operation. The southwestern coast—which had never been fortified because of its inaccessibility—and one small fishing port there could also be used for the landing of tanks if this should prove necessary.

Once a bridgehead had been formed, the Axis forces would be right in front of the Victoria Line, a row of fortified positions running across the island from east to west. In their breakthrough of the Victoria Line, the paratrooper and airlanding forces were to be reinforced by several Italian divisions landed by boat. The result would be an overwhelmingly large attack force combined with perfect air cover. Although British resistance on Malta would certainly be stubborn, all in all conditions could be regarded as far more favorable than they had been on Crete. The second wave of transport aircraft could reach Malta much more quickly and, because of the relatively short distance between the island and the base of operations in Sicily, four of five missions could be flown daily.

It could be safely assumed that British fleet units would not appear before the end of the first day of operations. Britain had too few aircraft carriers, and besides they would have represented far too vulnerable a target for the Luftwaffe forces around the island. In case of emergency, the Axis transport ships could always alter course to remain within running distance of Pantelleria or Tripoli. If British bombers were employed from bases in Africa, they would have to fly without escort and would be easy game for the German fighters.

It is Student's firm belief that German military leaders had every reason to count on the airlanding's being a success. The II Air Corps, the Second Air Fleet—with Kesselring as guiding spirit of the plan—and even Hitler himself were all of this opinion. Nor could there be any doubt as to the outcome of the landing of the forces transported by sea; the transport ships would be escorted by Italian warships and the long spring day would afford ideal conditions for providing effective air cover. Even without this landing, however, Student's original force—constantly reinforced from the air—would probably be sufficient.

But what was to happen next? The enemy had two alternatives; either he could defend the Victoria Line or he could attempt to push the landing force back into the sea. At that time there was no reliable information available as to his firepower. One thing was definite, however; no matter which course of action he selected, he would be forced to make his troops mobile, to occupy his firing positions, and to set up a system of supply lines. And, so far as it was possible to tell, he had no more antiaircraft artillery available to cover these operations. It was reasonably certain that all the antiaircraft artillery on the island had already been brought into action in order to protect the harbor of La Valetta and other important military and industrial installations against the German air attacks. If a part of this artillery (which had already been seriously weakened by German air attack) were diverted to cover the operations of the troops fighting in the interior and to combat German aircraft and tanks, then it would be too widely dispersed to be effective anywhere, and the entire island would be defenseless against the destruction wrought by German bombardment. In the last analysis then, it would have been the enemy's own defensive operations which hastened the downfall of the island.

It is certain that Hitler's aversion to the operation, like Goering's, was influenced by the fear that it could result in paratroop losses as high as those suffered in the Crete operation. The airlanding on Crete, however, had been followed by a mishap which Germany had learned to avoid in the meantime. Besides, Crete was much farther away from Athens than the target area in Malta was from the contemplated base of operations. In Crete, the landing force had operated at three widely-separated points of attack; in Malta there was only one, and the ultimate goal, La Valetta, was only about six miles away from the initial landing area. In the case of Malta, the Luftwaffe could even have established an airlift if it had been necessary.

The difficulty was that Hitler simply could not accept the necessity for the Malta operation. He could not bring himself to recognize its urgency. He let Italy take the initiative, despite the fact that it was German soldiers—not Italian—who were going to their death on the way to Africa because the British were sinking the troop transports—all too often left to fend for themselves by their Italian escort ships—with warships and aircraft based at Malta. Even if Hitler refused to entertain the thought of carrying out Operation Hercules without his Italian ally (because of his almost pathological loyalty to Mussolini), still he was skeptical enough of Italy's dependability and sense of duty that he was not quite willing to insist on Italian assistance at any price.

The Luftwaffe bombardment of Malta, in the end, was in vain. The fruit was ripe but it was never plucked. The island, which regarded its escape as a miracle, soon managed to recover its equilibrium. And as soon as its facilities had been restored to the point where British aircraft could land and British ships could utilize its harbors, the thorn in the Axis side began to throb again. Then in the fall of the same year the reversals suffered by Rommel at El Alamein and the Allied landing at Casablanca brought Germany and Italy into a situation they could no longer master. And as the fighting in Tunisia progressed, Malta's importance increased tremendously.

Again, it was the Luftwaffe which had to pay the price for Goering's senseless interference. Heavy losses and rapid attrition of materiel (in Naples-based operations to provide cover for the transport convoys), especially of the Ju-52 aircraft employed in air supply operations to Tunisia, were the results. If Malta had been taken in 1942, it is probable that Rommel would not have suffered defeat, and that the Allied landing in North Africa—if tried at all—would have come to an inconclusive end in the mountains of Algeria. Last, but definitely not least, civilian morale in the Axis nations would have been greatly bolstered!

As it was, however, Tunisia capitulated, Sicily was lost, Il Duce was deposed, and Italy withdrew from the war; Naples was lost—and with it the airfields at Foggia—then Rome, and finally, in April 1945, came the collapse of Germany's operations in the Italian theater of war. One catastrophe after another!

Victory in Malta—a foregone conclusion—would have certainly prevented this catastrophe, but Germany allowed this victory to slip through her fingers.

19
The Soviet Union

THE WAR AGAINST SOVIET RUSSIA clearly represented one of the most significant turning points for the Luftwaffe, as well as for the entire German Armed Forces. And all the important factors which made it so were present in its very beginning.

Since the German victory over France, there was only one enemy, England, to be faced in the West; to be sure, operations against England also required action on the high seas and, after 1940, in the Mediterranean as well. The decision to engage in war against Soviet Russia, however, meant the opening of a new and geographically enormous theater of operations. And for the first time since the end of the campaign in France, it was primarily a theater of Army and Luftwaffe operations. Army preparations for this new mission included the activation of a total of forty new divisions; this, in turn, represented an extremely heavy burden on Germany's armament industries. As a result, the Luftwaffe expansion originally planned for the same period had to be relegated to the background. Thus, while the Army was able to face the enemy in the East with a considerably strengthened force (still not strong enough, as events were to prove), reinforcement of Luftwaffe strength was limited to replacement of the losses entailed by the Battle of Britain.

If there was any justification for the momentous decision to start a war against Soviet Russia as a means of counteracting the potential threat of her entry into the European war, it could have been only the certainty that she could be conquered in another lightning campaign. But was this a certainty? It could be counted as such only if Germany were able, once again, to eliminate the danger of the time factor—as she had done in the campaigns in Poland, Norway, the West, and the Balkans (the latter campaign having been made necessary by Italy's boastful and bumbling intervention in Greece)—and this in an operational area of almost endless depth.

There were two ways in which the time factor might be fatal. In the first place England, still too weak to continue offensive operations at the moment, was pushing armament production as rapidly as possible, and America, standing behind her, was becoming progressively more unfriendly. In the second place Germany would not be in a position to attack until spring at the earliest (due to the Balkan campaign, the attack was not to begin until 22 June), and this would leave only a few months' time before the advent of the Russian winter, during which the Soviet giant would have time to recover his strength. If the time element could not be overcome by Germany, then the whole Russian campaign would be tantamount to stirring up a hornets' nest without having the means to destroy it.

From all possible viewpoints then, the risk entailed was a serious one. If Germany should not succeed in making the Russian campaign into another glorious episode like her earlier campaigns, then she was bound to be in for a life-and-death struggle, for she would be engaged in a destruction-bringing war on several fronts at the same time. It was obvious that the demands of such a war would raise Army requirements tremendously, with the result that Luftwaffe and Navy needs would be engaged in an action which permitted no respite, in a country whose airfields were definitely substandard and whose climate was barbaric.

In other words, the majority of the Luftwaffe units (which were, of course, committed in Russia) faced the certain prospect of continual attrition and depletion. And the situation of those units remaining in the West was not a great deal better. How could they expect to meet the British offensive which began at the same time as the Russian campaign and which would soon be strengthened immeasurably by the entry of the United States into the war? What chance did the Luftwaffe have of meeting the requirements for increased air strength in the Mediterranean? Not even Army strength was put to such a demanding test by the opening of the Russian campaign. The Army was still waging war in Cyrenaica, and its continued occupation of Norway and France, while it tied up a considerable number of troops, could be carried out by troops which needed a rest and which could prepare themselves for renewed commitment at the front in a country whose occupation required no further military action. It was the Luftwaffe, the majority of whose forces were called directly from the Battle of Britain to operations against Soviet Russia, which faced the most serious problems.

In view of this fact it was no wonder that it was the Commander in Chief, Luftwaffe, more than any other German military leader, who spoke out against Hitler's plans for a campaign against Soviet Russia. It cannot be denied that Goering had a certain intuition as far as political developments were concerned. And the fact that he, personally—as a conscientious husband and father, as possessor of valuable art collections, and as owner of a considerable amount of real estate—had a good deal more to lose than to gain from a new war, presumably served to sharpen his intuition. In any case it was not the Commander in Chief, Army, who spoke up against the Russian campaign, but the Commander in Chief, Luftwaffe, Hitler's closest confidant.

Goering's warnings against a campaign in the East were even more vehement than those of the Commander in Chief, Navy. Raeder did his best to distract Hitler's attention from the East by attempting to persuade him that if Germany's position in the Near East could be made strong enough, a war with Russia would be unnecessary.

When Hitler told him of his plans for Russia, Goering requested time to think it over, since he was somewhat surprised by Hitler's reasoning that it was imperative that Germany, "by means of a quick, tightly concentrated attack- . . . destroy" Russian military potential before America would be able to build up her armament and her forces. Goering states that he pleaded with Hitler on the evening of that same day "not to start a war with Russia, either then or in the near future." He begged Hitler to let the "danger represented by Russia remain in abeyance" for a while longer—after all, Hitler's genius had been responsible for the fact that Germany had had to wage war on only one front in the beginning. A conflict with Russia would mean the entry of a third world power in the war against Germany. Once more, Germany would stand alone against the whole world—and alone on two fronts for the neighboring states were inconsequential.

Hitler pointed out that by 1942-43, which—according to the information available to him—was the earliest date at which Russia would be fully prepared for war, "Germany would have either beaten England or have come to terms with her." But a good many more Luftwaffe attacks were necessary before this could be brought about and if Germany went to war against Russia, at least two thirds of Luftwaffe strength would have to be transferred to the East.

Goering made the consequences clear to Hitler: "The sacrifices made so far by the Luftwaffe in its attacks on England would be in vain; the British aircraft industry would have time to recover; Germany would renounce certain sure victories (Suez, Gibraltar) and with them the possibility of reaching an 'agreement' with England and, thereby, of guiding Russia's armament activity into another channel."

According to another report, Goering continued to "oppose Hitler's plan until the latter said to him: 'Goering, why don't you stop trying to persuade me to drop my plans for Russia? I've made up my mind!' "

Thus, the turning point for the Luftwaffe became inevitable. As Goering expressed it in his appeal to the Fuehrer, "My Fuehrer, the ultimate decision is yours to make. May God guide you and help you to prove your rightness in the face of opposition! I, myself, am forced to oppose your point of view in this respect. May God protect you! But please remember that I cannot be blamed if I am unable to carry out our plans for expanding the Luftwaffe!"

Hitler replied, "You will be able to continue operations against England in six weeks," whereupon Goering pointed out that ". . . the Luftwaffe is the only Wehrmacht branch which has not had a breathing space since the war began. I told you when we first went to war that I was going into battle with my training squads, and now they're all gone." Furthermore, said Goering, "I'm not at all sure that you can beat Russia in six weeks. The ground forces can't fight any more without Luftwaffe support. They're always screaming for the Luftwaffe. There's nothing I'd like better than to have you proven right, but frankly, I doubt that you will be."

The Russian campaign began on 22 June 1941. Its very beginning represented a race against time. And by the advent of winter on the Soviet front (between 6 and 12 December 1941), after which the Russians began their counteroffensive, it was obvious that Germany had lost the race. The beginning of the Russian campaign was a race against time in another respect as well, and in this respect too, Germany lost the race. On 11 December 1941, America officially declared war against Germany; in other words, Goering's fears became reality.

With the beginning of the Russian campaign, the Luftwaffe had a total of 2,000 aircraft in the East, broken down into twenty-nine and one-half bomber, nine and one-third dive-bomber, twenty single-engine fighter, two twin-engine fighter, and two close-support groups, and twelve long-range reconnaissance squadrons. To these must be added five air transport groups, with 150 aircraft, and eight liaison squadrons, with 80 aircraft. In addition, the Army had fourteen long-range reconnaissance squadrons (with 140 aircraft), forty-five short-range reconnaissance squadrons (with 450 aircraft), and eleven liaison squadrons (with 110 aircraft).

The following Luftwaffe strength remained in the West or was engaged in home air defense operations:

In the West: (Third Air Fleet; 660 aircraft)
twelve and one-third bomber groups, six single-engine fighter groups,

one and one-third twin-engine fighter groups, seven long-range reconnaissance squadrons.

In home air defense, Commander Center: (190 aircraft)
one and two-thirds single-engine fighter groups, four and two-thirds twin-engine fighter groups.

In the Mediterranean: (X Air Corps and Air Commander, Africa)
five bomber groups, three dive-bomber groups, one and one-third single-engine fighter groups, one and one-third twin-engine fighter groups, five long-range reconnaissance squadrons.

In Norway: (Fifth Air Fleet, less those units employed in Russia)
one and two-thirds bomber groups, one single-engine fighter group, four long-range reconnaissance squadrons.

As we have seen, Germany's air strength was already fairly widely dissipated. She was engaged in warfare on several fronts.

Heretofore, the Luftwaffe had always been able to cover itself with glory because the duration of its actions and the conditions under which it was operating were such that its weaknesses had no chance to take effect. During the Battle of Britain it had managed to hold its own in a hard fight; in Russia it was simply overwhelmed. The fact that there was no four-engine bomber which could reach and destroy the enemy's armament works (some of which were already located beyond the Ural Mountains), the scarcity of aircraft suitable for close-support operations, the lack of an adequate air transport fleet, the fact that air armament production had been far too small during 1939 and 1940 and had not been materially increased during 1941—all of these weaknesses began to make themselves felt as soon as the war became stationary or threatened to remain at the same stage of relentless, hard fighting.

Today it is a commonly accepted view among students of military history that the reason for Germany's defeat at the hands of the Russian giant was the fact that she made no attempt to carry out strategic air warfare.

The first successful blows which resulted in the destruction of those elements of the Soviet air force located in the vicinity of the front were not followed up by systematically planned and accomplished attacks. Nor was any concentrated attempt made to keep Russian armament works and the transportation network under continuous bombardment. The one time this was tried (in 1943), the forces employed were inadequate in number, and due to the critical situation at the front, soon had to be withdrawn. In any case, it was already too late in the game. On the whole, it can be stated that strategic air warfare played no role in Germany's campaign against Soviet Russia.

Why was this the case? To what extent did this sin of omission affect the subsequent course of events?

There are two things which make it absolutely certain that Luftwaffe leaders intended, from the very beginning, to utilize the newly created air arm in strategic operations in case of war.

In the first place, the Luftwaffe Field Directive on the Conduct of Air Warfare treats strategic air warfare as at least as important as the other two types of aircraft employment.

In the second place, we have seen that Luftwaffe leaders devoted much thought to the development of that type of aircraft which was indispensable to strategic missions. No less a personage than Wever had openly urged the development of a four-engine bomber. The fact that this model was known as the Ural bomber in Luftwaffe circles indicates the probable enemy in any future war.

When we consider the concept of distance implicit in the term Ural bomber, we can only conclude that the Luftwaffe top-level command must have been struck with total blindness when it ordered the project dropped shortly after Wever's sudden death on 3 June 1936—especially in view of the fact that both the Dornier and Junkers works had already built satisfactory test models (the Do-19 and the Ju-89). Shortly afterwards, the Heinkel works was asked to develop a long-range bomber, but the resulting model (the He-177) became buried in a morass of developmental alterations. And since its development was alternately pushed as rapidly as possible and completely relegated to the background, depending upon the political situation and events at the front, the Luftwaffe never had a satisfactory long-range bomber at its disposal, either at the beginning of the war or during any subsequent phase of it. It was true that the first two models, the Do-19 and the Ju-89, while perfectly satisfactory as far as fuselage design was concerned, had relatively weak engines. But this problem could certainly have been solved within the three years remaining before the beginning of the war; and by 1940, or 1941 at the latest, the Luftwaffe would have had its long-range, heavily-armored bomber.

Since the four-engine bomber had been scrapped, however, and the He-177 was hopelessly bogged down, the German Luftwaffe had no suitable instrument with which to carry out strategic attacks on the Soviet armaments industry beyond the Urals. Nor did·the Luftwaffe possess a suitably powerful long-range fighter. Despite the fact that Goering had expressly instructed Udet to push the development of a fighter capable of ranging over all of England (from bases in Germany!), the Messerschmitt plant, which had long enjoyed a virtual monopoly in the manufacture of fighter aircraft, was never able to produce one.

But it was not the lack of suitable instruments alone which was responsible for the fact that the German Luftwaffe, while piously mouthing Douhet, began to conduct the ground-support operations of World War II in a manner less modern than that used in World War I, when the BOGOHL's (bomber units of the Army High Command) were effectively utilized in support actions and were even committed in attacks over London.

Shortly after Wever's death, Jeschonnek began a meteoric rise in the circle of Germany's top-level military leaders. He was an avid champion of the dive-bomber concept as the surest and most economical answer to the problem of bombardment from the air. And it is obvious that the dive-bomber concept of attack could not be realized with a heavy aircraft such as a long-range bomber. Incorrigible until almost the end, Jeschonnek, with his inner aversion to the idea of a four-engine bomber, prevented the development of a long-range bomber. A devotee of tactical warfare from the very beginning, Jeschonnek's own instinctive preferences had been strengthened by his period of service as commanding officer of the Luftwaffe Training Wing, and by the time he joined the General Staff, he had left the Wever concept of air warfare pretty much behind him. It is amazing how soon after the death of the first General Staff Chief, the Luftwaffe turned away from the fundamental principles he represented!

There was another man, however, perhaps the most energetic personality in the entire Luftwaffe, whose words carried a great deal of weight, Baron von Richthofen. As former commander of the Condor Legion, von Richthofen possessed the advantage of firsthand experience in the testing of German aircraft models in combat against enemy air and land forces. His dive-bombers had led the Spanish to ultimate victory over the Communists, and he and Jeschonnek became very close friends. It is very likely that von Richthofen, the Luftwaffe's foremost specialist in close-support operations, did much to strengthen the young General Staff Chief's determination to make direct support of Army operations a decisive factor in achieving a rapid victory on the ground. Von Richthofen was undeniably the dominant personality in the relationship of the two.

The first four campaigns carried out by the German Armed Forces

(Poland, Norway, France, and the Balkans) were perfect examples of Hitler's ideal of the short-term, lightning war. In these campaigns the conduct of strategic air operations against the sources of enemy strength proved to be unnecessary, since the theater of operations was of limited extent. In fact, bombardment of the enemy sources of power would have been highly undesirable, since it would have resulted in extensive destruction in areas which Germany wished to exploit to replenish her own strength. These four campaigns placed the resources of Poland (those located in the German sphere of interest), Norway, the occupied area of France, and the occupied portions of the Balkan countries and Greece at Germany's disposal. Thus, all of these resources were then available to the German military economy and to German transport requirements.

Despite the experience gathered during the Battle of Britain in regard to aircraft range, Germany did not take advantage of its year of preparation for the Russian conflict to alter the organization of Luftwaffe units or to make any changes in the contemplated methods of their employment. The members of the Luftwaffe top-level command apparently were not gifted with sufficient imagination to visualize clearly the potential requirements of a war against Russia, with its enormous geographic extent, and consequently its sharply varying climatic conditions. They were going by established traditions, and the exigencies of administration left no room for new, creative thinking. In addition, of course, we cannot ignore the possibility that the General Staff Chief, blinded by his veneration for Hitler and his unreasoning faith in the latter's genius, may really have believed in Hitler's assurances that the campaign in Russia would also turn out to be a short-term operation.

Taken literally, however, established tradition called for a sudden surprise attack on the enemy's forces in order to paralyze them into inactivity, and an immediate follow-up in the form of direct and indirect air support of ground operations, in order to assure a quick victory for the Army.

The order to attack (Barbarossa) dated 18 December 1940 made the prior attainment of certain ground victories a prerequisite of strategic air operations. And then the Luftwaffe would be utilized only in order to hold enemy potential down to a minimum, *after* the ground campaign had already been won. The Barbarossa order, incidentally, spoke only of a "short campaign."

During the period 22-30 June, the blows which the German Luftwaffe directed against the enemy airfields lying within her reach were completely successful. The Russians allegedly suffered materiel losses amounting to 4,990 aircraft of all types; as a result, the Russian air forces were incapacitated for a number of weeks, at least in the areas assigned to the Army Groups North and Center. In these sectors then, the Luftwaffe had achieved air supremacy; in the sector assigned to the Army Group South, it had air superiority.

Considering the significance of this situation, together with the fact that the Soviet fighter forces were extremely cautious during the period immediately following, one is justified in concluding (without being accused of wishful thinking) that the attacks carried out by the Luftwaffe on those Russian aircraft works (or rather armament works in general) lying within its range were highly successful. At that time the Russians did not yet have the strong antiaircraft artillery with which they were later able to protect their industrial plants, power works, and railway stations.

On the whole, however, the Luftwaffe struck against the Russian air force rather than against the Russian aircraft industry. True, the Russians did sustain considerable aircraft losses thereby; however, the crews were not permanently put out of action. And the Russians were usually successful in managing to remove their aircraft plants (machines and other equipment) from those areas threatened by the German advance into regions where German air attack was out of the question because they lay beyond the range of the German bombers.

Production was soon resumed in the new locations and with it the first step was taken in the establishment of a strong Russian air arm; by the end of the war, its strength—at least in terms of numbers—was significant. This recovery would never have been possible if Germany had been able to accompany her attack on the Russian airfields (carried out by light and medium bombers) with a surprise attack with four-engine bombers against the Russian aircraft plants located near the front, particularly those in Moscow and Voronezh. The fairly desperate situation of the Russian air units assigned to the front must have been an indication of a similar situation in Russian industry. Even the American deliveries, which also would have been more vulnerable to attack by four-engine rather than by twin-engine bombers, would probably not have been able to help the Russians out of their difficulties.

As has been seen, however, the four-engine bomber had been dropped in 1937 and the long-range He-177 was nowhere near ready for employment at the front. In short, Germany did not possess the one weapon which would have had the range, bomb-carrying capacity, and armament strength needed in the present instance. Nevertheless, Germany's medium bombers could also have inflicted serious damage on

Russian armament works, power plants, and traffic centers lying quite far behind the front lines, especially if such bombardment had been carried out at the beginning of hostilities.

There are two commonly used excuses for why this was not done and neither of them is valid. The first of these excuses states that it would not have been possible to combine extensive air support of Army ground operations with the conduct of strategic air warfare. As has been repeatedly pointed out, Hitler's demand for direct air support of the Army in the East clearly implied that at least one tactical air command should be available for each Army group. The activation of these tactical commands, in turn, demanded that Germany's aircraft production (this time, single-engine aircraft) finally be brought up to a level commensurate with an all-out armament effort, in other words, that it be increased much more than was actually the case during the first months of the war and even throughout 1940 and 1941.

According to the plans for Barbarossa, four air corps were to be employed in Russia. Once the production of single-engine aircraft had been increased to the necessary level, the twin-engine aircraft (twenty-eight groups in all) could have been withdrawn and placed under a unified bomber command for commitment in strategic air operations. Even if a part of these twenty-eight groups had been deviated to indirect support actions for the ground forces, the remainder would still have been sufficient for strategic warfare requirements. And a clear separation of tactical and strategic air units, which would have been achieved by the reassignment of the twin-engine bombers, would have done much to clarify the problem of organization and that of the validity of existing concepts regarding the conduct of air warfare. The strategic units would have been freed of the necessity of providing direct support (as opposed to indirect support) for the Army, a mission which they were simply not equipped to fulfill; and at last there would have been sufficient units available which were specifically suited to air operations in the sense advocated by Douhet.

The second excuse given is that the Luftwaffe Field Directive No. 16 required the commitment of *all Luftwaffe strength* during the decisive battle. This is as invalid as the first excuse. Such commitment was rather to be spread over the entire campaign, beginning with the first day of operations and continuing until the campaign had been brought to a successful conclusion, presumably within three months. It is obvious that the Army would have received the all-out Luftwaffe support required by the Barbarossa directive despite the simultaneous launching of strategic air warfare, if armament planning and the training program had been carried out as has been suggested above. On the whole, the degree of support furnished the Army would have been even greater.

It might also be pointed out that a campaign of the contemplated duration (three months) could hardly be termed a decisive battle within the meaning of Directive No. 16. If the enemy's industrial plants were permitted to work on undisturbed during this period, they would provide, as indeed they actually did, a continual stream of materiel reinforcements for the Soviet Army at the front throughout the duration of the "decisive battle." This continuing reinforcement played a significant role in helping the Russian armies to hold out in one of the most decisive campaigns in the history of Russia.

A large Luftwaffe bomber command could and should have been set up! It goes without saying that a part of this large force could have been utilized to provide effective indirect support for the ground forces at points where it might be required.

This force of twenty-eight groups of medium bombers could also have been augmented by the 4th and 27th Bomber Groups, which the Commander in Chief, Luftwaffe, had been forced to retain in the West until the summer of 1941. They would have had excellent operating conditions in the East, especially after early August, when the German forces reached Smolensk. For a time at least, the Commander in Chief, Luftwaffe, would have had a force of thirty-four medium bomber groups at his disposal. Together with single-engine fighters, reconnaissance aircraft, and other special duty machines, there would have been nearly nine full wings, easily enough to form an additional air fleet.

We can hardly imagine what the commitment of a force of this size might have meant in 1941, when Russian antiaircraft artillery was not nearly so effective as it was in 1944, when the IV Air Corps carried out its attacks with frequent success. Each Russian tank, each gun, each airplane, each railway locomotive which could be destroyed while still in the factory saved the German Army serious losses.

The importance of this statement becomes clear when we consider that Soviet Russia, according to estimates made by Eike Middeldorf, produced a total of approximately 150,000 tanks during World War II. And while Russia could commit her entire tank production against Germany and Germany's weak allies (i.e. on a single front), Germany had to spread her production of approximately 25,000 tanks over Russia, the Mediterranean, the Balkans, and—later—the invasion front, not to mention the quota which went to her allies. German destruction of enemy tanks on the Eastern front was purchased at the cost of tremendous effort—by sacrificial commitment of German infantry, far too ill-equipped with armor-piercing weapons; or by the employment, invariably accompanied by heavy losses, of the Luftwaffe. In connection with the latter, the remarkable record achieved by Colonel Rudel deserves special mention—510 kills! In contrast, a single successful air attack on the Russian tank factories would have destroyed the product of several weeks' work all at once and would have been sufficient to stop any further production for some time. It is difficult to stop a rushing stream; its source, however, can be dammed up with relatively little effort.

The fact that the Barbarossa directive did not specifically require strategic air warfare along with direct air support of the ground forces was, admittedly, a serious error on the part of command, and the Army High Command cannot be absolved of at least a portion of the blame for it. If Germany's military leaders had recognized in time the need for a reorganization of Luftwaffe forces and a revitalization of the air armament program, the necessary resources would have been at hand when the need for additional activations became apparent.

It is completely beyond understanding, however, that the Luftwaffe General Staff Chief made no attempt to salvage the situation later on, for it must have been obvious by November 1941 at the latest that the war with Russia could not be concluded in a short campaign but was turning into a long-term struggle whose ultimate duration could not be foreseen. With practically no interference from Germany, Russia had been able to move her armament works out of the path of the German advance to safer locations far to the East. The few strategic attacks carried out by the Luftwaffe in 1941 were isolated incidents.

In Plocher's opinion, the proper course of action in October-November 1941 (when it must have been apparent that the blitzkrieg was doomed to failure) would have been for the Luftwaffe and Army General Staffs to submit a joint recommendation to the Commander in Chief, Wehrmacht, suggesting that operations be interrupted for the moment in order to prepare for an all-out strategic air offensive. During the winter of 1941-42, Plocher continues, a clear organizational delineation between strategic and tactical Luftwaffe units could have been effected, together with a clarification of the command channels involved.

From today's vantage point, the winter of 1941-42 seems to be a very late date for such basic alterations. Still it represented the last possible opportunity to prepare thoroughly for a decisive strategic air offensive.

Reorganization and the new activations which it entailed, represented difficult problems. Its concomitant result, however (increased production in dive-bombers, close-support aircraft, and fighters), would have provided Germany's air armament industry with a tangible goal and would certainly have served as a spur to Milch's ambition and energy. We can assume with a fair degree of certainty that the production goal could have been met at that time, despite the general military situation, without the necessity of Hitler's assigning the Luftwaffe a new priority rating for the allocation of raw materials. The Luftwaffe could have been ready to conduct strategic air warfare against Soviet targets by the fall of 1942. And the effects of strategic warfare would have made themselves felt in a very short time. For one thing, a good deal of Russian antiaircraft artillery would have been tied down far behind the lines and would thus have been kept from commitment at the front. The Luftwaffe close-support forces would have continued to provide even more direct and indirect support for the ground forces, while the long-range bomber wings could have gone on to attack the Russian armaments works and other sources of military strength. The spring of 1943 would have marked the climax of the effectiveness of strategic air operations, and in the meantime the German Army at least would have reaped a number of benefits.

Colonel Fritz Kless, first operations officer and later general staff chief of the Air Command Center (later to become the Sixth Air Fleet), was untiring in his efforts to persuade Luftwaffe leaders of the need for strategic air operations, until finally the Luftwaffe High Command agreed to permit the employment of bomber aircraft against the Russian rubber plant at Yaroslavl and the tank factory at Gorki, an indication of the fact that Jeschonnek had allowed himself to be persuaded shortly before his death. The organization of Luftwaffe forces suitable for strategic air operations into the IV Air Corps was not confirmed until 26 November 1943.

Understandably, no one wanted to admit that this action was being taken far too late to be of any real help. In the meantime, in a study dated 9 November 1943, the Luftwaffe Operations Staff had prepared a fairly realistic appraisal of the situation. Under Point 1, the following statement is made: "Up to and including the attainment of the Dnieper line in the fall of 1941, the German Luftwaffe was properly employed in the Eastern campaign. The defeat of the Soviet air forces and the providing of direct support in ground operations made a rapid advance possible."

From that point on, the study continues, at least a portion of

Luftwaffe strength should have been diverted to operations against the Russian railway lines far behind the front, in order to prevent the evacuation of enemy industry to the rear area, and against those factories still operating within bomber range of the front. The study goes on to say that operations of this sort, as well as the effective bombardment of Moscow and Leningrad, were rendered impossible by the need for continuing close-support actions for the ground forces. As a result, large-scale attacks on enemy industry could be carried out only sporadically (on Voronezh, Stalingrad, Saratov, and Grozny, for example, during the summer of 1943)—although with great success.

As the study indicates, the recovery of the Soviet air forces (as a matter of fact, their achievement of numerical superiority) and *the disappearance of the most rewarding industrial targets from Luftwaffe bomber range,* as a result of the German retreat, soon altered the situation. Point 4 of the study continues: "We have no choice but to admit that we let the most favorable moment slip through our hands; in the meantime the difficulties have become very great. Moreover, our Luftwaffe forces are now tied down more than ever in the East."

This was a bitter admission to make. The Luftwaffe Operations Staff still hoped to be able to "demolish at least the largest Russian armament works in the Moscow-Upper Volga industrial area" with "a relatively small force," a project which was to be given top priority and which would be executed through the employment of new aircraft types (He-177, Ju-290, etc.) which would have to be forthcoming "soon and in adequate numbers."

During the spring of 1944, the IV Air Corps carried out a series of attacks with what, in the words of some of the participants, was "very good success." Soon after the Russian breakthrough on the front sector assigned to the Army Group Center (on 18 June 1944), these attacks had to be discontinued, the 4th Bomber Wing flying its last bombardment mission during the night of 22-23 July 1944.

Strategic air warfare, begun far too late, had to be broken off because the Eastern armies, threatened with decimation, were beginning to scream for help, and the bombers were assigned to direct ground-support operations.

That was the end. All later plans for strategic air operations in the East—born of a hopelessly unrealistic optimism—were doomed to frustration.

Russian aircraft used in June of 1941 were then already obsolete. The loss of most of their front line planes during the first few months of fighting was largely a result of this obsolescence. As one German commander recalled, "At the beginning of the great German offensive in the East, the ground troops saw only flights of three or four reconnaissance planes, individual bomber squadrons, and only a few fighters. . . . They quickly became victims of German fighters." These massive losses might have proven disastrous except that the Soviet aircraft industry, wisely limiting its aircraft construction program to the models required for the defense and support of ground operations, succeeded in producing a large number of reliable, if not outstanding, aircraft. These planes were primarily fighters, ground-attack, and light bomber aircraft, all of which could be quickly constructed in mass.

As early as the autumn of 1941 the first IL-2 (Ilyushin) "Stormovik" ground-attack plane appeared at the front. This type, which soon became available in large numbers, was ideally suited, by virtue of its rugged construction and excellent armor protection, for air support missions. Frequently formations of Me-109's and even Fw-190's expended their entire allocations of ammunition firing at them without bringing them down. German antiaircraft commanders noted that the Stormoviks could be shot down by light and medium antiaircraft artillery only if direct hits were scored and soon began to make greater use of the heavy (8.8 cm) gun against Soviet aircraft. IL-2 planes were most vulnerable when fired upon from above or from the rear by explosive ammunition. The tail and control surfaces disintegrated readily if struck by gunfire. At ranges of 900 to 1,200 feet, light antiaircraft guns had little effect upon them, although successful hits were scored by medium or larger calibre guns which happened to strike the engines, tail assemblies, or control surfaces of these planes. The Stormovik was somewhat sluggish in performance; it might have been more maneuverable except for its weak power unit.

Fighter planes produced by the Russians during the war were generally good and were rapidly improved. They were simple in construction and in operation and were consequently very well suited for the training of Russian fliers, who normally had little technical knowledge. The handling and climbing performances of these planes were excellent at lower altitudes, although a very sharp decrease in performance was noted above 20,000 feet. In horizontal flight Russian fighters were vastly inferior to their German counterparts until the last part of the war.

After the autumn of 1944, fighters produced in the Soviet Union were equal in performance to the best planes in the German Air Force. The last fighter plane manufactured by the Russians during the war, the Yak-3, a fast single-engine fighter and ground-attack aircraft, was even superior to the Me-109.* Few highly advanced types of aircraft, such as the Yak-3, actually appeared over the front lines until the last months before Germany's capitulation. Some Pe-2** planes were observed as early as 1942, operating as tactical bombers. The Pe-2 was well constructed and definitely superior to the older twin-engine reconnaissance-bombers, the DB-3's. It met the most satisfactory requirements in speed, armament, and flight characteristics, and its great tendency to pick up speed rapidly during dive-bombing operations made it a "hot" aircraft. The Pe-2, being difficult to set afire and having good rear firepower, was one of Russia's most formidable planes. An improved type appeared somewhat later, the IL-4, a model patterned after the DB-3. In the closing months of 1944 a further, still more advanced model of this plane emerged, known as the TU-2, which could carry heavier payloads than the IL-4 and which, with a top speed of 348 miles per hour, was manifestly faster.†

Specific reconnaissance type aircraft were not seen on the Russian front during the early phases of the war since these missions were generally performed by the Pe-2, by fighters such as the IL-2, and by the American-made Douglas A-20 attack plane. The U-2, a slow but unusual type of aircraft, was a reconnaissance airplane, but was chiefly reserved for use in night nuisance raids because of its astonishing imperviousness to shellfire.

Besides their own planes, the Russians also utilized many makes of aircraft produced by their allies, thousands of which they soon acquired. The overwhelming part of this support came from the United States, most of the models received being the P-39 "Airacobra," P-63 "Kingcobra," and Douglas A-20.‡ These planes did not enable Russian pilots to achieve materially higher standards of flying performance. Disliking complex mechanisms, the Russians usually stripped the planes of all "superfluous" devices. Identical procedures were followed with respect to captured aircraft acquired from the Germans. Soviet leaders attempted, nevertheless, to secure fully operable and equipped enemy airplanes, especially the Ju-87 (Stuka), the Me-109, and later the

---

* The Yak-3 was absolutely superior to both the Me-109G and the Fw-190A at altitudes below 11,000 feet, but was greatly inferior to the Fw-190 at higher altitudes.

** The Pe-2 was a Soviet twin-engine reconnaissance dive bomber and bomber aircraft which saw widespread use during World War II.

† The TU-2 also had a service ceiling of 36,000 feet, which was about 6,500 feet above the service ceiling of the IL-4.

‡ Between 22 June 1941 and 20 September 1945, the Soviet Union received 15,000 airplanes from the United States. The "Kingcobras" were equipped, at Russian request, with direction-finding loop antennae.

Fw-190, which they intended to copy, a procedure in which the Russians were known to be highly successful.

The problem of spare parts was a matter of serious concern to the Soviet authorities throughout the war. This was largely the cause of the rather low number of Russian aircraft which were operational, a figure which was still further reduced by heavy demands upon combat air units. The continued use of wood and other inflammable materials in the construction and repair of their aircraft, stemming from acute shortages of aluminum and other critical metals, made a definite impact upon the morale of Soviet airmen, and gave the German fliers a great advantage for a time.

Russian airfields were generally primitive in construction with abnormally short runways. Many of them, scarcely comparable to the crudest German emergency fields, were devoid of most of the refinements found in even the simplest Western combat airfields. Barracks, steel mats, reinforced concrete or cement runways, or hardstands were unknown. Russian airmen expected this situation but it was a great novelty to the Germans.

Like other Russian arms, antiaircraft weapons were ruggedly constructed and simple in design. They were almost invariably used without radio range or direction-finding equipment and few of them possessed workable fire-direction devices. Soviet antiaircraft machine guns and light and medium artillery were equal in performance to German weapons, but their heavy antiaircraft guns were ineffective in comparison with their Western counterparts and were far from satisfactory, having severe range limitations which rendered them ineffective above 19,600 feet. The standard German heavy antiaircraft gun (*Flugabwehrkanone* or *Flak* (could fire up to 45,000 feet and was capable of highly effective fire at altitudes of 30,000 feet, all in rapid fire.

Every Russian Army Corps at the beginning of the war had, in addition to its normal complement of antiaircraft machine guns, one or two light or heavy antiaircraft battalions. A general reserve of eight antiaircraft regiments was also on hand consisting of battalions of three or four firing batteries each. Within the divisions, each artillery regiment possessed an organic light or heavy antiaircraft battery. Other army units had their own defenses against aerial attack, chiefly light and heavy antiaircraft batteries with antiaircraft machine guns. Besides these units, there were a few railway antiaircraft batteries, some armored railway trains with antiaircraft guns, some separate, permanently emplaced antiaircraft weapons, and a home force of fixed antiaircraft defenses. With the exception of the last two categories, only half of the Russian antiaircraft units were motorized.

Antiaircraft forces existing at the opening of the war were increased fourfold in accordance with the needs for a newly activated and expanding military organization. The Russian high command had begun the task of re-equipping its air and air defense forces at the opening of World War II.

The individual equipment of the Russian soldier was good to excellent in quality. Years of experience in an adverse climate had taught Soviet supply agencies to provide adequate clothing and boots for winter. Tools and uniforms were practical and well suited to combat requirements. With these assets added to the robust health and hardiness of the average Russian, the Germans had a formidable opponent indeed.

Russian air operations were monotonous and stereotyped in character, indicating a limited imagination in tactical matters and rather low standards in technical control facilities. Inflexible leadership made on-the-spot changes in air operations difficult, and the principle of blind obedience hampered things even more. Russian aeronautical weaknesses were not merely consequences of the devastating early blows by the Luftwaffe, but were also products of a weak affinity for aviation and an inadequate training program. Frequent absences of enlightened air staffs compounded the problems. An exaggerated emphasis upon close support also limited the scope of Russian air operations.

Soviet air missions were chiefly results of developing circumstances and expediencies rather than of deliberate planning by Russian leaders, many of whom knew little about the use of airpower but nearly all of whom were careful to observe the fine points of subordination to their superiors. Russian Air Force objectives were centered upon infantry and artillery positions and, late in the war, armored units. Because of this, German leaders like Galland never considered the Soviet Air Force to be anything more than an appendage of the Red Army, the artillery arm of the air.

Fighter operations were almost wholly defensive in character no matter what type of German air unit they might oppose; perhaps this was a manifestation of an acknowledged technical and tactical inferiority and of the principal missions of providing support for the army. Russian fighters attempted to establish local air superiorities by escorting ground-attack and bomber units, although they were seldom successful.

Doctrinal and tactical limitations of the Soviet fighter arm throughout the war indicated that it was incapable of embarking upon offensive operations. Fighters engaged in battle with German fighters only if they could not otherwise avoid it, preferring to pounce upon crippled, nonfighter aircraft. "Swarms" of Russian fighters, usually about five in a swarm, were frequently seen after 1941, flying in reasonably good order and with proper intervals, a possible indication that they had recognized the effectiveness of such formations in German air units. In general, however, their rather poor formation patterns enabled German pilots to identify them at long distances.

While Russian pilots appeared timid as individuals they could sometimes be daring in a group. In such cases some fighter pilots became so intent upon their targets and so stubborn in their efforts to bring down the enemy that they rammed German aircraft. Some Russians even developed a technique which enabled them to damage enemy planes with comparatively little damage to their own aircraft.

Large air strikes by forty bombers or more were rarely made by Soviet flying units, and even then the actual attacks were carried out singly. Retaliatory bombing, such as was seen in the West, was seldom attempted, and when it was its effects could hardly be compared with heavy German bombardments, and even less so with the massive, saturation bombing carried out by the Western Allies. The idea of saturation bombing appeared to be unknown to the Soviet Air Force. Russian bomber pilots used only a few simple formations because of their limited aviation skill. Once their formations were broken or the lead planes knocked down, the remainder of the units could be quickly scattered and eliminated.

In order to escape German fighters, Russian bombers began to attack German Air Force bases from altitudes above 16,000 feet. A single bomber, or perhaps two, would appear after daylight in the morning or well before sunset in the evening, dropping a few fragmentation bombs. Sometimes small groups of bombers would participate in such flights. Few of the bombs fell near the targets and, in several instances, they dropped within the Soviet lines. Night bombing attacks by the Soviet Air Force were equally ineffective. Carelessness in the bombing runs and poor marksmanship characterized both bomber and fighter-bomber operations of the Russian Air Force. Most Soviet fliers tried to release their bombs as soon as possible over the German air bases in order to flee as the German antiaircraft guns opened fire. Such piecemeal, unsystematic efforts made little impression upon German Air Force personnel.

German leaders were continually amazed that Russian ground and air units never singled out Luftwaffe searchlight and directional centers for attacks. They interpreted this as an indication of a failure of Russian commanders to appreciate the significance of such stations to the overall campaign. Soviet leaders also lagged in producing antitank aircraft, presumably because they were slow in learning the procedures for attacking armored equipment. This failure permitted German tanks to operate in relative safety from air attacks throughout most of the war.

Among the many missed opportunities of the Soviet forces, none was more striking than the failure of the Russian Air Force to follow up the retreating German forces in the withdrawal from Moscow during the winter of 1941-42. Any sort of systematic assault upon those retreating columns, which were then choking the few available traffic arteries, would have dealt a heavy blow to the Wehrmacht.

The great initial successes of Germany in Russia were partially due to the failure of the Soviet long-range reconnaissance arm. Following the early damage of 1941 upon the Russian air forces, their tactical reconnaissance units were the only organizations capable of fulfilling combat missions. But even this service was deficient in many respects. Training of reconnaissance pilots was basically faulty and technological and operational weaknesses plagued reconnaissance units until the closing part of the war. Long-range reconnaissance flights usually were not carried out in sufficient depth to provide good intelligence data, while photo-interpretation work was so poor in the Soviet Air Force that missions were seldom made solely on the basis of this information. For example, in April of 1944, a Russian Pe-2 reconnaissance plane appeared over Daugavpils, Latvia, and was humorously dubbed "the reconnaissance duty officer" by German airmen because of the regularity of its arrival between 0700 and 0800 hours. This plane obviously made a practice of scouting German airfields and installations near the Dvina River, but despite the frequency of these visits no air attacks or bombardments followed.

Another area of Russian deficiency could be found in the unfavorable flying techniques employed by Soviet liaison pilots. Russians often used their liaison aircraft to transport important partisan and military personnel, which made these planes prime targets for the German Air Force. Painted to match the landscape, the planes were difficult to observe from above, but without fighter cover they were extremely vulnerable to German attacks. So many of them were soon shot down that Russian generals switched to fast bombers or fighters with fighter escorts for their personal transportation. Luftwaffe leaders noted that Soviet liaison pilots invariably used railroad tracks as their guides, flying along with their left landing gear above the right-hand line of track. Although this mode of operation became widely known among German air units, with the consequence that hundreds of Russian liaison planes were shot down, especially by Fw-190 fighter-bombers, Russian liaison pilots continued to stick to the railroad tracks without fighter cover.

At the outbreak of the war, the Soviet planes were largely obsolete and the older models were rapidly destroyed by the German Air Force. The situation was so bad that a single German fighter, if well handled, could ward off large numbers of older Russian fighter planes. The line fighters in the U.S.S.R. in 1941 were the I-15 and the slightly improved I-153 biplanes, stemming from a 1932 design. With top speeds under 200 miles per hour they were no match for the Me-109's of the Luftwaffe. Another radial-engine plane, the "Rata" I-16 low-wing monoplane (derived from a Boeing design), which had been employed in large numbers during the Spanish Civil War, was widely used and became the mainstay of the Soviet fighter arm in 1941. They were highly maneuverable planes, but their speed left much to be desired, and since only the best Russian pilots could fly well enough to take advantage of their fine turning qualities, the Germans made short shrift of them. Most serious of all was the fact that these models caught fire easily if struck from above or from the side. Efforts to fireproof them by applying coats of artificial, fireproof resin to the surfaces were unsuccessful.

American P-40's were as maneuverable as German fighters, but since they were inferior in speed and climbing performances Soviet pilots did not favor them. The Bell P-39 Airacobra and the P-63 Kingcobra were capable fighters and were highly popular with Russian pilots. During the last two years of the war, Russian fighter planes were generally superior to those sent to them by their Western Allies under lend-lease, but they remained deficient in climbing power and maneuverability at higher altitudes and never overtook Germany's top fighters in diagonal diving speeds. Considering their fine handling qualities they were about equal to the German planes in the field in 1944. In fact, the Yak-3 was superior to German planes at low and medium altitudes. Few of these planes appeared on the front, however.

Russian bombing missions were carried out by IL-4, Mitchell B-25, Douglas Boston A-20, and Pe-2 aircraft. These planes were maneuverable and well suited for medium bombing activities, but they were far too light for strategic purposes and therefore were used mainly for tactical purposes.

The standard ground-attack plane for the Russian Air Force was the well-armored IL-2 Stormovik, which was highly vulnerable to fighter attacks from the rear, although its armor protected it very well against ground fire. It might have been a more effective aircraft had not Soviet leaders persisted in doubling its payload of bombs so that its good flying characteristics were considerably diminished.

The aircraft instruments used by the Russians, such as bombsights, radio direction-finding equipment, generators, and compasses, were as crude as their flares and ammunition, and most of them were obsolete. Even the American delivery of innumerable radio units and the American outfitting of meteorological stations failed to cause a sudden improvement in Russian communications. This was principally the result of a critical shortage of personnel capable of manning such stations and equipment. Control tower installations were unheard of in Soviet ground organizations and radio and electrical apparatus were usually nonexistent. When units took off it was reminiscent of the old flying squadrons of World War I, which operated from primitive flying fields and communicated by a wave of the hand or a tip of the wings. Even normal field telephone equipment was absent from most Soviet airfields.

The best-known large transmitting station was at Moscow. Russians continued to make broadcasts from this station long after it had been identified by the German Air Force, and kept it in operation until the latter part of the war. In the meantime it was used as an orientation point by German fliers.

When Russian squadrons were finally outfitted with radios, they came under the control of air-direction teams. Air-to-air communications were notably absent in Russian units, but transmissions in the clear by air-direction teams were not necessarily helpful. Because of notoriously poor radio discipline among Russian air and air-direction units, the appearance of German fighters invariably caused a medley of communications, profuse with mutual recriminations.

In summary then, the Soviet Union was badly surprised by the speed and power manifested by Germany in its blitzkrieg defeat of Poland in 1939. As a result, the Russians immediately and furtively inaugurated a program for the modernization of their army and air force. Soviet fears and anxieties were demonstrated by their sudden seizure of a number of independent adjacent areas—Finland, the Baltic States, and portions of southeastern Europe—and by their efforts to remove and revamp the entire Soviet war industry. When the first units of the German Wehrmacht rolled across the Russian frontiers, the Soviets had already taken steps to improve their air and ground defenses.

Russia's early losses were enormous. In aircraft alone she lost more than 4,000 in the first week of the war. The carnage continued all through the late summer and autumn, raising the tolls of Russian prisoners and destroyed equipment to incredible figures. In late October Hitler mistakenly announced that the Soviet Union was in its "death throes." The arrival of an early and exceptionally cold winter soon brought the situation into better perspective. The Soviet Union had indeed suffered heavy losses but these losses were not decisive. The reactions of Soviet air and ground units to German air attacks had made many of its enemy's victories costly and time consuming, and time was of the essence for the German Army and Air Force. Possessing a thorough knowledge of their home terrain and a mastery of the arts of camouflage, deception, and improvisation, Soviet troops were able to keep their own forces in the war and to have them at least partially intact for later offensives. The Germans, fighting in an environment about which they knew little, under conditions for which they were grossly unprepared, and against an enemy which they had seriously underrated, found themselves forced to adopt many of the Russian techniques for their own protection and survival.

Soviet leaders learned to compensate for their deficiencies by arranging their air and ground operations within a framework of conditions which tended to favor their comparatively untrained but expanding armed forces. Russian reactions to air attacks seemed to the Luftwaffe to be of minor importance when Wehrmacht offensives were in full swing, but as these drives bogged down, Russian measures could no longer be ignored, even on a local basis. With the lengthening of the Russian campaign, German Air Force leaders grudgingly admitted that they faced an extremely clever, ruthless, and able opponent, who cunningly understood how to equalize his chances against an enemy possessing greater tactical and strategic sophistication.

Many of the Russian reactions to German air power were copied from German tactics, and were valuable in helping Soviet forces to nullify enemy air transport, combat, and even air defense operations. As a result, when the Russian ground forces went over to the offensive their advances were even more rapid than they would normally have been. The Luftwaffe then found itself caught up in a giant cause-and-effect circle. Offensives of the Red Army resulted in the conquest of scores of German air bases and forced German bomber squadrons still farther from vital strategic targets. At the same time, Soviet advances threw the

German Army into a series of critical situations requiring immediate air support, which tied the German Air Force even more closely to ground operations and tactical problems and hampered any serious strategic efforts. Yet, even those support operations were unsatisfactory in many cases because of heavy personnel and equipment losses within the Luftwaffe.

Since neither the Russian Army nor Air Force had been decisively defeated in the field, both were able to regain the initiative, and even relatively weak Russian air organizations continued to affect German operations in the East. Russian air units supplied partisans, coordinated Red Army operations, and when conditions permitted, harassed the Luftwaffe. It would, however, be a grave mistake to assume that the defeat of the German armed forces was largely a result of Soviet air power, since World War II was a period in which the Russians were just awakening to a realization of the potentialities of air power. Even the Germans were principally concerned with the operations of armies and army groups on the battlefield, where the major decisions were unfolding. The Russian Air Force was, nevertheless, a factor which materially contributed to stem the tide of battle and start Germany on its road to defeat.

It should be borne in mind that many Soviet operations were timed to coincide with the blows landed by the Allies in the West and in the Mediterranean area. The three-front war could only have the effect of dissipating the German armed forces. Despite the pressing need for air support by army units on the Eastern Front, the Luftwaffe, after 1942, was even more urgently required for the defense of the homeland against the massive air power of Great Britain and the United States. Having failed to stifle the influx of lend-lease equipment into the Soviet Union or to destroy the Russian war industry (especially the aircraft industry), the Luftwaffe was obliged to face more formidable odds as the war progressed, unfortunately at the precise time when Germany's demands for air defense became most critical.

These factors combined to thin out and eventually nullify the best efforts of the German Air Force. During the latter stages of the war its operations were sporadic in character and extremely temporary in effect. The Luftwaffe, harassed on three fronts and over the Reich, almost isolated from its sources of petroleum—with the exception of the heavily damaged synthetic industry—short of aircraft, and suffering grievous personnel losses, was compelled to commit its remaining fliers in hundreds of futile air defense actions against enemies with overwhelming numerical superiorities. It thereby lost its only available group of capable pilots, many of whom had, until then, survived the war from its inception in 1939.

Because of Soviet camouflage, deception, and improvisation the German Air Force was unable to stop the steady flow of arms and equipment to the Russian forces at the front, the infiltration of Russian troop units into German occupied areas, and the menace of partisan activity. Active and passive Soviet defense measures prevented Luftwaffe units from accomplishing needed logistical support of entrapped German units and increased the steady rate of attrition within the German Air Force. The success of Russian reactions is attested by the German employment of fighter cover for all bombing, dive-bombing, destroyer, and airlift operations, in the call up of reservists and instructor personnel to fill the gaps in the Luftwaffe in the East, in the increasingly urgent demands for fighters at the front to counter Russian actions, and finally, in the transition of the German Air Force to an almost purely defensive arm as the Soviet Air Force achieved air superiority.

As events show, Russian reactions to German Air Force operations, however primitive and makeshift in character, and however crude they might have first appeared to be to their more enlightened Western opponents, proved throughout the course of the war to be highly efficient, effective, and ultimately an important factor in the defeat of Germany.

20
Stalingrad

THE HISTORY OF OPERATIONS at Stalingrad will always remain a psychological and military riddle.

Since the end of August 1942, fighting had been going on for the possession of Stalingrad, where the German Sixth Army was involved in a difficult frontal attack against a large city which became all the more impenetrable as its factories and apartment houses were turned into ruins that provided ideal cover for the defenders. The Germans were unable to control the Volga, and the Russians continued to bring supplies and reinforcements to their hard-pressed units by way of the river. German forces were unable to penetrate into the area east of the Volga. Those units which had marched so proudly over the Don at the beginning of August made no attempt at all to disrupt supply lines to the defenders of Stalingrad by sending a task force over the Volga—or perhaps they were no longer strong enough to do so.

In the meantime, in its third month the battle for Stalingrad raged on without bringing a decision in the form of incontestable possession of the city. Strangely enough, the battle of Stalingrad failed to remind either Hitler and his advisors or the officers most intimately concerned, Generaloberst von Paulus, Commander in Chief of the Sixth Army, and his General Staff Chief, General Arthur Schmidt, of the action at Verdun in 1916. There, Germany's Western armies were sacrificed on the altar of bloody frontal attack. Memory of Verdun certainly should have served as a warning at Stalingrad. Generaloberst Freiherr von Richthofen, of the Luftwaffe, seemed to be the only one who was unduly disturbed by what was happening at Stalingrad.

Somehow, one cannot escape the feeling that the Germans were paralyzed like rabbits before a snake, in the face of coming events in the East.

After all, had not the Commander in Chief, Luftwaffe, been informed of the fact that a large Russian force was gathering east of the Don River? What did he order in the way of countermeasures? Is not Plocher perfectly right when he points out that the establishment of the Luftwaffe Command Don, ostensibly created to come to the aid of von Richthofen's Fourth Air Fleet in the Voronezh area, was approved in reality in order to provide Korten—in high favor with the Luftwaffe High Command—with an appointment as commanding general? Strange that personal vanity could still play a role in the face of the danger approaching from the Russian steppes! According to estimates made by Plocher, the Luftwaffe High Command could have given the Fourth Air Fleet a few more reinforcements in its battle to hold the Don front, if the Luftwaffe Command Don had not been established for Korten.

To be sure, Plocher's estimates took even half-groups into account, as indeed they had to, for the original estimates made during 1939 and 1940 had been far too low. Germany's armament, as a result, was worse than inadequate. During the Russian campaign Germany simply did not possess the necessary materiel and personnel reserves which must be held in readiness, prepared for immediate action in just such critical situations. Inasmuch as Germany had entrusted Rumanian, Italian, and Hungarian troops with operations on sectors of the front which were of vital importance to the southern wing of the German Army, the least she could have done would have been to provide these troops with effective air cover. Ideally, such cover should have extended far beyond the front into enemy territory, and should have been capable of so dispersing enemy troop assemblies that they had no chance to develop into the serious threat which they represented on 19 November 1942.

The Luftwaffe High Command had administered; it had not led. Apparently it had relied completely on Hitler's proverbial good fortune and on the uncanny intuition which had already brought Germany so many victories. In any case, the Luftwaffe—assigned the mission of providing air cover for the entire southern wing of Germany's Eastern armies in two opposing directions (the Caucasus and Stalingrad), and this with a single air fleet (the Fourth) and the relatively weak Luftwaffe Command Don—found itself in a desperate position between the catastrophe taking place at the bend of the Don and the growing threat of disaster all the way along the line to the Caucasus, where another German army group was already involved in heavy fighting.

To outline the individual events very briefly:

The Russian breakthroughs at Serafymovich and Kletskaya on 19 November, followed by successful storming of the line held by the Rumanian Fourth Army south of Stalingrad, resulted in the encirclement of the German Sixth Army, completed by the afternoon of 22 November. The Sixth Army had remarkably little on hand in the way of food, medicine, and ammunition supplies; moreover, although the danger of a Soviet breakthrough along one or both of the Rumanian-held flanks must have been recognized as ever-present, the Sixth Army had made no definite plans to go into effect automatically in the case of such a breakthrough.

The clear-sighted Commander in Chief of Army Group B, Generalfeldmarschall von Weichs, suggested to Hitler immediately that the Sixth Army should fight its way out of encirclement. It was up to Hitler to make the final decision. Unfortunately, the Sixth Army Command was playing with the idea of digging in for the winter and having itself supplied from the air. In any case, von Weichs' eminently reasonable recommendation for an immediate breakout found no clear echo on the part of Sixth Army leaders.

It is totally irrelevant for this study whether it was Goering or Jeschonnek whom Hitler consulted first in regard to the Luftwaffe's ability to keep Stalingrad supplied from the air. The fact remains that a top-level Luftwaffe commander committed the Luftwaffe to air supply operations for Stalingrad instead of pointing out firmly at the very beginning that such operations could not be carried out.

In the long run, the frightening thing about this decision is that it could have been made without a single qualified dissenter raising his voice. If von Weichs and Zeitzler had found firm and articulate support for their recommendations, then Hitler might have been saved from the pitfall into which he stumbled at Stalingrad—namely the temptation, in his subsequent conduct of the war, to override or ignore the advice of expert counselors.

The Luftwaffe, which after all was the agency most affected by the decision, certainly ought to have derived sufficient warning from its earlier air-supply actions at Kholm and Demyansk. It ought to have had on hand, for immediate reference, lists of the losses incurred by those two actions; it ought long since to have prepared a study of all the pros and cons, with appropriate documentation. If this material had been available, the Luftwaffe would have been in a position to give an unqualified and well-documented "no" as answer (unless, of course, an air-supply mission were ordered as a "must"), if Hitler had not been willing to accept a categorical "impossible!" from Goering. It may well be asked why the Commander in Chief, Luftwaffe, maintained a military history branch!

The origin of the disaster at Stalingrad, however, was inherent in the personnel makeup of the Luftwaffe long before the Sixth Army was given up for lost. Goering, made uneasy and insecure by Hitler's growing bitterness at the Luftwaffe's failure to stop the highly successful British night raids, was all too easily tempted to promise anything in order to prove that the Luftwaffe was ready and able to perform. Jeschonnek's idealistic concept of the Luftwaffe's highest mission as unreserved obedience to Hitler's will kept him from following the dictates of his own common sense and simply refusing to agree to the Stalingrad operation. Even von Richthofen, one of the most realistic men in the Luftwaffe, when he was informed of the decision to attempt what he considered to be an impossible airlift operation, had only the following resigned comment to make: "We have only one chance to cling to; so far the Fuehrer has always been right, even when none of us could understand his actions and most of us had strongly advised against them."

Despite heroic efforts, the Luftwaffe was unable to keep the promise made by its Commander in Chief. Only one time, on 19 December, did it succeed in bringing as many as 289 tons of supplies into the encircled area with a total of 154 machines. Otherwise the tonnage figures are considerably lower, apart from the fact that there were days on which weather conditions or military developments prevented any aircraft from approaching Stalingrad. The significance of these figures becomes clear when we consider that the Sixth Army needed delivery of 550 tons each day if it was to maintain itself at all. During the period 22 November 1942 through 16 January 1943, an average of approximately 100 tons per day was flown in. If we extend this period to 31 January or 2 February 1943 (the final tragedy of the Sixth Army), the average is even lower—due to loss of the airfields at Pitomnik and Gumrak—despite the untiring energy of Milch, who was placed in charge of the Stalingrad airlift on 15 January and given all-encompassing authority to carry it out.

Its heroic efforts in vain, the Luftwaffe lost nearly 500 aircraft (total loss) during the period 24 November 1942 through 2 February 1943. This figure was made up of the following:

266	Ju-52's
42	Ju-86's
165	He-111's
9	FW-200's
5	He-177's
1	Ju-290

Personnel losses amounted to approximately 1,000 men (flight crew personnel).

The VIII Air Corps, previously so successful, met its first defeat in attempting to carry out air supply operations for the encircled Sixth Army. All in all, the Fourth Air Fleet retired from Stalingrad sadly chastened and considerably depleted in strength.

The training program suffered enormously from the loss of aircraft and even more from the loss of qualified instructional personnel, many of whom failed to return. Those officers who had recognized the mission's utter futility from the beginning, but who had had a hand in the tremendous sacrifices made in the desperate effort to accomplish it, were depressed and discouraged beyond words.

It should now be considered just why the catastrophe at Stalingrad, which resulted in the loss of an entire German army, was a turning point for the subsequent course of the war and just why it was so significant for the Luftwaffe.

Military history contains countless instances in which entire armies were destroyed without making ultimate victory impossible for their fatherlands. The Russians themselves, whose armies survived far more serious catastrophes during 1941, are perhaps the best example of this. The history of antiquity provides still another example, the Battle of Cannae.

Just what are the factors which determine whether a catastrophe is to become a link in the chain of ultimate disaster or—as was the case at Cannae—a first step upwards towards the winning of the war? The determining factor would seem to be, more than anything else, the way in which the catastrophe is received, i.e., what conclusions are drawn from it.

To return to the example of the Battle at Cannae: the reaction of the Roman Senate and the Roman people to the defeat at Cannae will always remain one worthy of emulation. Without any loss in dignity, all possible preparations were made in order to avert the worst effects of the catastrophe. Steps were taken to mobilize every ablebodied man; changes were made in the traditional methods of command; a singleness of purpose became apparent in the government of the state. In short, the Roman people went forth out of the crucible of catastrophe to a new victory, transformed, hardened, and purified.

As far as Germany was concerned, this is not what happened after Stalingrad. There were no measures designed to effect total mobilization; the ineffective system of command—whereby officers were manipulated like marionettes from the Rastenburg headquarters—was not curtailed but confirmed. The Stalingrad catastrophe had indeed awakened Hitler's distrust—unfortunately not towards his own policies but towards the generals of his armies. Stalingrad could have created a transformation in Hitler and his military staff; there is no evidence that it did so.

If Germany's leaders had been cognizant of all the ramifications of Stalingrad—this strategic error, this source of indescribable suffering and bitter unhappiness for so many—then they might have realized that the German people, if properly guided, still had it within their power to develop a tremendous potential energy. At the same time, they might have realized that it was time to turn the Russian campaign into a crusade to liberate the Russian peoples—as well as the Estonians, the Latvians, and the Lithuanians—from Bolshevism. One cannot begin to imagine how far-reaching the effects of such a crusade might have been!

And the Luftwaffe?

Is it possible that Goering and Jeschonnek could have failed to be aware of the urgent necessity for an all-out effort in the air armament and pilot training programs, or of the crying need for the establishment of a reserve force? Must it not have been obvious to them that without these steps the Luftwaffe was irrevocably doomed to disintegration? Can they have failed to realize that their only hope lay in being scrupulously realistic in the advice and information they gave to Hitler, even if it meant their becoming personae non gratae? Why did they make no attempt to present their Supreme Commander with tangible documentation of the impossibility of carrying out air-supply operations for the Sixth Army? Why did they not make it absolutely clear to him that the Luftwaffe could not possibly survive another airlift action—especially one which was not really justifiable in point of its potential effectiveness? Would it not have been better for them to risk the loss of prestige and position than permit themselves to become responsible for another costly disaster?

Under existing conditions, such an attitude of self-sacrifice was unthinkable; the spirit prevailing within the Luftwaffe command hierarchy would have to have been an entirely different one. True comradeship and a genuine spirit of leadership would have been possible only if Luftwaffe leaders had succeeded in banishing the prevailing attitude, at best one of indifference and at worst one of active dissatisfaction and dissension. Instead, as the reader may be surprised to learn, precisely during the weeks of the Stalingrad airlift, Jeschonnek and von Seidel were barely on speaking terms. As a matter of fact, all through the war the Quartermaster General (von Seidel) and the Chief of the Luftwaffe

General Staff met only when it was absolutely necessary! Strangely enough, Stalingrad was never visited by Goering, Jeschonnek, or von Seidel. Instead, from 15 January on, Milch—placed in charge of all the air-supply operations by Hitler—stood alone at the front, a sort of whipping boy for the others.

Did the Luftwaffe High Command make any changes in its strategic planning as a result of the tragedy at Stalingrad? There is no evidence that this was the case. Apparently, not even Stalingrad was sufficient to awaken in Luftwaffe leaders a determination to provide Germany with such an impenetrable air cover that her armament program and the lives of her citizens would be safe.

We know that Goering was overcome by a fit of hysterical weeping as the reports of the Stalingrad debacle reached him. This is presumably an indication of the sympathy, and perhaps guilt, which he felt in the face of the sufferings of Germany's soldiers. Far more significant than sympathy, however, would have been a manly deed of resistance, requiring the sacrifice of personal prestige, a willingness to renounce certain comforts and to accept certain inconveniences. The Commander in Chief, Luftwaffe, in his blind selfishness and moral weakness, was incapable of such resistance. Nor did Jeschonnek find in the events at Stalingrad an inspiration to rise above himself and to enforce a spirit of cooperation among Luftwaffe leaders. To be sure, it was late in the day; yet true singleness of purpose might still have saved the Luftwaffe in the crises to come.

In summary, the events at Stalingrad did absolutely nothing to improve, or even to change, the situation existing within the hierarchy of the Luftwaffe command.

Not only did Germany's military leaders fail to draw positive conclusions from the Stalingrad airlift, they even drew some negative ones. And this is what made it an evil omen for Hitler and the Luftwaffe.

Hitler, in his desperate eagerness to prevent the Russians from recapturing any sector of the front for fear that he might lose what territory he had already won, ordered his troops to hold out until it was too late for them to escape encirclement. And once a force was encircled, he invariably ordered defensive operations to the last man rather than an immediate attempt to break out. It is interesting to observe the changes apparent in the Soviet and German conduct of operations during 1942 and afterwards. During 1941, the Russians sacrificed entire armies to enemy encirclement with the categorical order to hold out at all costs. By the time the Germans launched their summer offensive in 1942, Soviet military leaders had already abandoned this disaster-inviting tactic.

Instead, Russian troops learned to withdraw into the depths of their rear area in plenty of time to avoid encirclement. As a result, the German advance—although it penetrated quite deeply—did not take nearly so many prisoners as it should have. The same thing was true of the otherwise highly successful German maneuver to recapture the city of Kharkov in 1943. While the Russians tended more and more towards greater mobility in their conduct of operations, German military policy became steadily less flexible after Stalingrad.

And what about the Luftwaffe?

Hitler never reproached Goering publicly for the fact that he was the one responsible for Stalingrad; still, if Goering had not given his casual assurance that air-supply operations were feasible, then Hitler would probably not have issued his fatal order to the Sixth Army to hold out. Although he did not make a public issue out of it, Hitler's faith in the good judgment of his erstwhile first advisor had suffered still another setback. Goering's reaction was to become even more immediately acquiescent to Hitler's every whim in a desperate effort to regain the latter's confidence. His original independence of mind was replaced by complete intellectual submission to the Fuehrer until he was soon nothing more than "his master's voice," as the last General Staff Chief called him. It is obvious that a yes-man like Goering could not protect the already exhausted Luftwaffe from being exploited beyond the point of endurance.

Goering's reaction to the Stalingrad catastrophe then was diametrically opposed to what it ought to have been. Instead of taking counsel with his conscience and resolving to make up for his years of neglect by settling down to intensive and intelligent work, he persisted in his attitudes of absolute submissiveness towards Hitler and nagging jealousy towards Jeschonnek, and permitted nothing to interfere with the continuance of his own comfortable existence, untouched by the exigencies of war. The seeds of disaster, sown long ago, were beginning to bear fruit.

21
The Defense of Germany

WHEN THE BATTLE OF BRITAIN was broken off, German air warfare in the West was already on the defensive. To be sure, those few night-fighter units still available for home air defense operations were able to combat the British attackers successfully, although the latter had already begun (in July 1941) area bombardment on residential sections with incendiary bombs. The British attacked in waves, the participating aircraft carrying out individual bomber runs during both the approach and departure flights. As long as the British continued to utilize these tactics Kammhuber, chief of Germany's night-fighter operations, was able to combat them to a certain extent with the "four-poster" method, whereby the fighter aircraft were stationed in air standby areas and were then directed from ground radar stations to the enemy bombers. Thanks to Kammhuber's night fighters, the Royal Air Force—despite its delivered bomb load of 35,000 tons—could not book a total success for 1941.

The German night fighters were employed in a line extending from the island of Sylt to the mouth of the Scheldt River, ranged in front of the antiaircraft batteries. Enemy aircraft approaching over Holland automatically ran into some nine to twelve night-fighter stations. Since this was too little to be really effective, at the end of 1941 an attempt was made at combined night-fighter operations, i.e. the integration of fighter aircraft and searchlights within a tightly limited area, the whole directed from a central ground station. Sixteen of the stations along the Sylt-Scheldt line were utilized for "dark-night" operations; a belt of stations immediately behind this line (thus stretching from the Danish border to Aix la Chapelle), as well as a number ranged before Berlin, carried out "illuminated night-fighter operations," and a total of nine stations were committed in the combined operations described above.

The limitations of this system became obvious, of course, as soon as the enemy was in a position to send over a really sizable bomber fleet.

For example, only thirty-six night-fighter aircraft could be employed over the Ruhr District in accordance with the methods outlined. And it could hardly be expected that each one of these thirty-six would manage to down an enemy bomber though, on the other hand, there were fighter aces who chalked up several kills for each mission. In any case, there was no doubt but that the number of fighter aircraft employed was not sufficient to inflict more than token damage (less than 15 percent) on an enemy who was even fairly strong.

The night-fighter command directed a goodly number of recommendations to the Commander in Chief, Luftwaffe, most of them requiring an unrealistic increase in the available production facilities and none of them capable of immediate fulfillment. For the cost of any one of the suggested projects the night-fighter command could have financed the operations of at least two more aircraft from each standby sector. It is open to question whether any one of the recommendations would have resulted in a substantial increase in the number of enemy bombers downed.

Long-range fighter operations (i.e. fighter operations over British airfields) were carried out by the I Group and 4th Squadron, 2d Night Fighter Wing, during 1941, until the transfer of the I Group to the Mediterranean made continuation impossible. Hitler was not particularly impressed with the potential effectiveness of such operations—quite apart from the fact that they could have little or no value in bolstering civilian morale, inasmuch as they could not easily be followed from Germany. After a short period of experimentation, these operations were discontinued, though Kammhuber was personally convinced of their potential efficacy.

Grabmann has the following to say in this connection:

> In view of the highly complicated and weather-sensitive takeoff and landing maneuvers practiced by the Royal Air Force in its steadily increasing nocturnal bombardment activity, a well-developed system of German long-range fighter pursuit would have had an excellent chance of success. The fact that Germany neglected to develop this weapon as long as she had the chance to do so must be counted as one of the gravest sins of omission on the part of the night-fighter command.

Britain, as a result of such sins of omission, was able to build up her strength without interference.

Although British air attacks during 1941 could not be counted entirely successful, in the spring of 1942 the Royal Air Force brought off a successful area bombardment raid on Luebeck (during the night of 28-29 April), which was followed by several similar attacks on Rostock. The night attack on Cologne (30-31 May), carried out by some 1,000 British bombers, was alarmingly effective, as were the subsequent attacks on Essen (on 1 June) and Luebeck (25 June). German night-fighter defenses at Cologne accounted for no more than thirty-six British bombers—slightly more than 3 percent of the attacking force. This was hardly a record which could be expected to deter a stubborn, strongly-industrialized enemy from further attacks. There was no doubt but what German night-fighter operations were sadly ineffective.

It is completely beyond comprehension that Goering, faced with the mounting effectiveness of the RAF raids, failed to insist upon the immediate issuance of special instructions designed to achieve a rapid and disproportionately large increase in Germany's manufacture of air armament equipment. On the other hand, since Germany's bombers were committed on the Eastern front, Hitler's policy of meeting terror with terror could only be implemented sporadically. Under these conditions, Germany's raids against England gradually disintegrated into pinpricks, or what the British called "baby blitzes."

Thus, Germany's only hope lay in a strengthening of her antiaircraft defenses—including the fighter aircraft arm—especially since the intervention of American bomber units was obviously imminent. Fighter aircraft and modern radar equipment were the answer! Yet, in 1941 Jeschonnek declined Milch's offer to raise fighter production to 1,000 units per month. The General Staff Chief explained that he had no use for more than 360 per month since he had only 170 crews to man them.

At this point an illusion inherent in the term so often applied to Germany's part in World War II should be dispelled; the term in question is "the poor man's war." It can only be used accurately, however, when comparing Germany with a power like the United States. Germany's potential was not inconsiderable, however—and this is a point which is all too frequently ignored—it did not develop completely until it was too late for it to be effective. Armaments production, for example, reached its peak during the first six to eight months of 1944 (July and August were the peak period). If the same goals could have been attained during the first half of 1942, then Russia would have been very hard put to maintain herself in the air and at sea, and an Allied invasion of France—despite America's military might—would never have been possible. It must not be forgotten that a full mobilization of

Germany's armament potential in 1942 (and such mobilization was within the realm of possibility) would have resulted in a very considerable increase in overall war potential during the following years. One neglected opportunity after another, including the chance at a negotiated peace.*

We know, at least to some extent, why these opportunities were not utilized. In the armament industry, for example, Udet and Todt did not have anywhere near the same degree of influence as did their successors, Milch (for the Luftwaffe) and Speer and Saur (for all other armament sectors). In addition, the many requests for special weapons development prevented the Speer ministry from turning its attention to conventional armament programs, including that of the Luftwaffe, until 1944. As far as command was concerned, Germany's military leaders simply failed to see the possibilities inherent in strategic air warfare against Russia, and they completely ignored the necessity of building a strong fighter aircraft arm for employment in home air defense operations.

The story behind these two wholly inexplicable errors is one of the most perplexing cases of self-delusion in all history.

First, right after the beginning of the Polish campaign Hitler was still hopeful that England and France would not declare war on Germany.

Second, once the Polish campaign was concluded Hitler was firmly convinced that England would be ready to sue for peace, inasmuch as a final decision had been reached (i.e. the territories in question—about half of Poland—were in German hands) and the motivation for the war had been removed—further bloodshed was unnecessary.

Third, after the conspicuous success of the campaign in the West, evidenced by France's capitulation, Germany's leaders were convinced that the war was already won, that England could finally be forced to make peace, and that this goal could be achieved by any nation willing to sanction the continued existence of the British Empire (and Hitler felt that the empire should be preserved).

Thrice the victim of self-delusionment, Hitler clung ever more firmly to the conviction (which was soon to become an obsession) that Germany had already won the war, including the war against Russia—and this despite the setbacks suffered during December 1941. Firm in his belief that the German offensive in the summer of 1942 (which really seemed to be off to an excellent start) would bring about the final col-

---

* The Allied decision to insist on unconditional surrender was not announced until January 1943.

lapse of Soviet Russia, it is quite probable that Hitler and his devoted disciples (and this group very definitely included Jeschonnek, Chief of the Luftwaffe General Staff) really believed that the German bombers would return victorious from the East to avenge the injuries inflicted by the British night raids and to make further offensive operations by the English impossible.

In summary, Germany's leaders were first betrayed into inaction by their unrealistic hope for peace, nurtured far too long; afterwards they were so blinded by rapid and relatively effortless victory that they failed to take advantage of the time given them for armaments production. As a result, Germany simply drifted along, her leaders always convinced that final victory was imminent, until they found themselves suddenly on the brink of disaster. By the time they recognized the peril and plunged the nation into hectic armament activity in an effort to make up for lost time, it was already too late.

It was not the poor man who lost the war, but rather the man who refused to face reality.

The British tactic of the bomber stream was the undoing of Germany's night-fighter defense system. During 1942 England carried out a total of seventeen large-scale attacks. And on 17 August 1942 came the first daylight attack by American four-engine bombers. The American aircraft had particularly efficient armaments in the tail region, which was the "classical" point of attack for a fighter aircraft.

The daylight attacks, of course, represented a far greater danger to Germany's antiaircraft defenses than the night raids. The majority of the former were carefully planned attacks—like the first of its type on 27 January 1943—and since the bombers traveled in close formation, it was extremely difficult for the German fighters to get in near enough to strike an effective blow against the heavily armed and heavily armored B-17's and B-24's. Needless to say, American losses were very slight.

The American system of target selection was fairly predictable, and the American attacks—insofar as their targets lent themselves to nocturnal bombardment—were usually followed up by British raids carried out as area bombardment missions by bomber aircraft guided by the pathfinding Mosquitos. The German submarine arm was the first top-priority target for the Americans—submarine bases, factories, diesel engine works, and shipyards. The German aircraft industry, including auxiliary parts factories, ball-bearing works, and assembly plants, was the next one. This was followed by the Ruhr District, various rail centers, and finally Berlin (because of its electrical industry).

Only after a great deal of experimentation were the German fighter aircraft able to work out an effective method of attack for use against the four-engine bombers. In recognition of the serious threat represented by these bombers, it was decided in July 1943 to replace the single-engine fighter units on the Western, Eastern, and Southern fronts with twin-engine fighter units. The single-engine fighters were then to be used to reinforce the home air defense units. It was high time.

The British raid on Hamburg (24-25 July), which was followed by an American daylight attack (an effective technique, incidentally, and one which the Allies often employed throughout July), resulted in very serious damage to the Hanseatic city. In addition, the British succeeded in paralyzing the German night-fighter and antiaircraft defenses by jamming their radar equipment with aluminum foil strips (the process known as "dueppeling," after the village of Dueppel). Gradually, the night-fighter forces learned to function effectively in spite of enemy jamming; the antiaircraft artillery, however, dependent upon its electrical aiming equipment, never fully recovered.

On 17 August, the German day-fighter forces (somewhat increased in the meantime) succeeded in bringing down at least sixty of the 315 American bombers participating in an attack on the ball-bearing works at Schweinfurt; as a result the enemy refrained from attack for ten days. This minor success was sufficient to awaken the optimism of Goering and Milch without, however, inspiring them to do everything possible to preserve Germany's newfound defensive strength at its present level by introducing measures designed to increase aircraft production (such as the seventy-two-hour week).

The peak of day-fighter effectiveness was reached on 14 October 1943, when sixty-six out of an attacking force of 295 B-17's were shot down over Schweinfurt. The October average for enemy aircraft downed was 12.4 percent, contrasted with a loss of only 4 percent for the defending fighters. Even during this peak month, the minimum figure of 15 percent was not attained.

And from November on, the situation changed radically. The enemy began to schedule his attacks for periods of bad weather, having noticed that the German fighters (due to the lack of adequate pilot training in instrument flight) were completely helpless. In addition, the American bombers were often escorted by heavily-armed long-range fighter aircraft whose radius of operations soon covered the entire German Reich. Not only were the England-based bombers of the American Eighth Air Force becoming more and more dangerous, but towards the end of 1943 Germany began to notice the effects of the assignment of the American

Fifteenth Air Force to the Italian airfields at Foggia (captured by the Allies on 28 September). From the Italian bases, the American bombers were able to attack southern Germany and the eastern portions of the Reich, as well as targets located in the Balkans. This served to dissipate German air defense forces even further.

The German single-engine fighter aircraft were incapable (as a result of the inadequate training of their pilots on the one hand and the inadequacy of their equipment on the other) of attacking in loose formation an enemy bomber stream approaching above a closed cloud cover. Nor was it possible for the twin-engine fighters to be effective in an attack of this kind. Moreover, German antiaircraft artillery was fairly useless in view of the flight altitude of the enemy bombers, quite apart from the fact that its instruments were extremely vulnerable to enemy jamming.

Thus, in 1944 the German fighter aircraft forces were unable to combat effectively the enemy air attacks, which were systematically directed towards the destruction of the sources of German military strength. This was true in the case of the February attacks on the factories producing airframes, as well as of the carefully planned attacks—begun in the spring and continued relentlessly—on the gasoline hydration plants in central and eastern Germany.

Beginning with the American bomber attacks in 1944, with their strong fighter escorts, Germany's day-fighter defenses were doomed to operations which resulted in heavy losses and yet failed to inflict any appreciable damage. The night-fighter forces were in an equally critical position, since the British bomber stream tactic had robbed the fourposter method of its effectiveness. Moreover, the British jamming of radar equipment, as introduced during the attack on Hamburg, presented a very serious problem.

In this situation Goering was willing to grasp at any straw. The first was a suggestion made by Major Hajo Hermann on 27 June 1943 concerning the possibility of illuminated night-fighter operations. These were to be operations by single-engine fighters, utilizing the illumination provided at the scene of attack by burning buildings as well as searchlights to simulate daylight conditions and thus to obviate the danger of "window." In spite of initial successes, this method did not continue to justify the hopes placed upon it.

On the other hand, realization of a suggestion made on 29 July 1943 by Colonel von Lossberg proved to be of great assistance to Germany's night-fighter forces. Basing his recommendations on a study by Major (Engineer) Guenther of the Technical Office, von Lossberg suggested that the night fighters should infiltrate the enemy bomber stream during the approach and return flights, should be reinforced as much as possible, and should then carry out individual pursuit operations. By combining Hermann's and von Lossberg's suggestions within the framework of the fourposter method, it ought to have been possible to guide three times as many fighters against the enemy bomber stream. Lossberg's method of individual pursuit was most successful during the British attack on Nuremberg on the night of 30-31 March 1944, when a total of 107 bombers was shot down,* a record which had never before been achieved and which was never again to be equalled, even by the day-fighter forces.

This "triumph of the pursuit method" was possible only because the majority of the night-fighter aircraft were equipped with the Li-SN-2 radar instrument. The enemy, however, far superior to Germany in the development of radar equipment, continually invented new methods of jamming German radar. By October 1944, the British had found a way to jam the SN-2 completely, and German night-fighter operations were on the wane. During October the night fighters managed to destroy only 6.6 percent of attacking enemy aircraft; in November the figure dropped to 1.5 percent; in December to 0.7 percent; in January it rose to 1.3 percent; and in February dropped back to 1.2 percent. Needless to say, these losses were insignificant for the enemy. During the month of March, the gasoline shortage was so acute that only top-ranking crews were permitted to fly. Operation "Gisela," during the night of 4-5 March, represented one last success for the German night-fighter forces. In carefully planned operations, the fighters slipped into the enemy bomber stream and by individual pursuit and aerial combat over Chemnitz (the scene of the attack) they managed to bring down seventy-five four-engine bombers.

It may well be asked whether German military leaders made any attempt in early 1944 to create more favorable conditions for the day-fighter forces. Milch certainly made every effort to support the hard-pressed day-fighter units by increasing aircraft production as much as he could. On 1 March 1944, when it seemed clear that the February air attacks had almost completely destroyed the German aircraft industry, one last attempt was made to save the situation by the establishment of the Fighter Staff. Its missions were the reconstruction of the industrial facilities destroyed by the enemy, the achievement of the fighter production goal established by Milch in 1943, and the removal of air arma-

* The British estimated their losses at 94 bombers.

ment works to safer, underground locations. This entire project was entrusted to Saur, Speer's most powerful assistant, and was given top priority. Soon thereafter, the Luftwaffe armament program was made an integral part of the activity of Speer's ministry. As usual, purposeful action came far too late.

Even so, the Fighter Staff did manage to bring about a considerable increase in the production of single-engine fighter aircraft. However, the fighter forces were still restricted to traditional models, which—despite the gradual improvements being made in them—were no match for the enemy. This might not have been the case if Hitler had not obstructed for so long the development of the Me-262, and if Milch had supported—in time—the further development of the Do-325, a new Dornier fighter with a speed of 435 miles, which never reached the mass production stage. An increase in fighter production was no longer sufficient, and an increase in quality was apparently either beyond Germany's capabilities or came too late to be of any use.

Obviously, the production of thousands of single-engine fighter aircraft made a difference in the operational readiness of Germany's fighter arm. On 2 November 1944, for example, there were 695 day fighters available for employment, and on 28 November, 684 night fighters. These figures represented the climax in operational readiness for the fighter forces.

The German fighter pilot's inferiority to his American counterpart—in number, in the standard of the training he had been given, and in the performance qualities of his aircraft—was bound to have an unfavorable effect on his morale, particularly since he knew his often heroic efforts were wholly unappreciated by Goering. This may well have been one of the reasons for the Luftwaffe's failure to increase its strength materially in spite of the tremendous rise in aircraft production figures during the period of the Fighter Staff. Another reason for this failure can be traced to Germany's highest-level commanders who were making plans which were to result in the dissolution of the reserve force which had been slowly building up and which the General of the Fighter Forces planned to utilize in a large-scale offensive against the American bomber streams.

The first such instance was in June 1944, when the Allies landed in France. Hitler ordered the majority of the fighter forces to France where the successes they achieved were really insignificant in terms of overall events, but where their lack of familiarity with the airfields and the difficult conditions under which they were forced to operate against an enemy far superior in number caused enormously high losses.

The second instance of such wasteful employment occurred during the Ardennes offensive. This ambitious operation had been carefully prepared. With Goering's concurrence, plans had been made to withdraw the day-fighter units from action long enough for their personnel and materiel strength to be restored. As soon as this point had been reached, and weather conditions were favorable, a force of 2,000 single-engine fighters was to be sent up in aerial combat against the enemy in the hope of inflicting such heavy losses that the Allies would refrain from further strategic air operations. As a tentative goal, the destruction of 400-500 four-engine bombers and at least as many enemy fighters had been established. The Luftwaffe had completed its preparations by the first week in November and Goering had even addressed a personal appeal to the fighter forces (7 November). Then, in contradiction to these plans and in spite of vigorous protests on the part of Galland, Hitler ordered the fighter forces to be transferred to the Western theater for employment in the Ardennes offensive. Weather conditions were extremely unfavorable for fighter operations, losses were high and success nil.

The third instance, Operation "Bodenplatte" (Ground Plate), carried out on 1 January 1945 and directed against fifteen Allied airfields in France, Holland, and Belgium, used up what was left of the reserve force. In a surprise attack costing 150 German fighter aircraft and their crews, the Luftwaffe managed to destroy 800 enemy machines on the ground. Grabmann calls it "a Pyrrhic victory paid for by destruction of the last reserves of the Luftwaffe."

22
The Legend Exposed

NEARLY ALL of Germany's difficulties during World War II can be directly or indirectly traced to the lack of a central command organization. Thus, the first prerequisite must be the establishment of a central instrument of command—an armed forces general staff. Within the framework of constitutional policy and procedures, this staff should have authority over all civilian and political agencies in all questions relating to the defense of the nation; it should have the status of a superior staff for the general staffs of the service branches making up the armed forces. In the event of international alliances, an overall planning agency should be set up during peacetime and entrusted with the authority and missions on a supranational basis which the armed forces general staff exercises on a national basis.

In keeping with the importance of its missions, the armed forces general staff should be made up of the best qualified General Staff officers from all branches of the service and of outstanding personalities from public life, and these two groups should then be given joint training for their roles in the accomplishment of a joint mission. This training should be carefully designed to orient the members of the armed forces general staff concerning the problems involved in the conduct of a global war and those aspects of global warfare which are bound to affect the life of the nation—or nations in case there is a coalition—in time of war. The nation's best-trained minds should be set to work to evaluate conditions in potentially hostile countries; the men selected for this task may be either active or reserve members of the armed forces general staff; rank or civilian profession should not be permitted to influence the choice. Outstanding representatives from the field of scientific research as well as from all other fields of public endeavor should also be given a seat and a voice on the staff.

The problem of the integration of all these various persons into the work of military preparations and the conduct of military operations is one which will require a great deal of study—a possible future war would be impossible to conduct without these persons. Any nation which buries its best minds in subordinate jobs during wartime merely because they happen to belong to people who have no military rank is guilty of wasting an important part of its best military potential on meaningless activity.

The points which have been discussed above in connection with the armed forces general staff are also applicable, on a smaller scale, to the general staffs of the individual service branches of each nation. The missions assigned to these staffs should be specifically limited in nature and should be determined by the overall armed forces general staff. Within the restricted framework of these missions, however, the subordinate general staffs will also require the help of prominent representatives of those fields of civilian endeavor which have some bearing on the mission of their particular branch. In this connection one need only recall the lack of contact between the Luftwaffe General Staff and the agencies responsible for armaments research and development, and the unfortunate results it had on the course of the war. The only possible conclusion to be drawn from this is that the decentralization of the various aspects affecting the conduct of war, as it was practiced in the Third Reich—except by Hitler himself—and, strangely enough, earnestly furthered by Goering, must inevitably lead to a weakening of the overall command apparatus. The establishment of a central command and planning agency is now more necessary than ever before. The military exclusiveness of the traditional General Staff, at any rate, can no longer be justified.

Those principles which are accepted as applicable to the conduct of war on its overall scale should be equally applicable to the conduct of operations in each individual theater of operations. During the course of World War II, Germany often placed an Army or Luftwaffe commander in command of operations in a particular, remote theater of war (Africa, Norway, Finland, etc.). In most cases these commanders had only their own staffs to assist them, and no matter how well-versed they might be in the affairs of their own particular branch, they were bound to be limited in outlook. Occasionally, liaison officers from the other Armed Forces branches were also available, but these had no command authority over the troop units belonging to their service branches. Ordinarily, the commander had direct authority only over the units of his own service branch, while all other units received their orders from their own local command headquarters. So long as all the parties concerned were convinced of the need for close cooperation, this method was perfectly feasible; in practice, however, one cannot always rely on the goodwill of all the parties involved. As a matter of principle, remotely located theaters of war should always have a superior operations staff, detached from the armed forces general staff, in order to assure a certain degree of uniformity in the employment of the available forces.

The frequent changes in organizational structure with which the Luftwaffe General Staff had to contend both before and during the war proved most unfortunate. The troop general staffs, however, were only slightly affected by them. There was never time for the responsibilities of the Staff to become as firmly established as the successful accomplishment of its mission required. Some of the disadvantages arising from this situation have already been discussed. Nevertheless, there would seem to be no doubt but that general staffs ought to be retained in the individual service branches, provided that these staffs restrict themselves to their proper missions of operational command, organization, and training, and that they receive their instructions in this respect from a superior armed forces general staff. The fact that the individual Armed Forces branches were often able to develop their own plans and pursue their own goals during World War II must be attributed to the lack of an Armed Forces command agency capable of issuing competently prepared and unequivocal orders; this lack was bound to lead to a blurring of the lines of authority and responsibility and to a dissipation of forces.

The general staffs of the individual service branches, like the executive agencies of other public service institutions, should be nothing but executive instruments for the armed forces general staff. Their influence on the conduct of war should be limited to those specific operations for which they have been assigned responsibility, for too broad a delegation of command authority tends to weaken the overall strength.

One very important responsibility of the individual service general staffs would be the selection of their representatives to the armed forces general staff, as well as the careful pretraining of younger candidates for these positions. The officers selected for service on the armed forces general staff should not be too young; they should very definitely have had some experience in the planning and command of operations within their own particular service branches. The experience of the Luftwaffe General Staff during World War II is indicative of the fact that extremely young and inexperienced officers on high-level staffs are capable of doing a great deal more damage than they can later rectify. On the other hand, of course, the officers selected for the armed forces general staff should not be so old that they are no longer capable of thinking in terms of new and larger problems.

In order to be eligible for promotion to the rank of a general officer, a man should be required to have proved his fitness for service on the armed forces general staff, or better still, have served successfully with that body. A general officer in any service branch cannot be considered capable of directing the operations of a large number of troops unless he is thoroughly familiar with the problems involved in the overall conduct of operations and with the potentialities and requirements of the other service branches. The criticism levied at many an otherwise highly capable German general can certainly be attributed in part to his lack of experience outside his own service branch. It is equally certain that a great many of the German generals would not have gone along with Hitler if they had had access to full information, and had thus been truly aware of the overall situation.

An article appearing in Volume 8 of a publication on world politics of the Arbeitsgemeinschaft Demokratischer Kreise (Study Group, Democratic Societies) contains some interesting comments regarding the future relationship between statesman and military leader:

. . . In the future, too—in fact, in all probability particularly in the future—there will be general staff officers. These men will have to be familiar with all the many and varied ramifications of military affairs, and will also have to possess a certain degree of familiarity with the equally complex ramifications of developments in the political sphere. Their frame of reference must encompass the entire world; otherwise they will be incapable of filling their posts as competent advisors and aides. The organizational structure of the general staff of the future will be closely akin to that of the political organization of the larger defense areas. Narrow national barriers would only be a danger to the successful accomplishment of its mission. The traditional concept of military service as duty to the nation—or supranational unit—must remain.

The statesman, who quite correctly claims the right to establish goals for the strategic employment of the nation's armed forces and to place certain limitations on their activity, will have to give ground on one point; he should avail himself freely of the advice and recommendations of the military leader, but he must not, under any circumstances, interfere in matters of strategic or tactical command. These must remain the province of the military leader, who will employ them as he sees fit in order to achieve the strategic goals established by the statesman.

True cooperation between the statesman and the soldier—indispensable to the successful achievement of their common goal—is possible only if the statesman is capable of thinking constructively and realistically in regard to strategy, i.e. the overall conduct of military operations. The statesman, too, should be at least somewhat familiar with the basic principles of military affairs. Above and beyond the demands of his own particular field, the military leader—particularly at higher level—must be sufficiently at home in the political sphere to comprehend the broad ramifications of developments in politics or diplomacy. He must, of course, be very careful to see that his personal ambition does not lead him into a position of noncritical acceptance of the political regime.

The same thing is true of the members of the general staff.

There are certain basic guidelines whose acceptance will be decisive for the future. We mention them in closing in the hope that they may become firmly entrenched in the thinking of both statesman and military leader.

The political leader, or statesman, bears the responsibility for the fate of his nation. This cannot be otherwise. Thus, the political leader must be granted the right to make the final decision in matters of preparing the nation for defense or of waging war.

Once the decision has been taken, however, and the political leader has established the overall objectives, the military leader must take over and must apply his knowledge and experience to the achievement of these objectives.

If the political leader is objective in his evaluation of the nation's position, and if he is confident of the wisdom of the course he is pursuing, then any attempt at warmongering will be doomed to failure. The political leader will do well to remember that there is a healthy tendency towards pacifism in the makeup of every responsible military man. A soldier knows war and knows what suffering it means for the nation and the armed forces alike. For this reason, he will do his best to avoid war if at all possible. . . .

Precisely in connection with the above remarks it might be well to point out that Hitler's "Basic Directive No. 1" was catastrophic in its effects. Because of this directive, no one in a position of military responsibility was ever informed of the ultimate aims of the Fuehrer, and no one—not even the members of the Armed Forces High Command—was given access to sufficient information to construct an accurate picture of the overall situation. And no military leader, whether he be a member of the general staff or in charge of some other important military function, can fulfill his mission effectively unless he is informed of the ultimate objectives of the political leader and is familiar with the overall situation. Otherwise he is like a hen who pecks about in the dark and occasionally manages to find a grain of corn.

The selection of individuals to fill the top posts in the political and military life of the nation must be handled with great care so that there will be no risk of the abuse of military security regulations.

As regards the post of Chief of the General Staff, in the sense which was usual within the German Armed Forces during World War II, one can only conclude that it was an unfortunate one for the Chief of the General Staff as well as for the chiefs of subordinate staffs within the troop organization. The post was adopted from the rich tradition of the past. No attempt, however, was made to give it the traditional authority which might have justified its existence.

If the wisdom is conceded of giving the commander of a unit, or even of a fairly large segment within a service branch, full responsibility for directing the operations of the troops under his command, then there would seem to be no need for a Chief of the General Staff. It is difficult to justify the employment of such highly-qualified officers in a post which is practically devoid of responsibility. One remedy would be to consolidate the position of the Chief of the General Staff— of an armed forces branch, a troop general staff, etc.—with that of the deputy commander. In this way, the Chief of the General Staff, by serving at the same time as deputy commander, would have control over the entire element rather than only over portions of it. Administrative functions, as well as any other functions which are not directly concerned with operational command, could be made a specific responsibility of this position. The authority of the commander would thus be secure, even in the eyes of the troops, and the ambiguity of his authority over the staff would be once and for all dispelled. The deputy commander, of course, would have to be a general officer and his training and experience would have to be such as to qualify him for his position in the eyes of the armed forces general staff. All the other officers on the troop general staff could be members of the general staff corps of their particular service branch.

The officers selected for general staff training should be men who have proved their ability and their strength of character; they should not be chosen on the basis of their ability to march correctly, their talent for sports, their skill in aerial combat, or their social accomplishments. Stupidity and vain ambition in the command organization can do more damage than a defeat in battle, for they can undermine the confidence which the troops must feel in their leaders. Experience with the troops and proven ability in action should be made prerequisites for service on the general staff. Spotty or limited training of the officers occupying high-level positions can also result in the loss of troop confidence. The fallaciousness has been recognized of the view that young, inexperienced, and untrained holders of war decorations are more suited for general staff service and operational command than the carefully selected and thoroughly trained general staff officer, unless of course, these younger men possess the same qualifications as the latter. The experience accumulated by the Luftwaffe General Staff in this respect is as unequivocal as it was unfortunate.

One other important lesson taught by Germany's experience should be mentioned. Events have proved beyond any doubt that the rapid turnover in General Staff chiefs was a catastrophe for the Luftwaffe General Staff. It is probable that the development and expansion of the Luftwaffe and its General Staff would have been far more satisfactory if the first General Staff Chief, Wever, had been permitted to carry his mission to completion. It lies in the nature of the situation that any new general staff chief—provided that he is a man of character and personality—will try to impress his own personality on both command organization and troops. If he is then removed from his post before his ideas have had time to take effect, he leaves behind an indeterminate structure, and his successor has no alternative but to start experimenting from the beginning. When a general staff has too many chiefs within a relatively short period, as was the case with the Luftwaffe General Staff, the result is proverbial: "Too many cooks spoil the broth!"

The collapse of the German Air Force revealed dramatically that the Luftwaffe had really been all along precisely what Heinz J. Rieckhoff suggests, not "a phantom but a bluff," a force which stumbled along behind the Army in training, development, and organization. The wonder of it all is not how the Allies were able to bring about the Luftwaffe's downfall, but how the Luftwaffe was able to carry on for so long against such formidable odds.

Index